WILD LIFE

BRAD WILSON

WILD LIFE

BRAD WILSON

Foreword by Desmond Morris

PRESTEL
Munich • London • New York

CONTENTS

"There is grandeur in this view of life, with its several powers, having been originally breathed into a few forms or into one; and that, whilst this planet has gone cycling on according to the fixed law of gravity, from so simple a beginning, endless forms most beautiful and most wonderful have been, and are being, evolved."

Charles Darwin, *On the Origin of Species*

WILD LIFE
DESMOND MORRIS

Since the world's first photograph was taken in 1827, photography has grown into a refined new art form. Studio photography has become technically so advanced that it is hard for anyone to introduce new innovations. The only way to do it is to come up with a completely outrageous idea and then carry it out fearlessly. This is what Brad Wilson has done in his new body of work entitled simply *Wild Life*.

Of course, wildlife photography has become a major preoccupation of many fieldworkers—photographers who set out to capture the look of an animal in its natural environment. Ecological considerations have become a dominant theme of this work. Animals in artificial zoo enclosures have long ago ceased to be of interest. They are fake because, in modern zoos, they pretend to be natural but they are not. So the intrepid photographer must spend days hidden in a hide in some remote forest to capture the moment that a baby bird first ventures from the nest, or an industrious parent brings home a tasty morsel for its young. These field studies had become so prominent as a photographic style that it was hard to see how anyone could find a new way of capturing exciting images of wild animals.

This is where Brad Wilson stepped in and demonstrated that there was. His audacity was to reject ecology and the natural environment totally, deliberately setting out to make a series of studio portraits of wild animals using completely plain backgrounds. By removing the natural background in this way, he forces the viewer of his animal portraits to see the creatures as astonishing pieces of sculpture. In their stark isolation, every minute detail of their anatomy is exposed to us. By treating each one as if it were a great movie star, a fashion icon, or a head of state, he takes us closer to an intimate contemplation of the facial details of these wild beasts than has ever been achieved before.

The practical problems involved in achieving this are huge. Even the greatest diva from the world of music or cinema could not be more demanding than, say, a giraffe, when it comes to welcoming one to your photographic studio. And how do you take a close-up studio photograph of an adult tiger or a mountain lion? The answer, inevitably, is that you must work with trained animals, and these are increasingly difficult to find these days. Circuses are being swept away into history. Zoos no longer try to tame any of their animals. Movies are now carefully supervised by animal welfare organizations imposing severe restrictions on what the directors may and may not do with live animals. It would have been easier for Brad Wilson if he had attempted to make his portraits in the 1920s or 1930s, when attitudes to captive wildlife were very different. But in those days his photographic equipment would not have been so refined. So, to get his technically perfected animal portraits, he somehow had to find trained animals of a very special kind. Fortunately for him a few of these do still exist.

Young animals abandoned by their parents are occasionally rescued and hand-reared from a very early age. This makes them tame, even as adults. I was once taken into the enclosure of an adult grizzly bear where the owner put a banana in my mouth and told me to sit still. The bear came up and ate the banana with great delicacy, taking care not to hurt me. I can still remember the heat of its breath on my face and the expression in its dark eyes. It could have killed me in a few seconds, had it wished to do so, but was more friendly and gentle than a family dog. In Thailand I was persuaded to lie on the ground and let an adult elephant give me a body massage with one of its front feet. Again, it was unbelievably delicate in its actions.

It is animals of this kind that Brad Wilson had to find for his portraits. If he had failed to do so, even once, his wonderful book might have been a posthumous publication. But he was fortunate in finding experienced animal trainers who knew what they were doing and were able to pose their wild beasts long enough for the camera to click, and click, and click. Watching film of these proceedings I was surprised to see Brad use flash. Animals dislike flash, and if they are nervous or on edge the blinding moment of light can be enough to startle or anger them. I did notice a few twitches, starts, and blinks when the flashes went off, but no more than that. These were wild animals with a remarkable tolerance for being treated like fashion models.

Brad's pictures fall into five classes. There are the three-quarters "head-and-shoulders" portraits, the head-on full-faces, the profiles, the small details, and the unusual angles. To my surprise, it is the head-on full-faces that I find most appealing. I say I am surprised because I usually have a strong reaction to the composition of a photograph, and these symmetrical, close-up full-faces are notable for their lack of any composition whatsoever.

But it is the immediacy and the confrontational impact of these full-faces that is so electrifying. It is as if you and the animal are staring hard at each another, trying to assess the innermost feelings of the creature staring back. Looking at them for any length of time eventually becomes mesmeric and afterwards, when you have looked away, you feel that, now, at last, you truly know that particular animal's essence in minute detail.

Another special quality of these portraits is the way they allow you to appreciate the texture of the sitters. Because of the very high technical quality of the images, it is possible almost to feel the softness of the kangaroo's fur, or the leathery harshness of the elephant's ear. Or the knobbly hardness of the reptilian skin.

Take a close look at the dark, expressive eyes, especially those of our closest relatives the monkeys and apes. Surprisingly they all lack one important feature that is highly conspicuous in our own, human eyes. There are no whites to their eyes. Where our eyes are white theirs are brown. Having visible white to the eyes is a uniquely human quality that evolved in connection with the importance, in social groups, of spotting who was glancing at whom. In social groups we look more often at the dominant individuals than we do at the weaker ones. So, by evolving whites to our eyes that highlight glance direction, we can be much more socially sensitive.

If a sidelong glance in a chimpanzee is inconspicuous, in an owl it is non-existent. The huge eyes of owls in Brad's photos seem to fill their heads—and that was the problem they posed during evolution. They had to be very big because of the owl's nocturnal lifestyle, but two huge eyeballs would leave no room for the owl's brain. So evolution took another path. The result is that modern owls have no eyeballs—instead they have tubular eyes. This means that, if they wish to look to one side they must turn the whole head. Aiding this, changes to the neck took place and today it is possible for an owl to turn its head right round so that it can look backwards. But glancing up or down, this way and that, with only the eyes, is completely beyond it.

One of the problems human beings have when looking at the faces of animals is that it is hard not to see them as caricatures of human faces. We have a deep-seated reaction to seeing any pair of eyes above a nose and a mouth, and this reaction has, at its core, a standard set of proportions that we expect to see. If a face has the eyes a certain distance apart, the nose a certain length and the lips a certain size, we recognize these combined features as a typical human face. If someone has unusually large eyes, or a very long nose, or very full lips, we react by seeing these dimensions as distortions of what our brain tells us is the average face. In this way we come to recognize and remember hundreds of individual faces.

This mental process of classifying faces is hard to switch off when we look at, say, the face of a chimpanzee. We cannot help seeing it as a distorted human face, rather than the face of another species in its own right. It is important, when looking at Brad Wilson's animal portraits, to try and suppress this tendency. If we feel that an animal's face is frowning, smiling, or glaring at us, the chances are that what we are seeing is simply the anatomical arrangement of the features of that particular species. To get the most out of these animal portraits we should try to forget human facial proportions for the moment and see each animal on its own terms. A heavy brow may simply be the result of a more powerful bony protection for the eyes, rather than a sinister, angry frown. And sneering lips may simply fall into that shape because of the large teeth they are covering. It is not easy to avoid an anthropomorphic response to these animal faces, but if it can be done, then they will have an even greater visual impact.

I think of Brad Wilson not as a photographer but as a portrait artist, and one who, through his undeniably risky labors, has brought us a collection of unforgettable, iconic images that will linger in the mind's eye long after the pages of his book have been closed.

“A man’s work is nothing but this slow trek to rediscover, through the detours of art, those two or three great and simple images in whose presence his heart first opened.”

Albert Camus

AFFINITY
BRAD WILSON

I have always been interested in that precision which creates beauty—the exact instant when mood, stillness, and composition align to make something common suddenly uncommon, something expected suddenly unexpected. In many ways, my entire life in photography has been about trying to find those few elusive moments and capture them. The path to those moments, however, has seldom been straightforward. For me, the primary obstacle is always familiarity. It gives rise to a special kind of blindness—one that prevents me from seeing anything artistically compelling in the repetitive scenes of my everyday life, or along the roads I've already traveled. I need journeys into the unknown to restore my vision. This project with animals, and all that it encompassed, was one of those journeys.

For as long as humans have been on this planet, we have had a remarkably complex and constantly changing relationship with the wildlife around us. At times, animals have been our allies, our enemies, our gods, and our food. Often these roles have existed simultaneously across many different cultures and continents. Our destinies have been, and will continue to be, inexorably linked. Perhaps this long shared history is one significant element of the powerful affinity we feel for them. It is impossible to stand a few feet away from an elephant, a tiger, or a chimpanzee, with no barriers between you, and remain unmoved. There is something deeply resonant about this type of encounter that is profound in the moment and primal in its roots. This was the rare and fragile territory I entered as the project began.

From the start, there was something immensely challenging and inspiring about working with these creatures. Up to that point, I had spent my career photographing subjects I largely controlled: professional models, actors, or other noteworthy people. In general, I told them exactly what to do and they did it. Now suddenly I was facing subjects, who, for the most part, did what they wanted with no regard for me or my artistic agenda. Specific verbal directions were replaced by patient waiting and observation—a kind of meditation in the middle of organized chaos. That in itself was exhilarating, but there was something more. What I discovered was a world that we, as humans, have largely abandoned—a place of instinct, intuition, and present moment awareness—a fully natural world, distinct from the increasingly urbanized and digitized landscape that surrounds us. In the midst of our modern human civilization with all its technological complexities, animals still remain stark symbols of a simpler life and a wilderness lost. Perhaps these images can stand as a testament to this other fading world, and remind us, despite the pronounced feeling of isolation that too often characterizes our contemporary existence, that we are not alone, we are not separate—we are part of a beautifully rich and interconnected diversity of life.

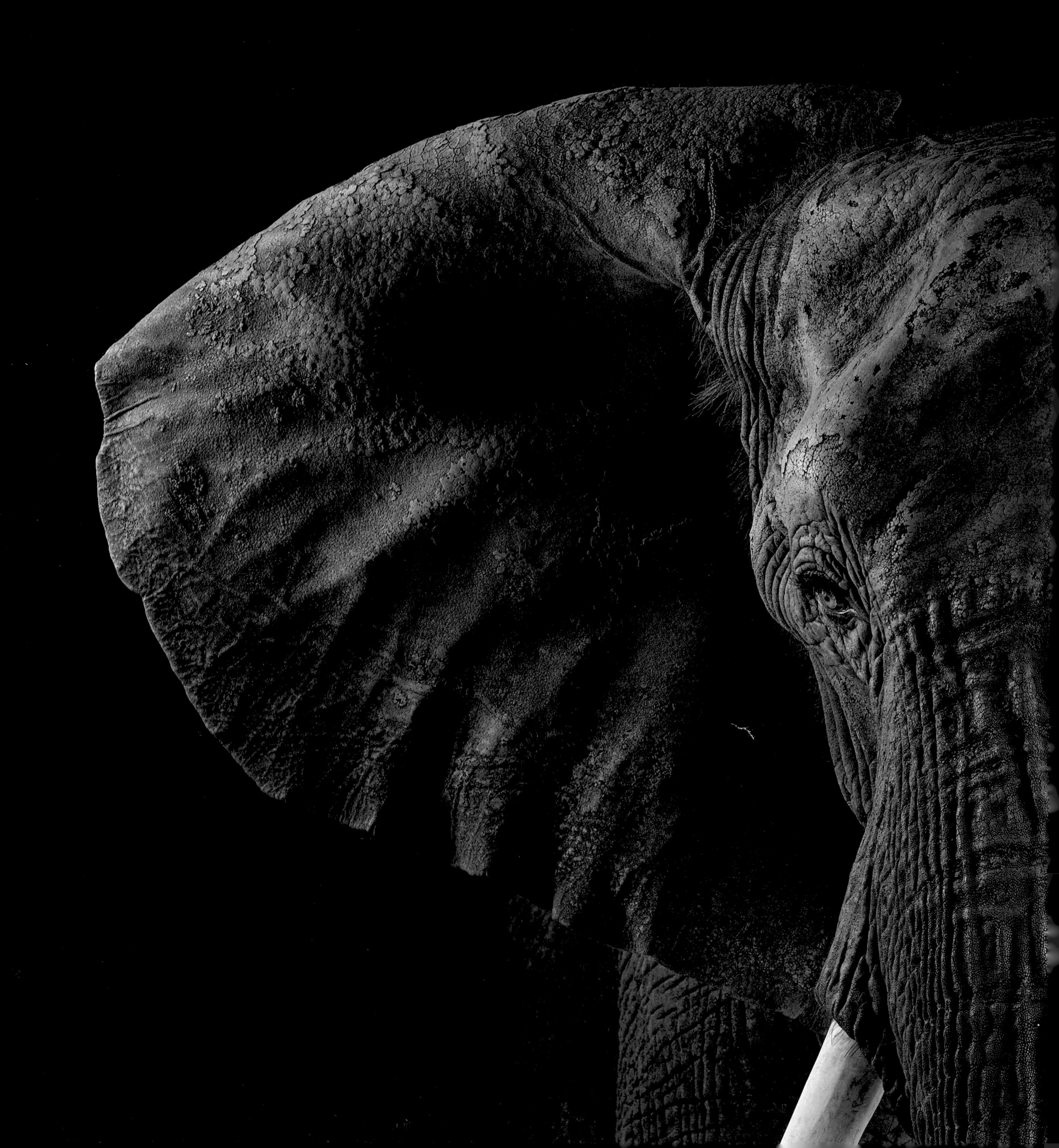

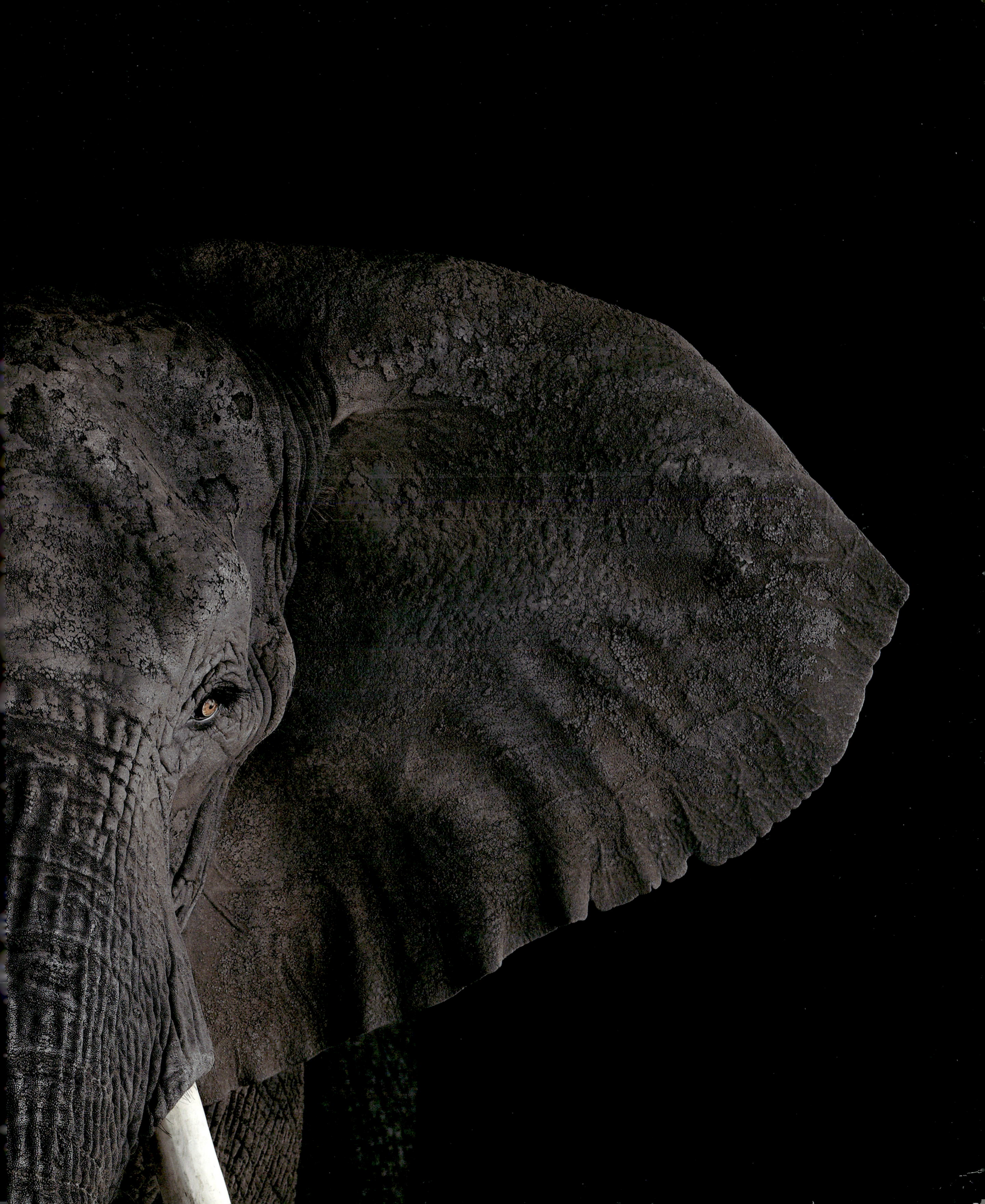

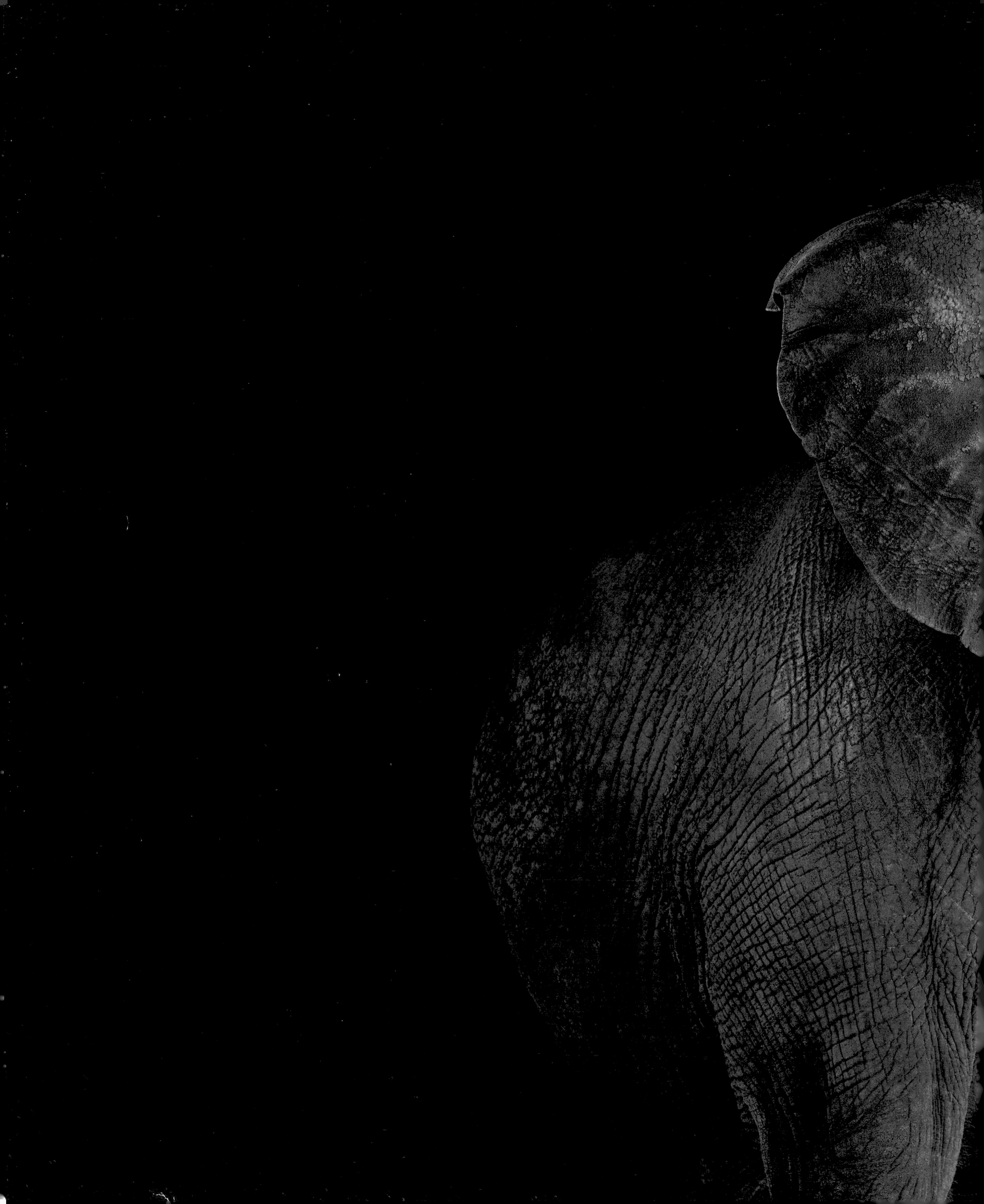

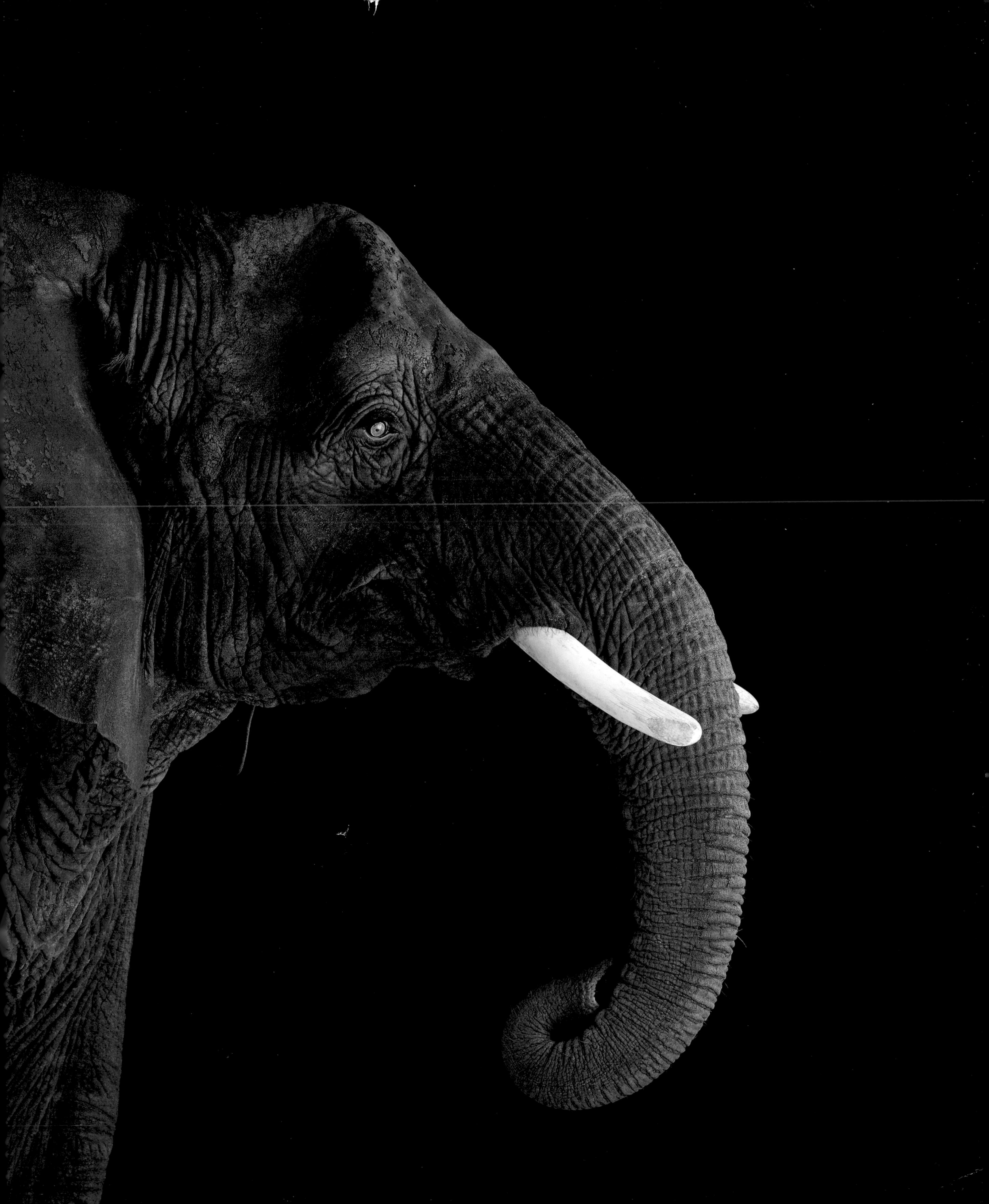

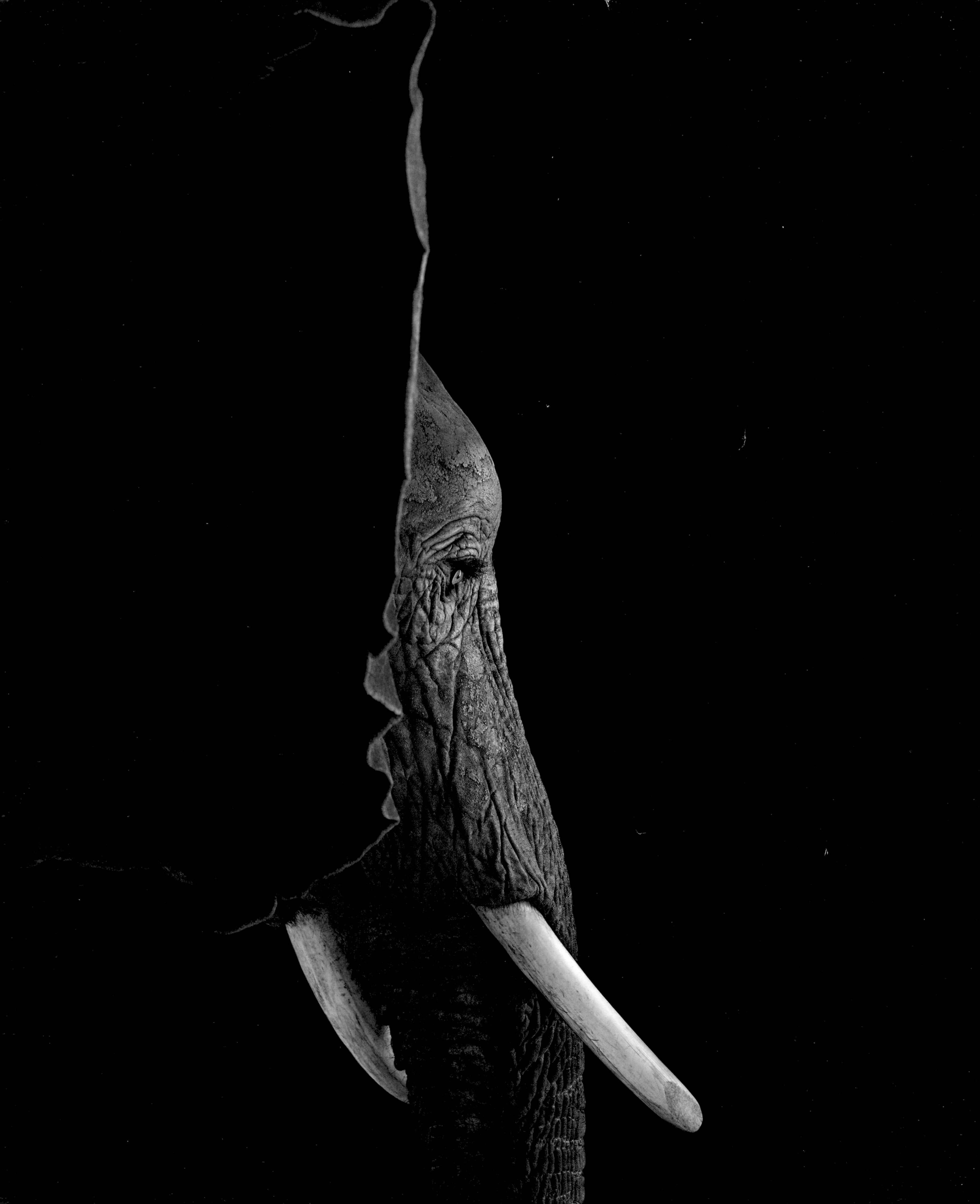

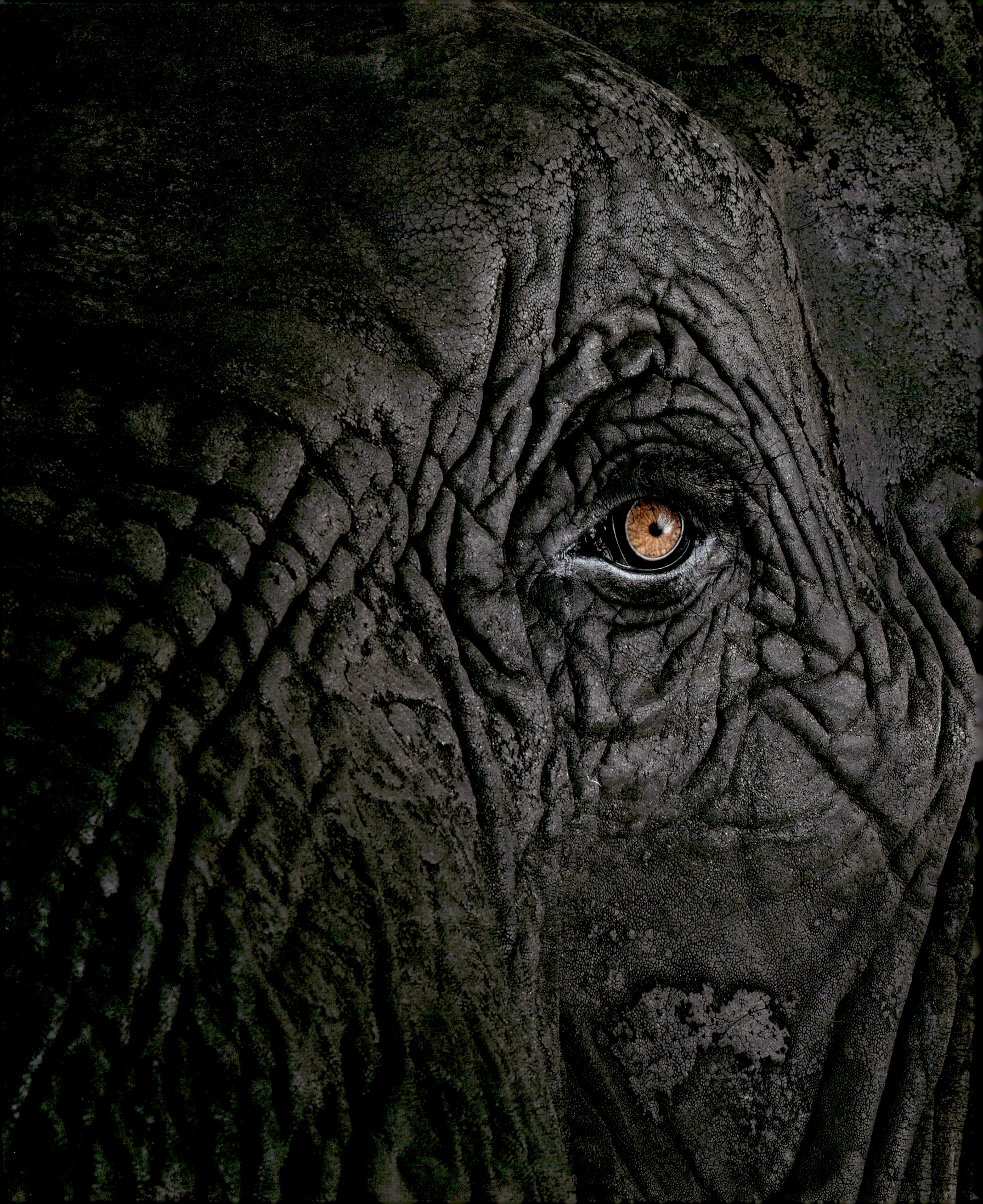

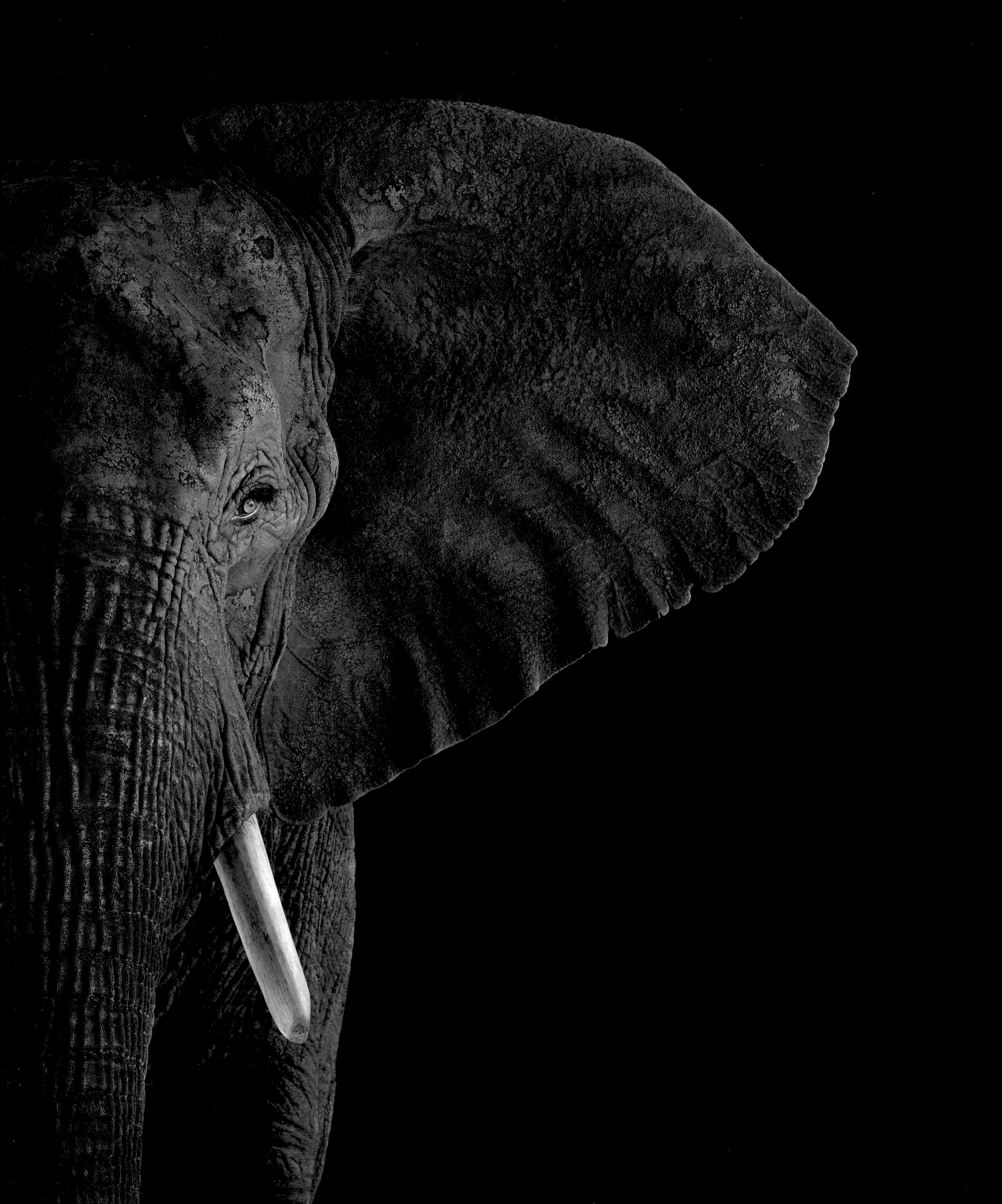

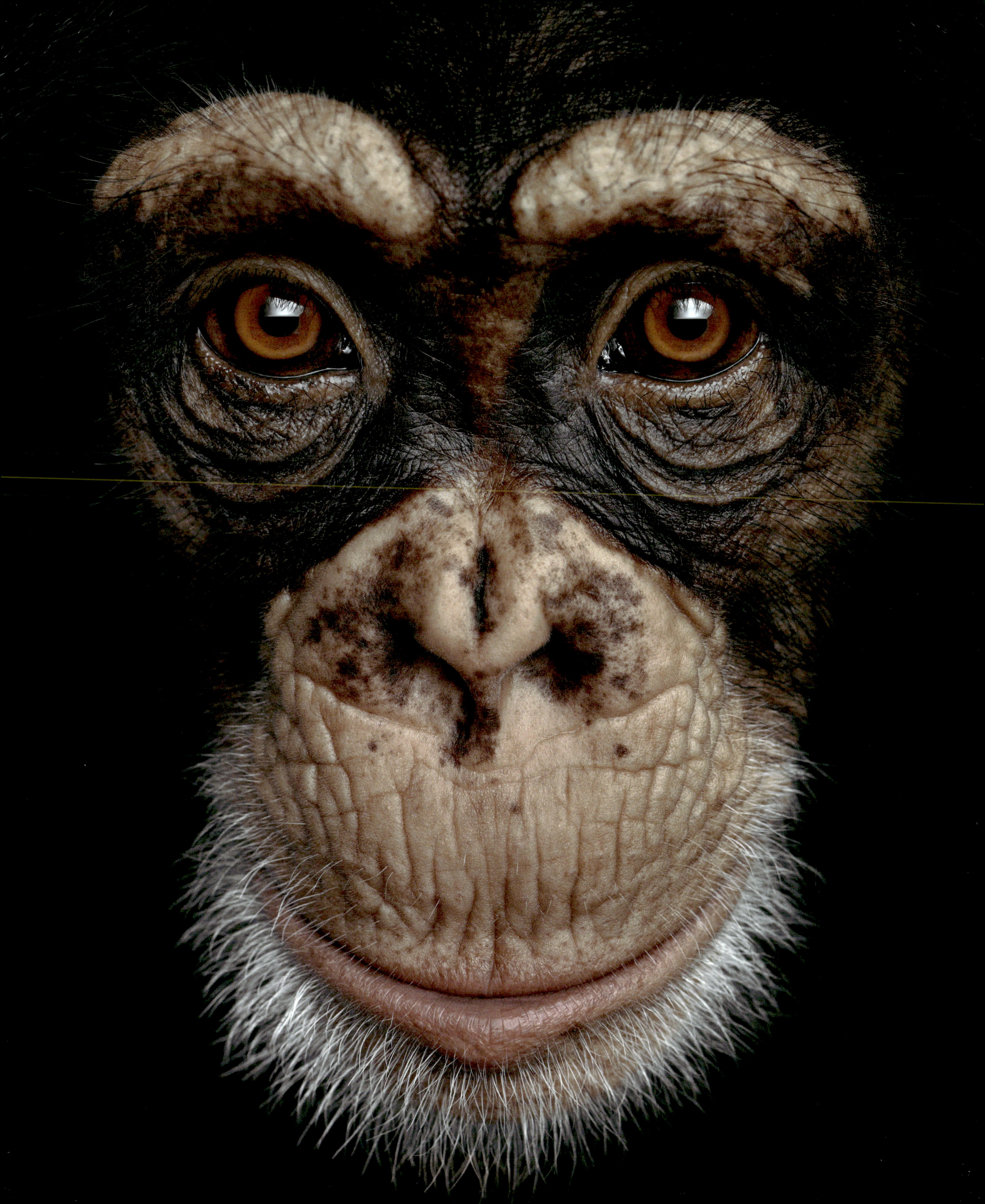

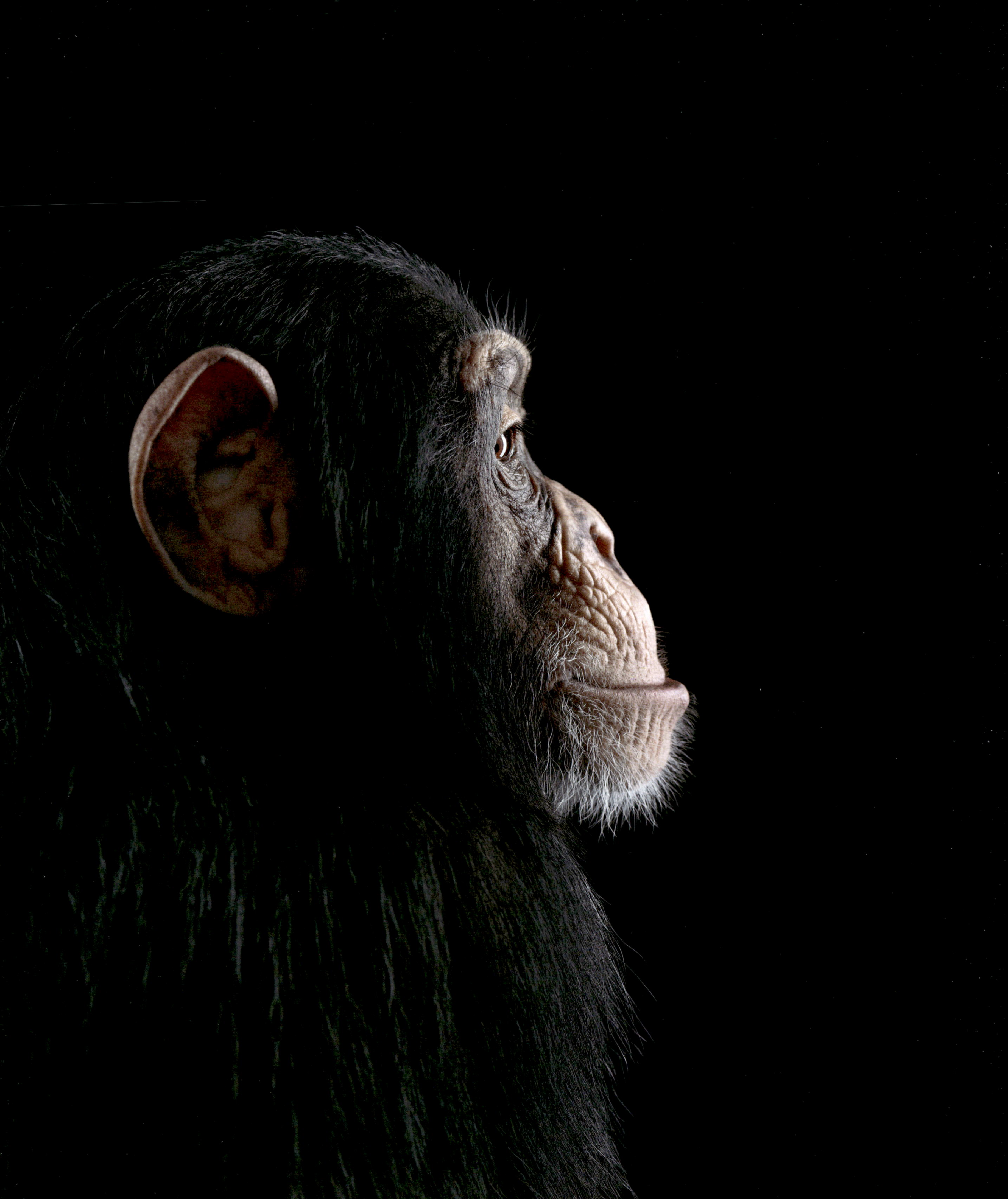

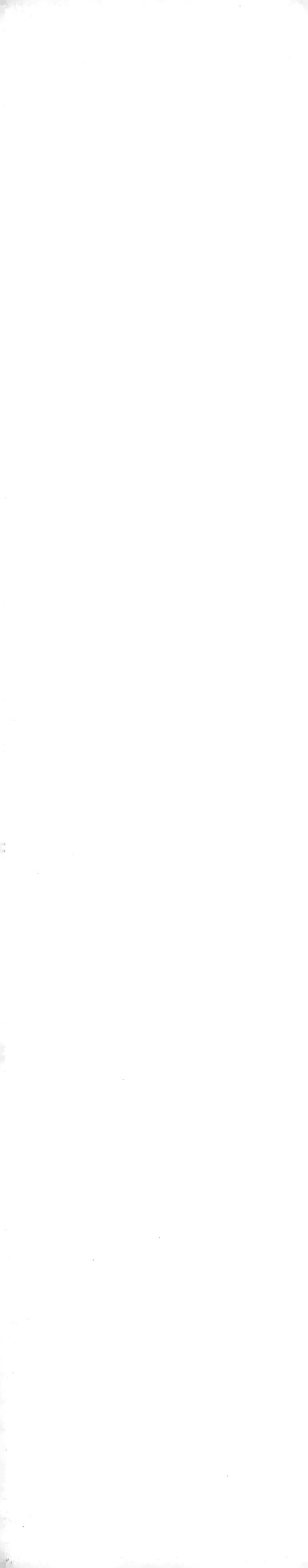

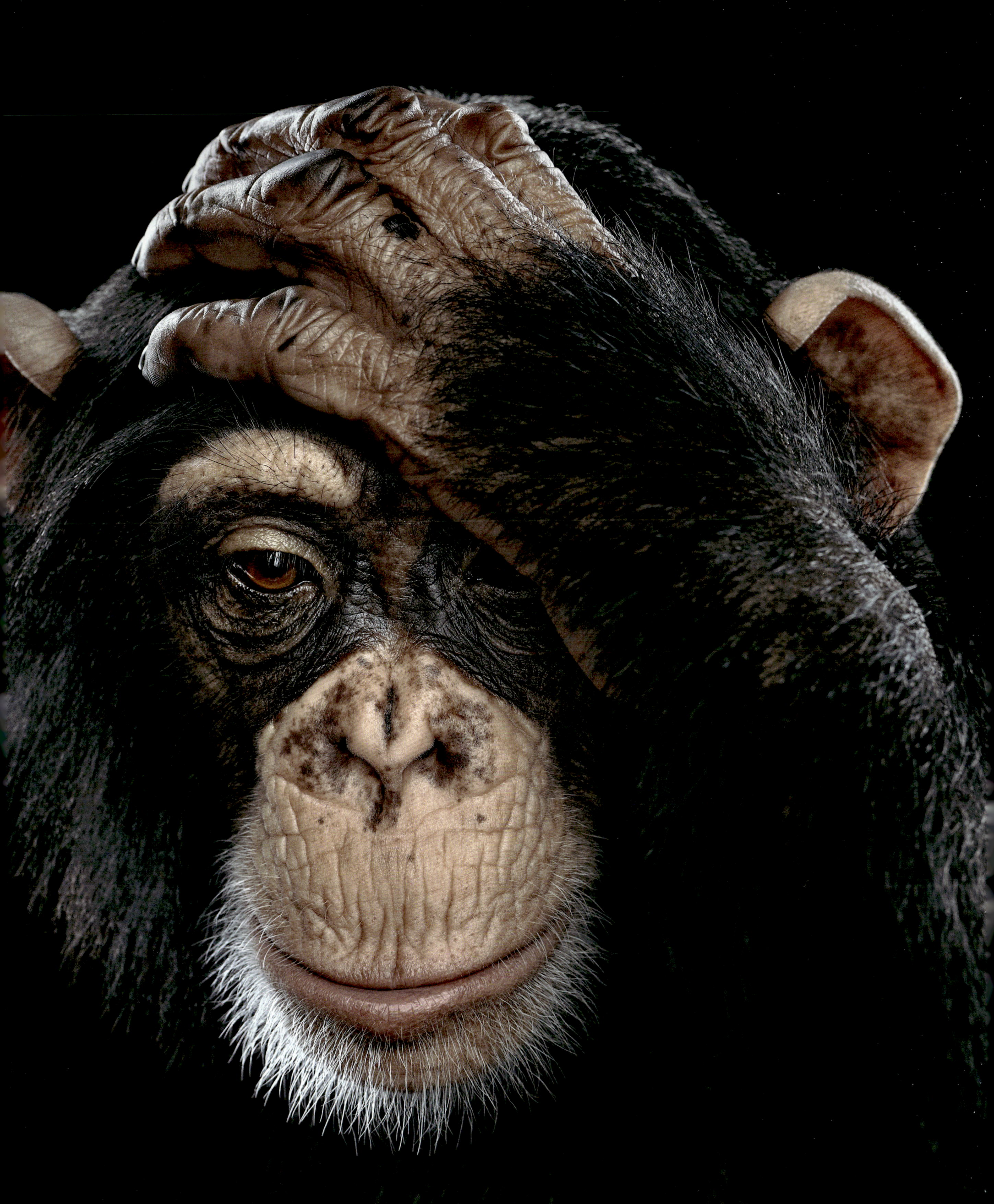

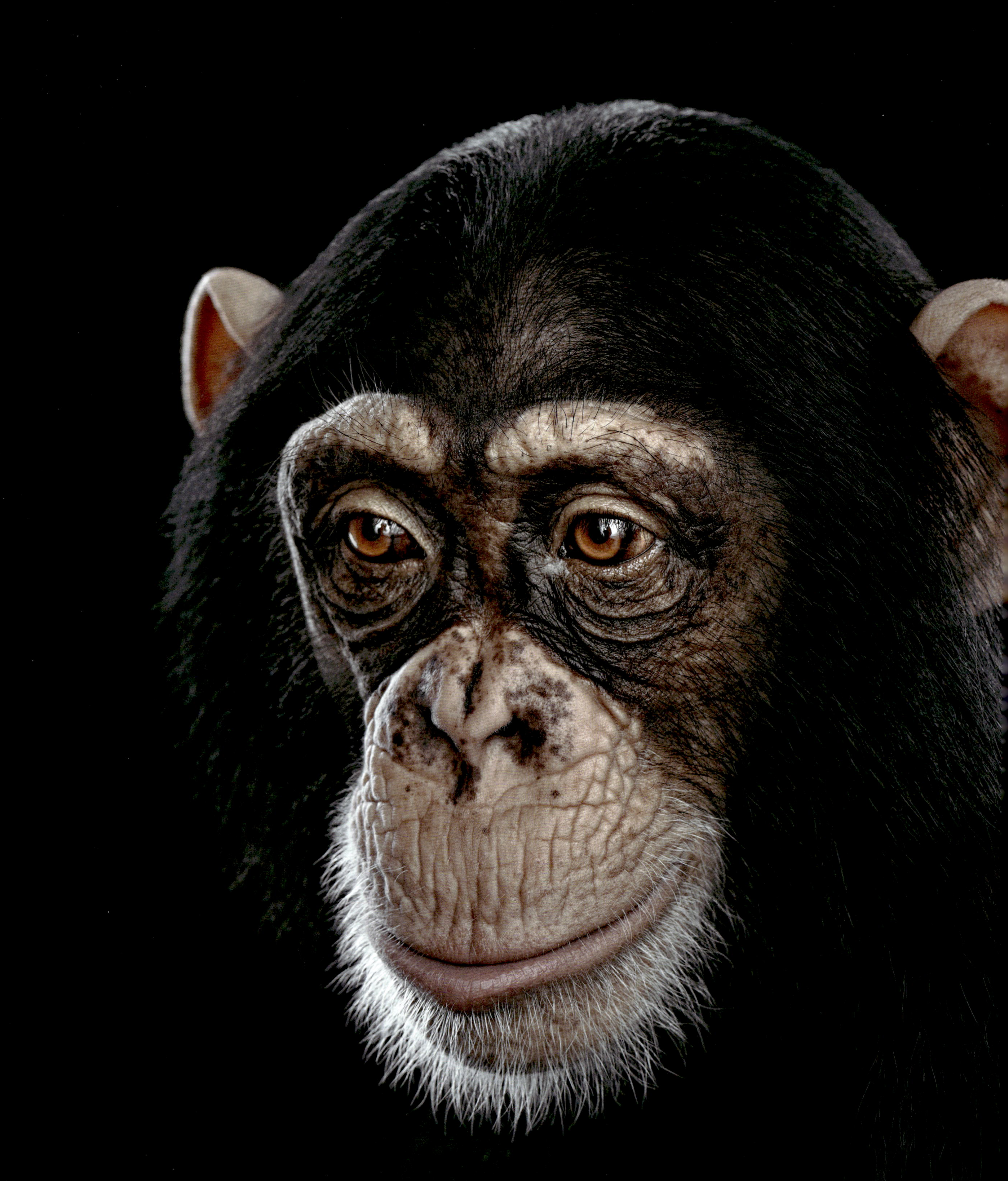

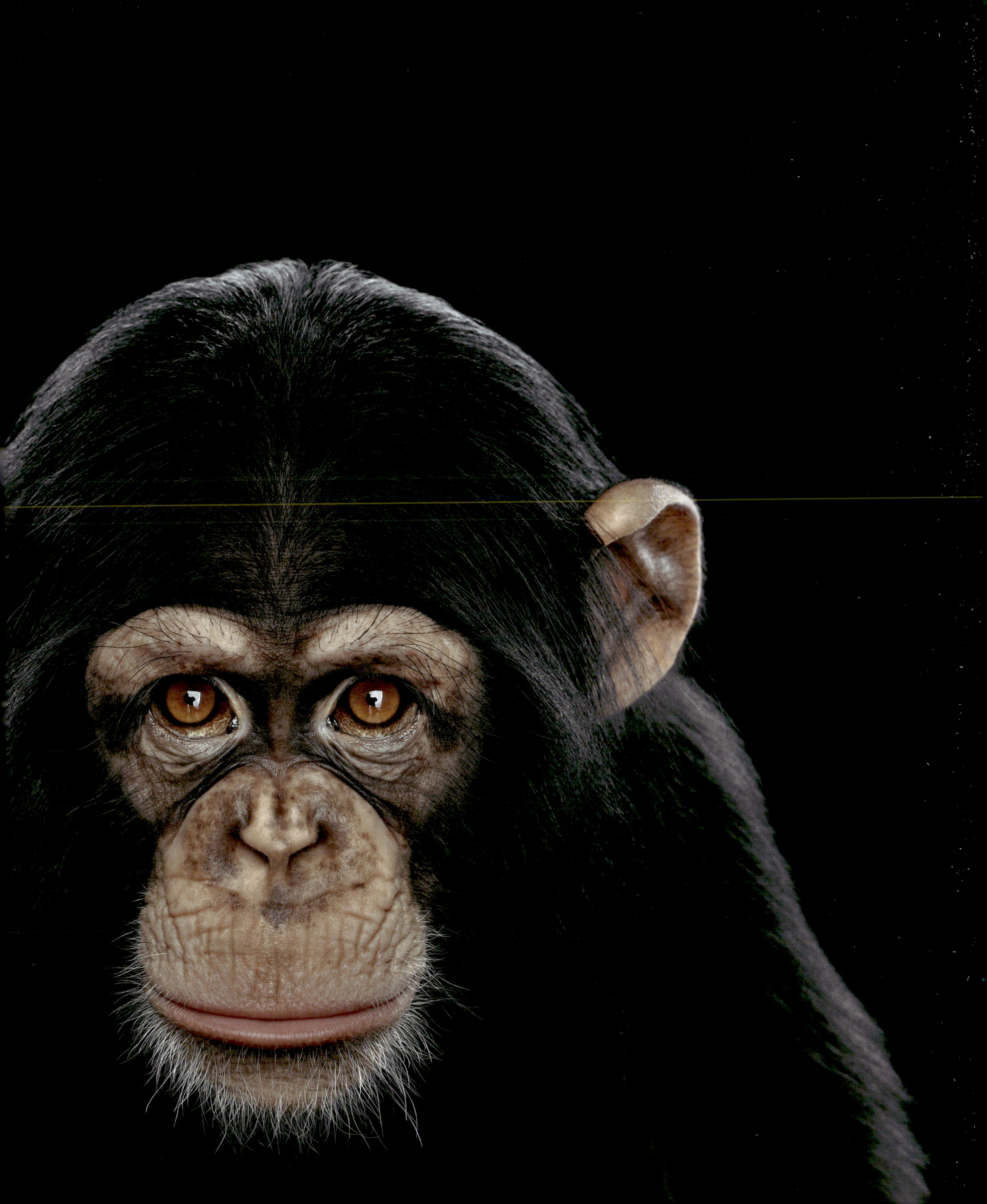

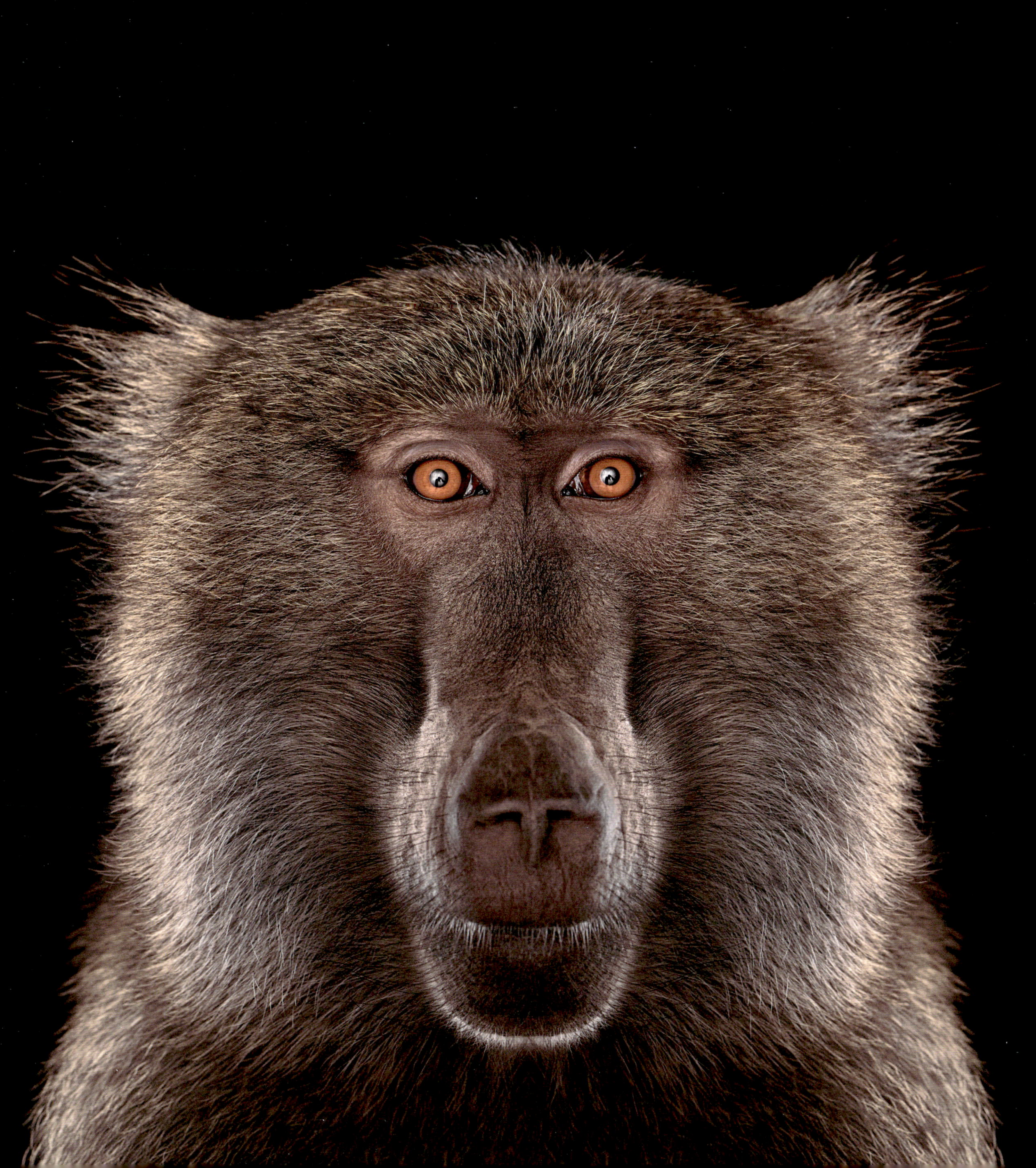

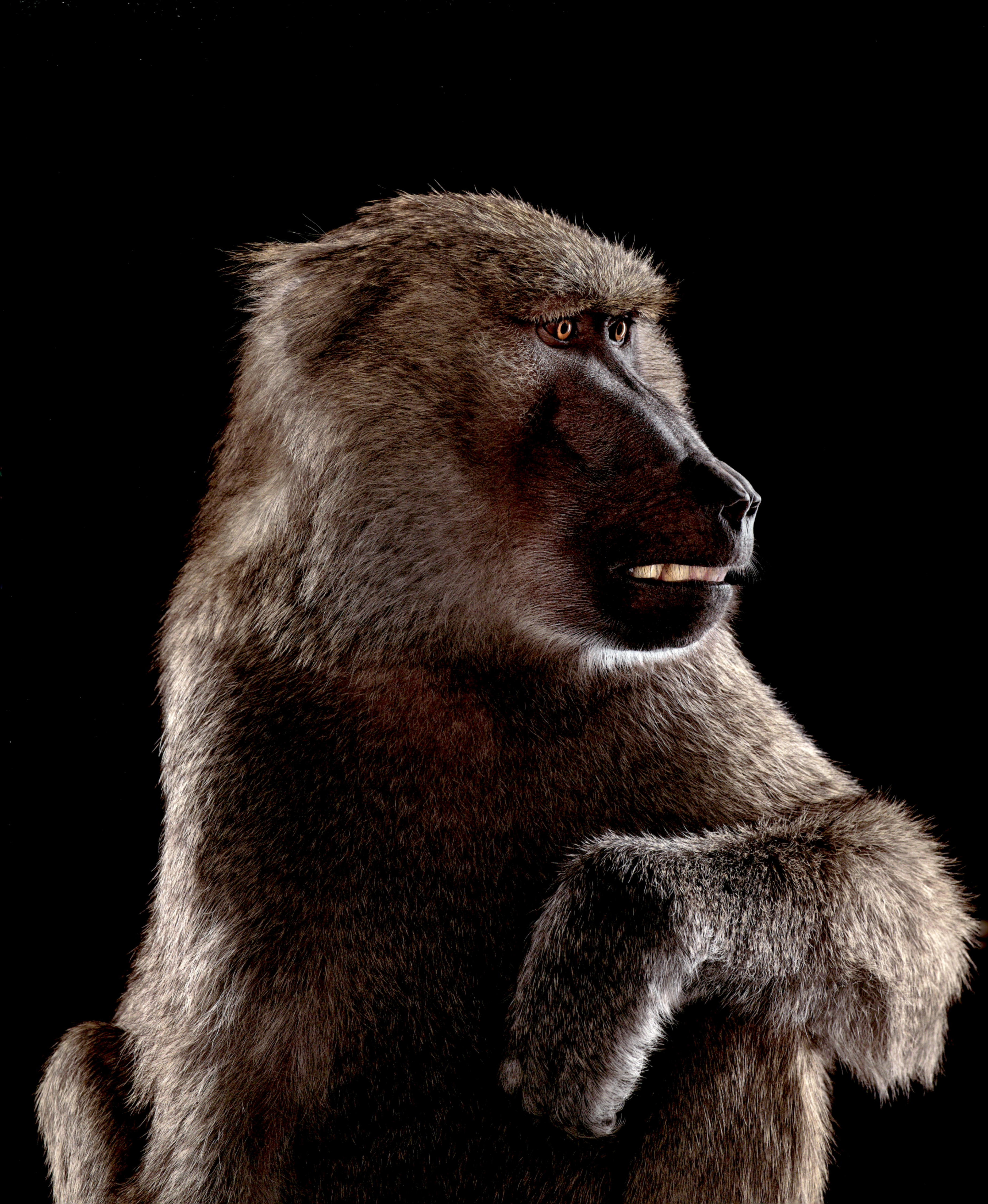

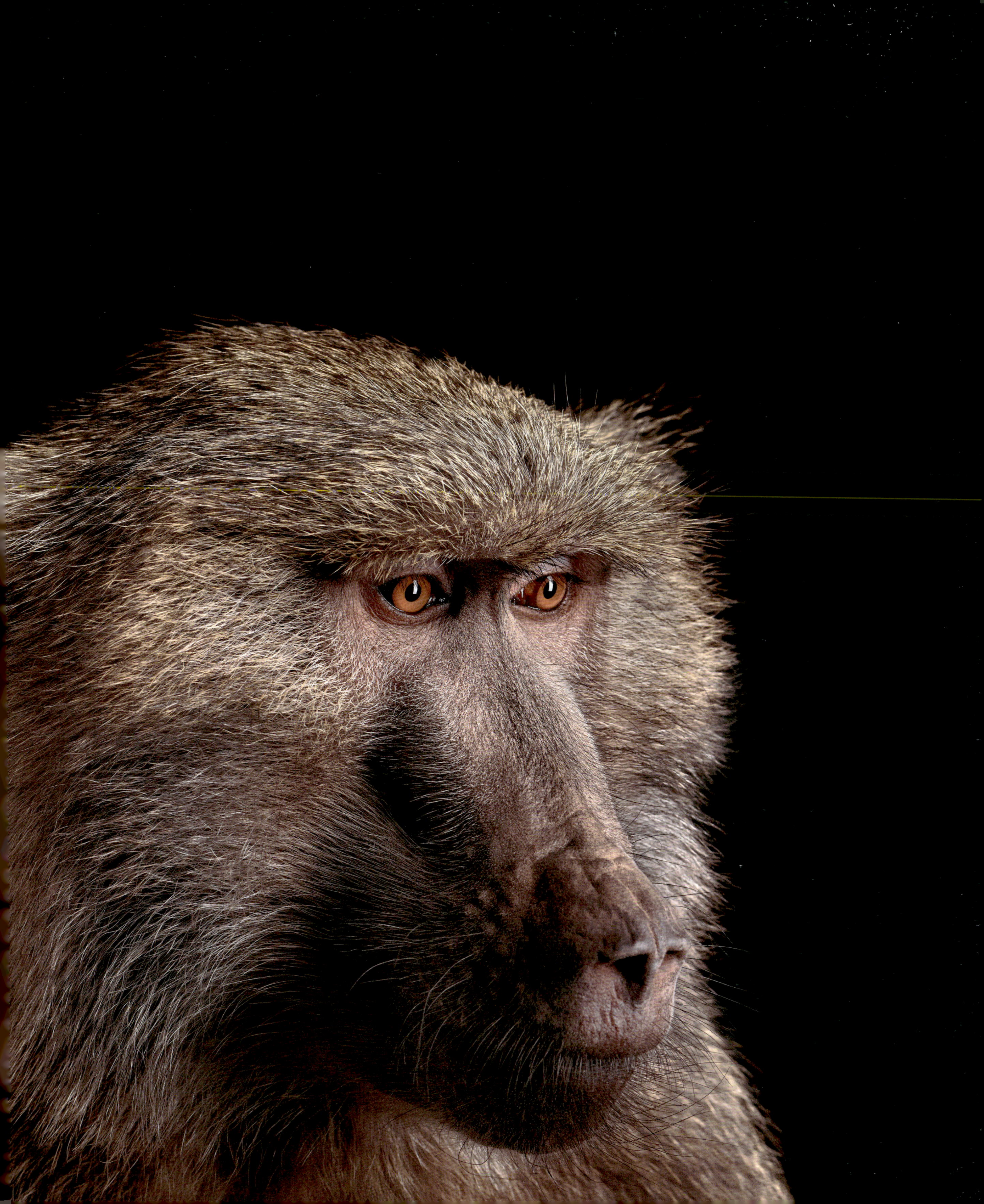

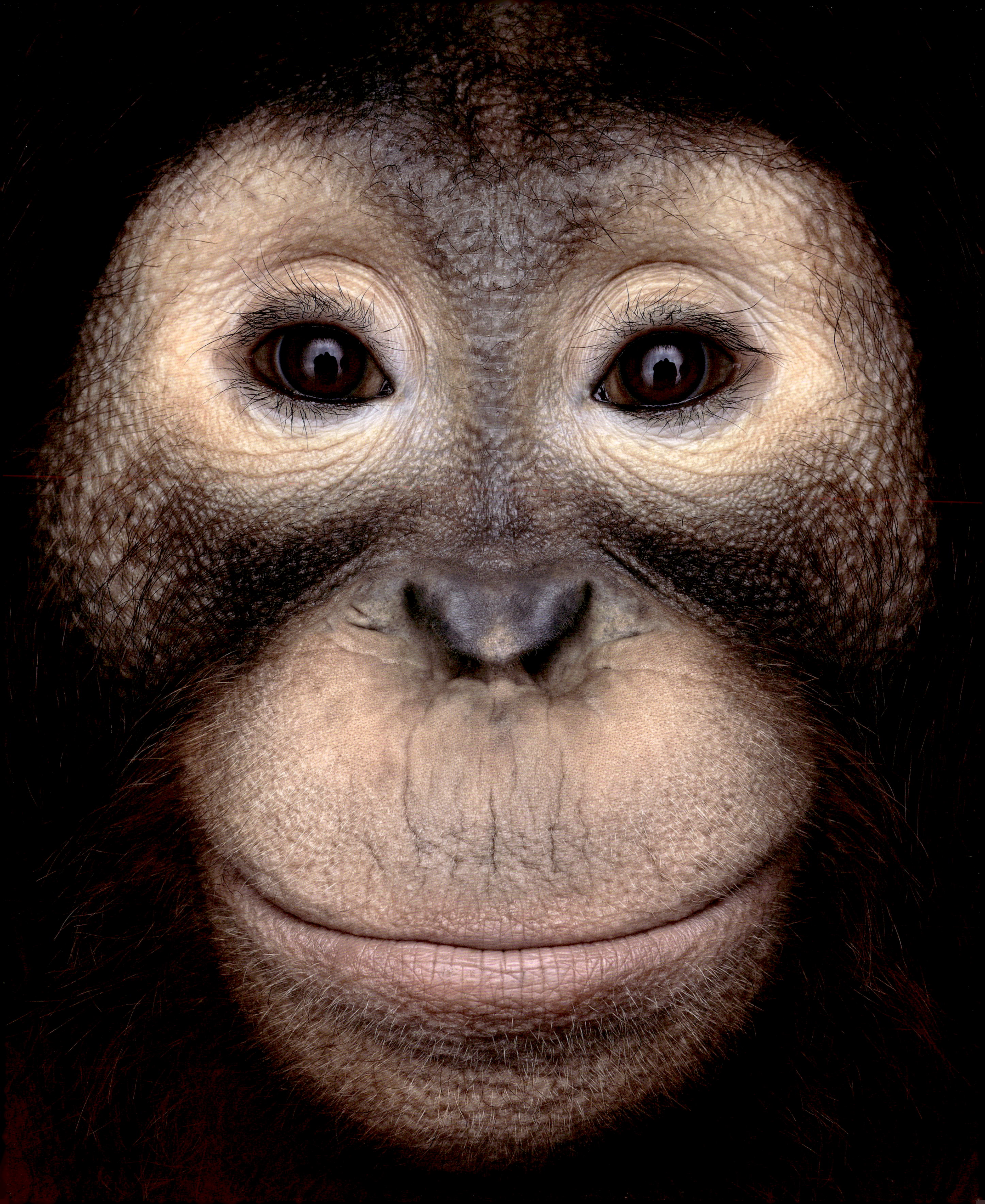

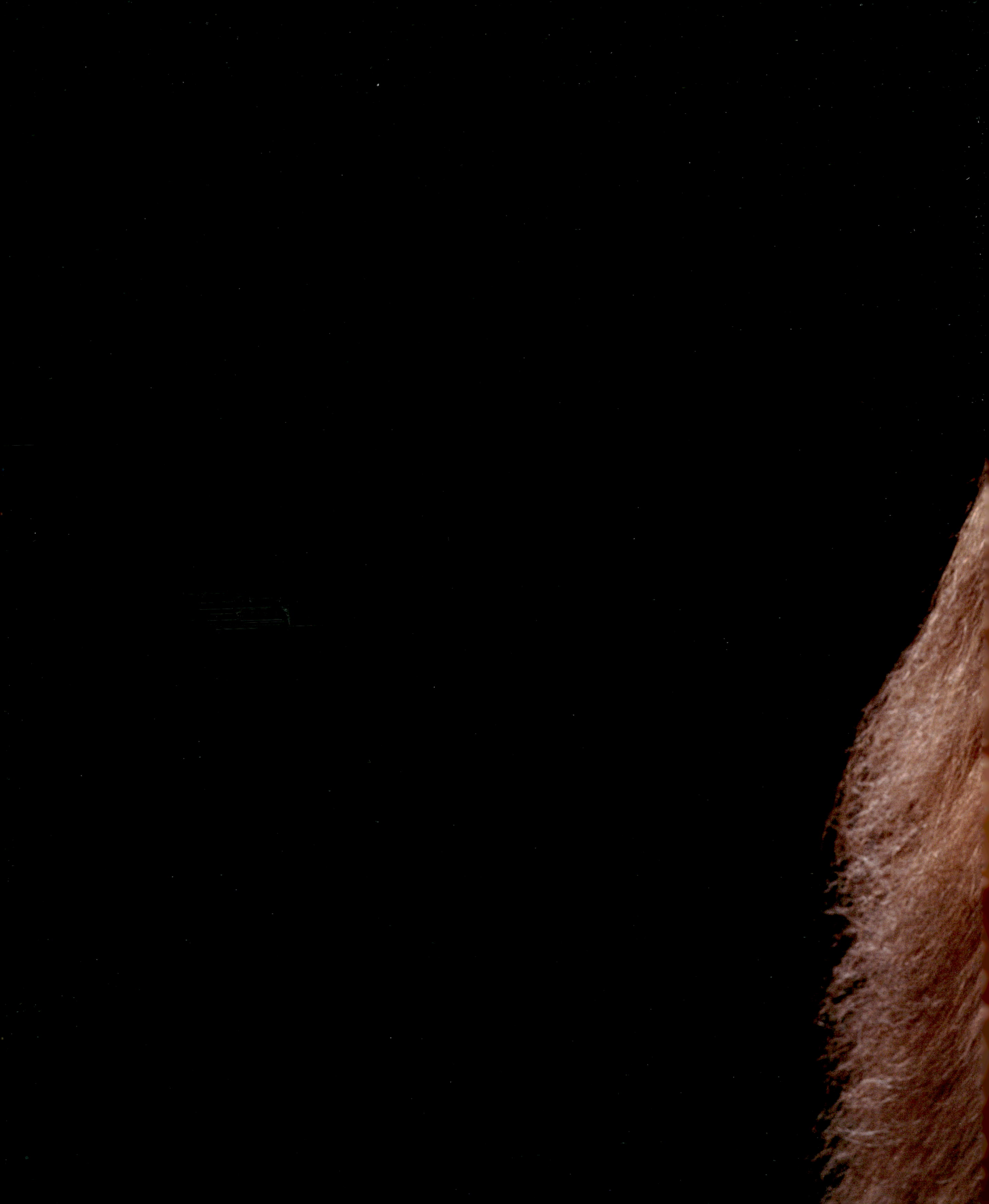

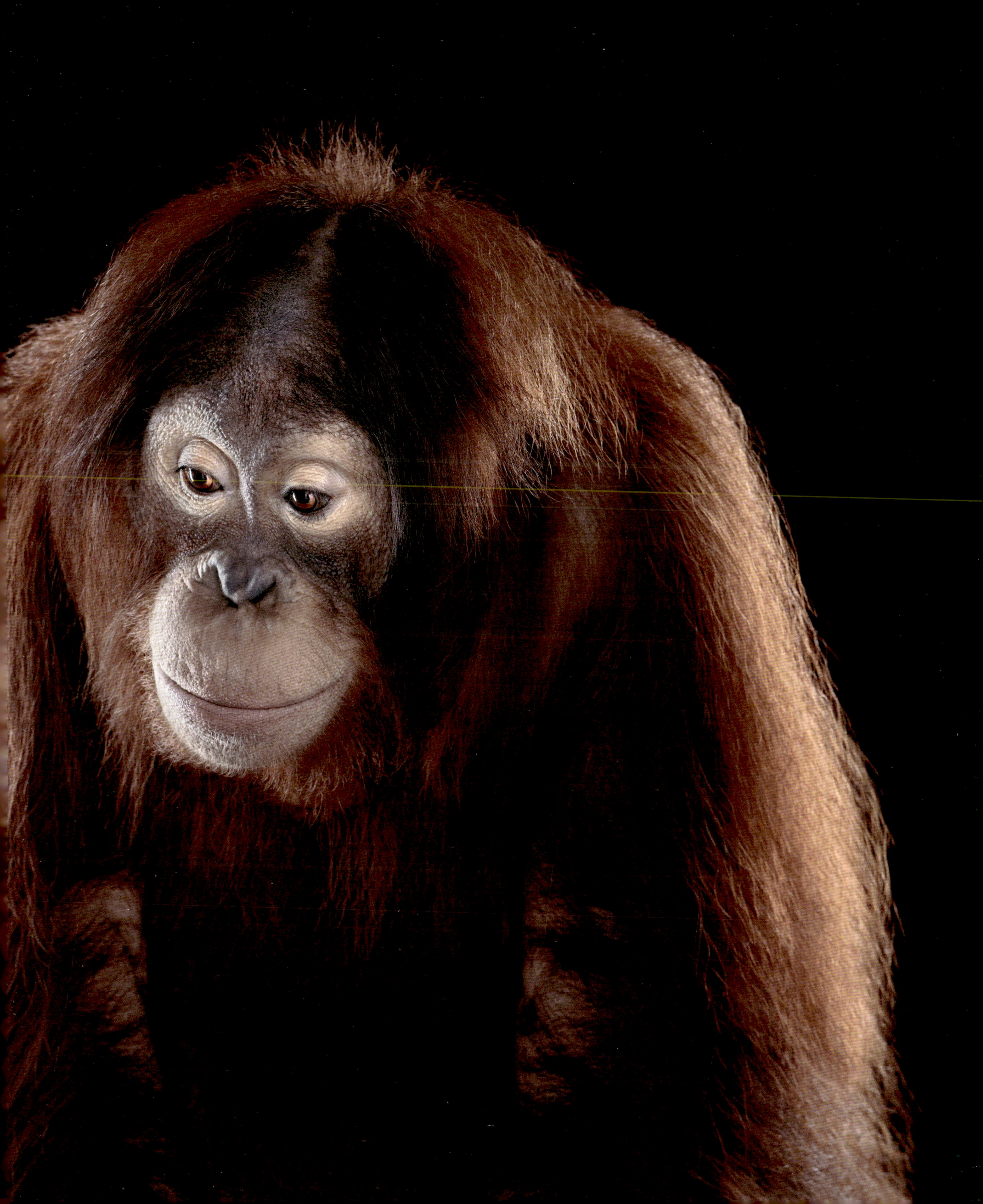

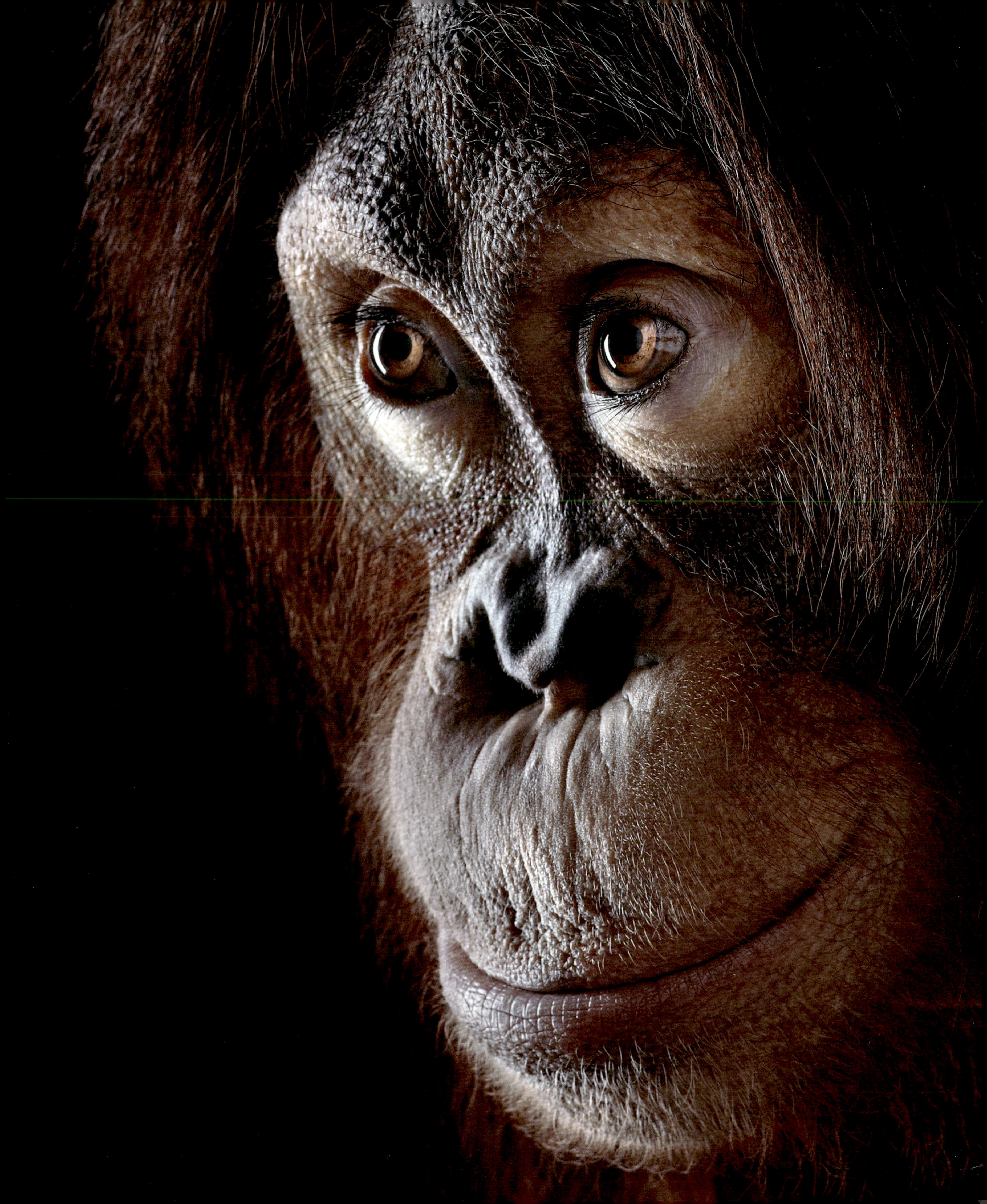

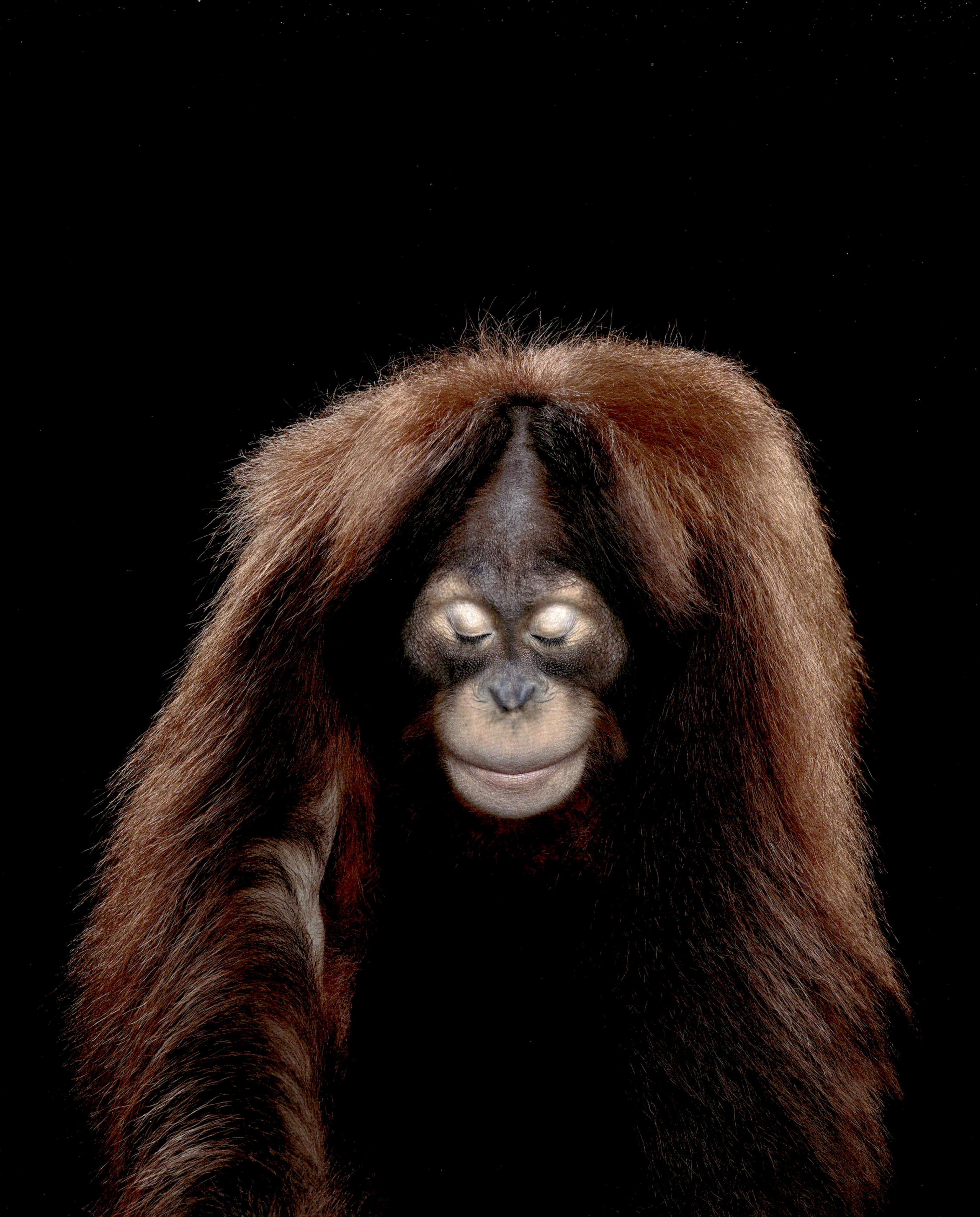

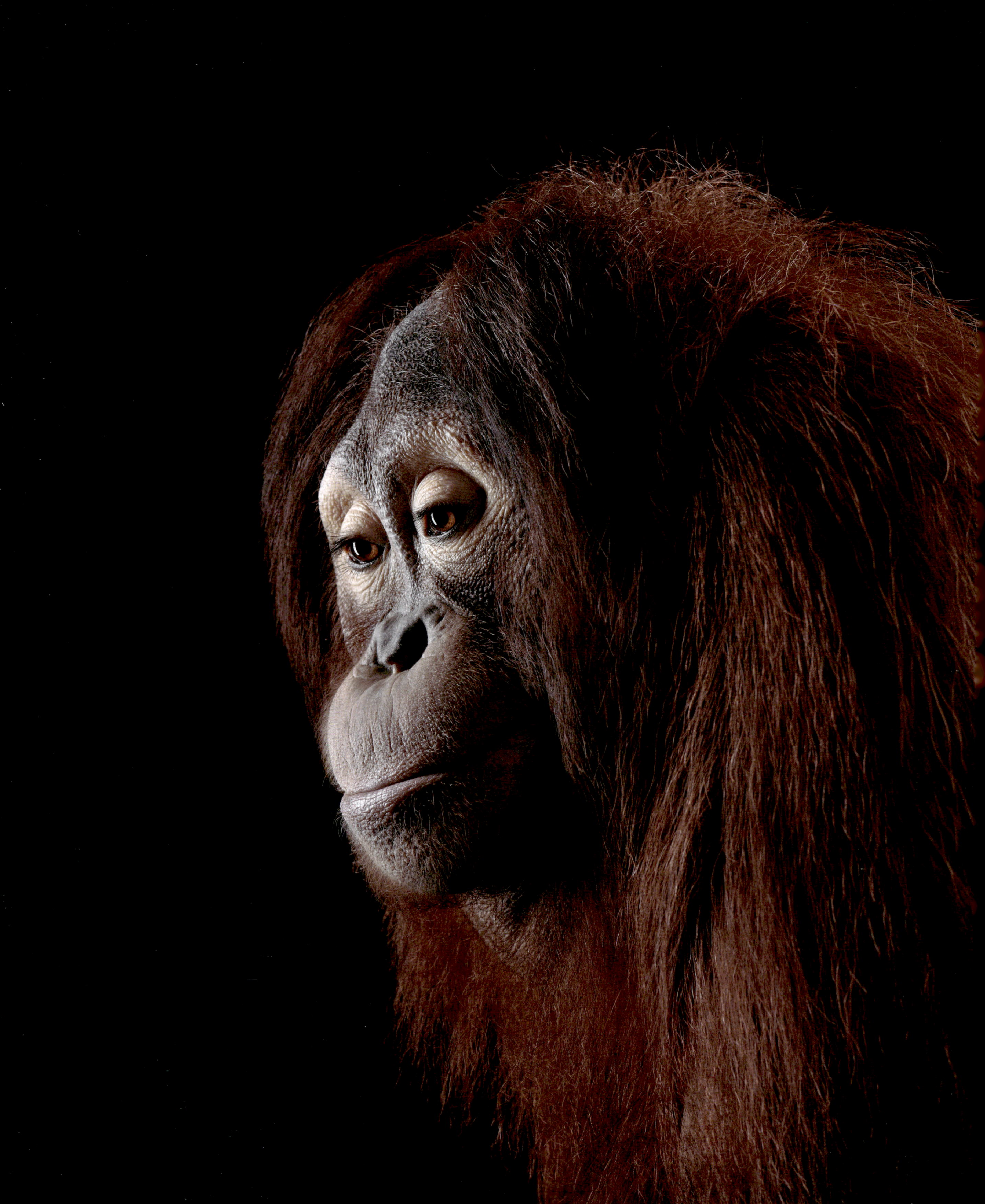

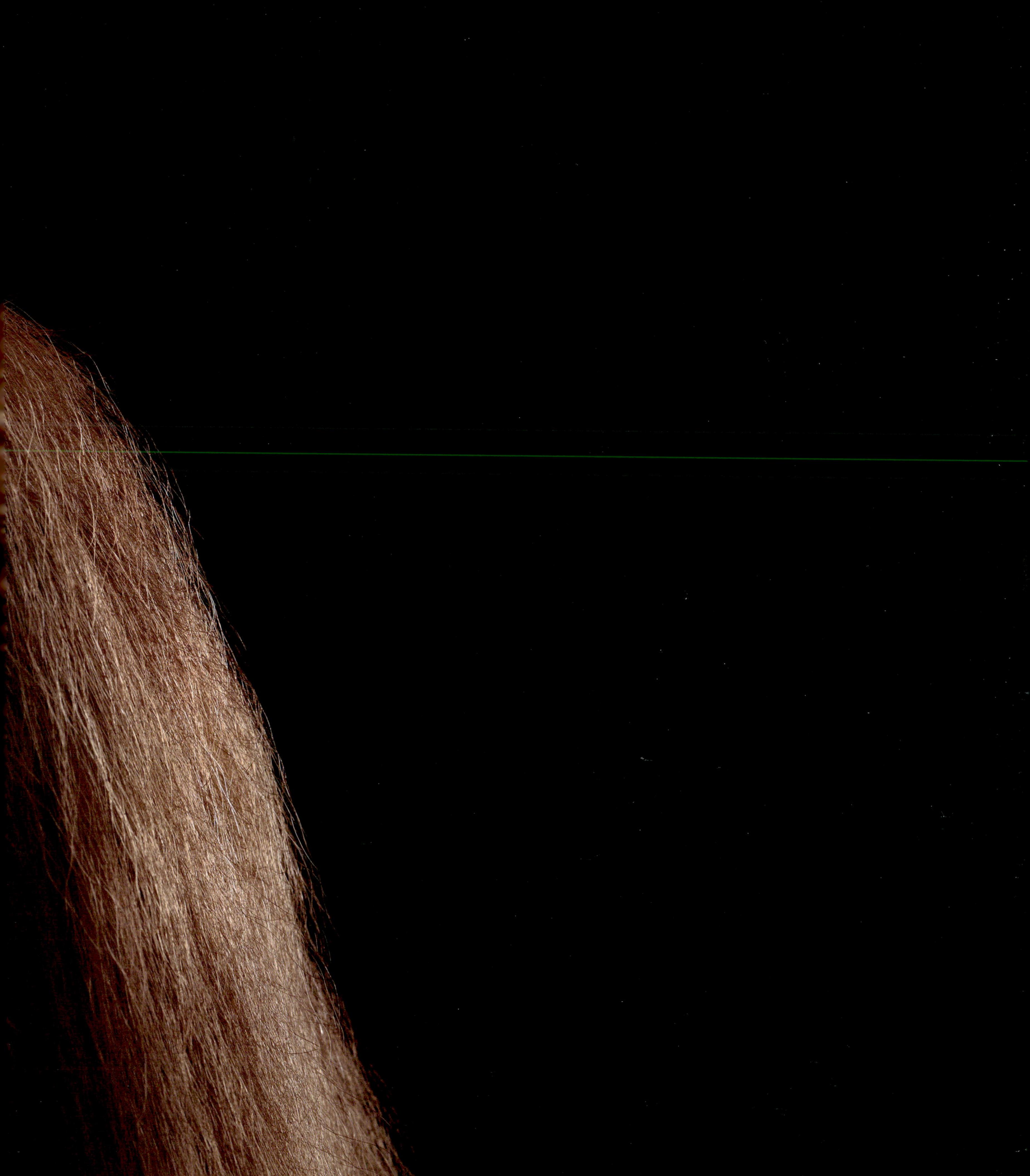

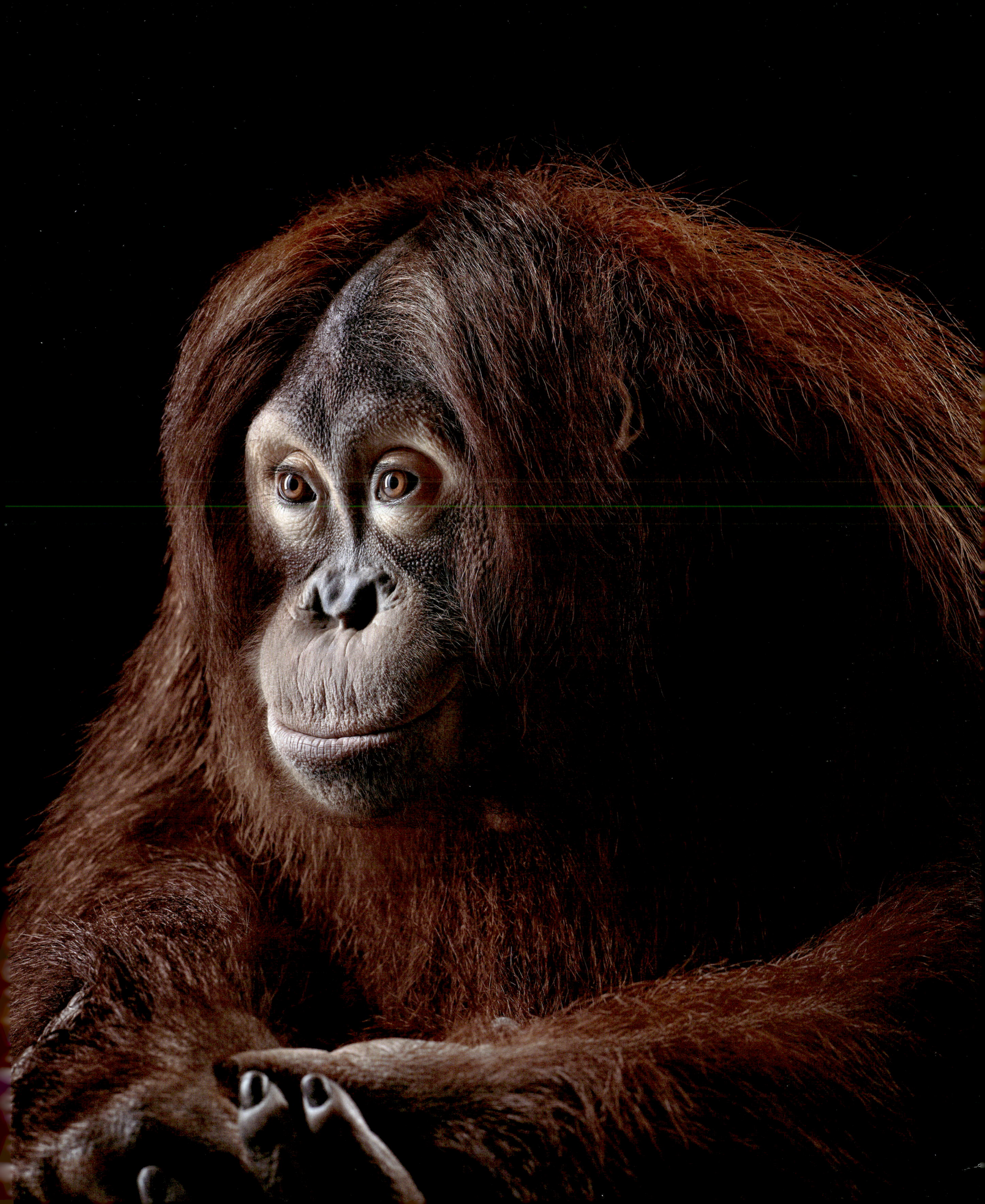

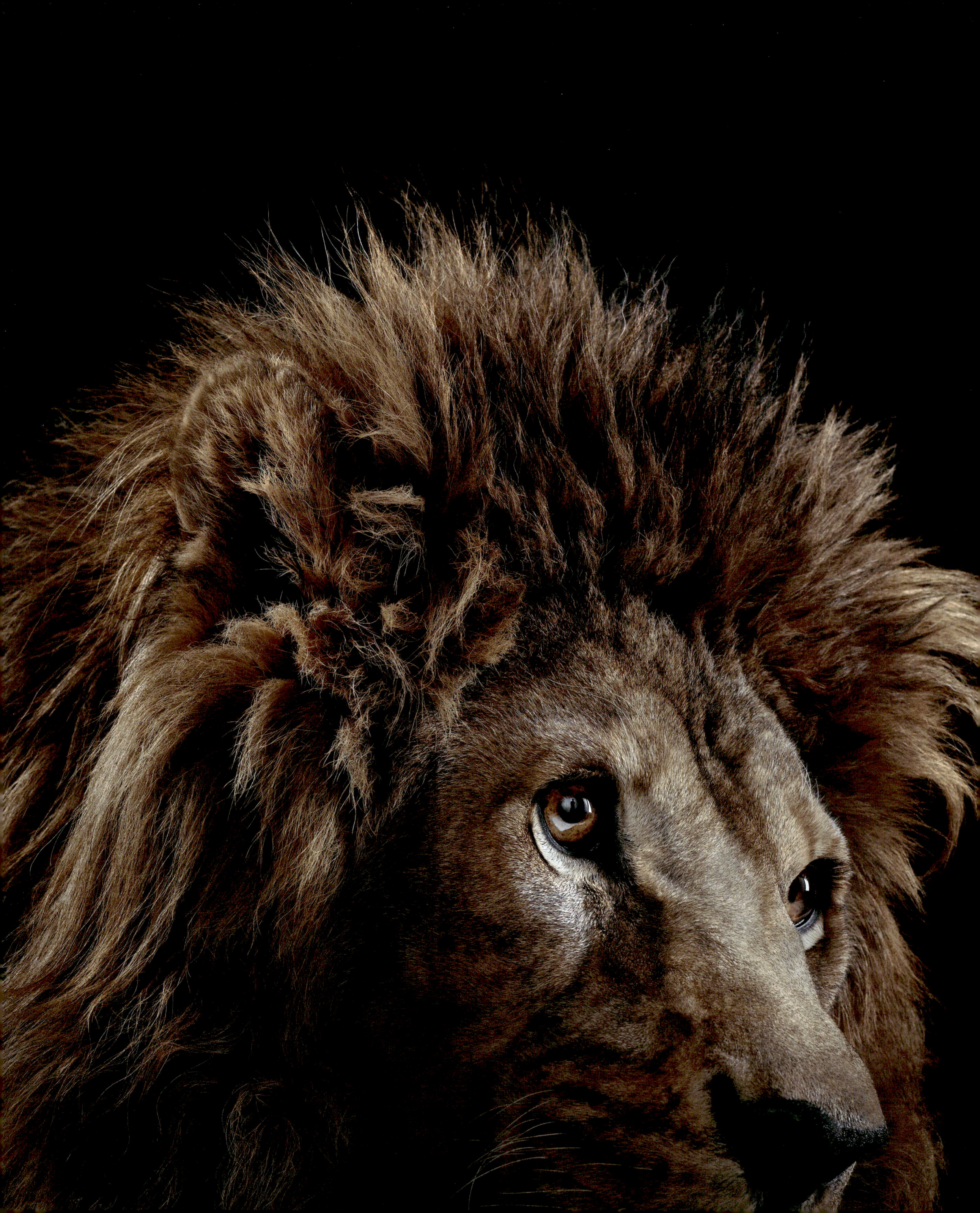

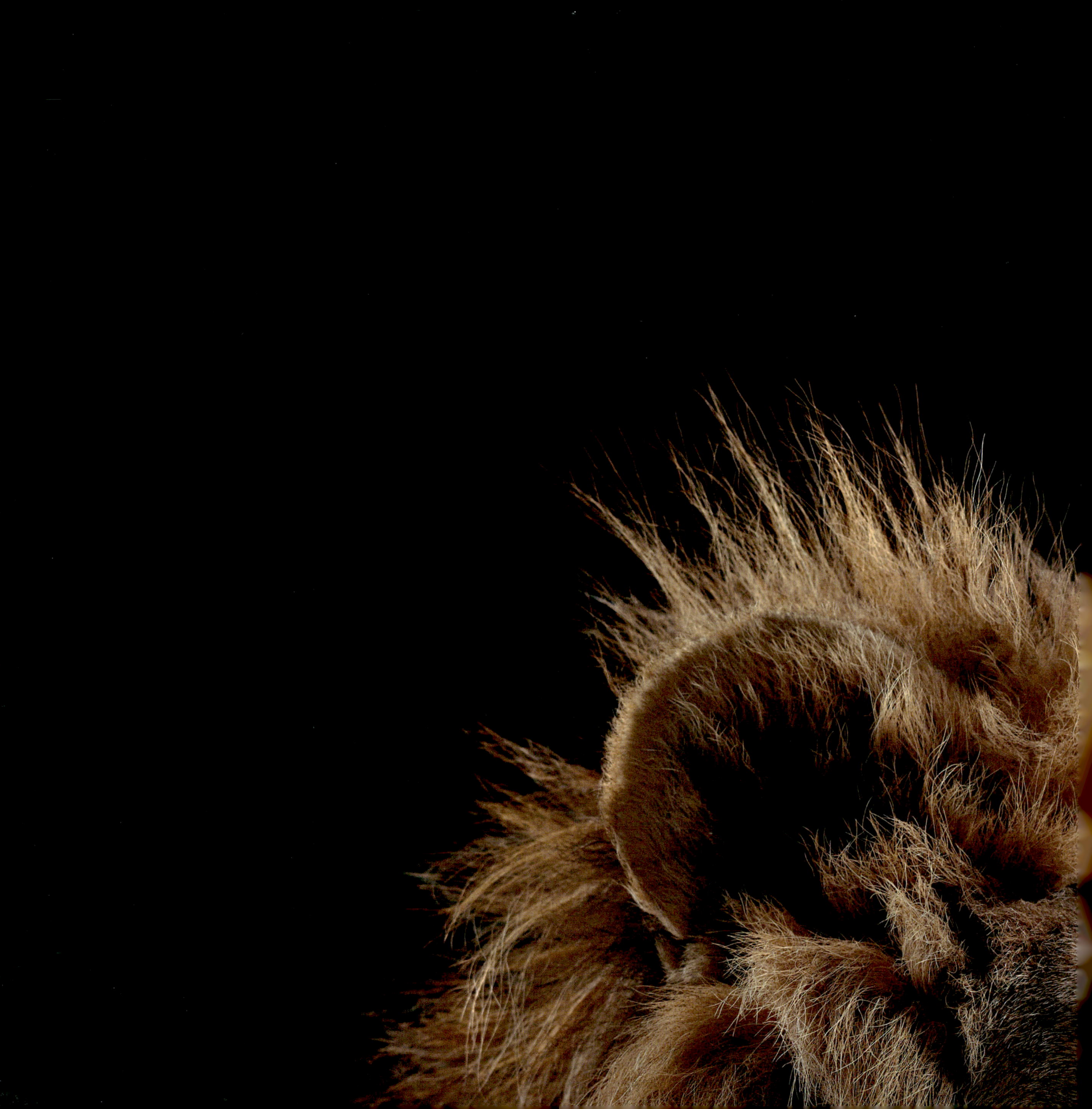

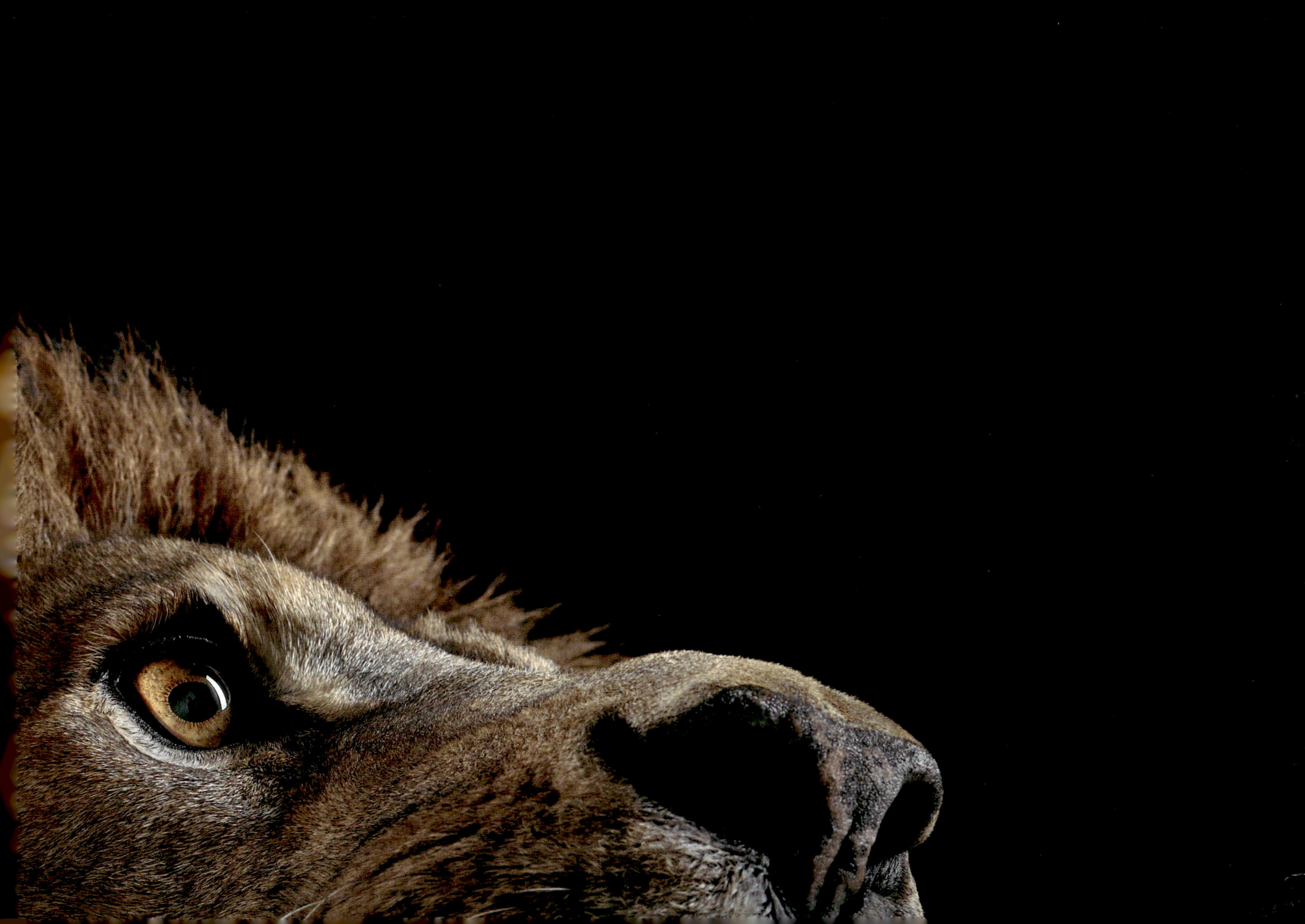

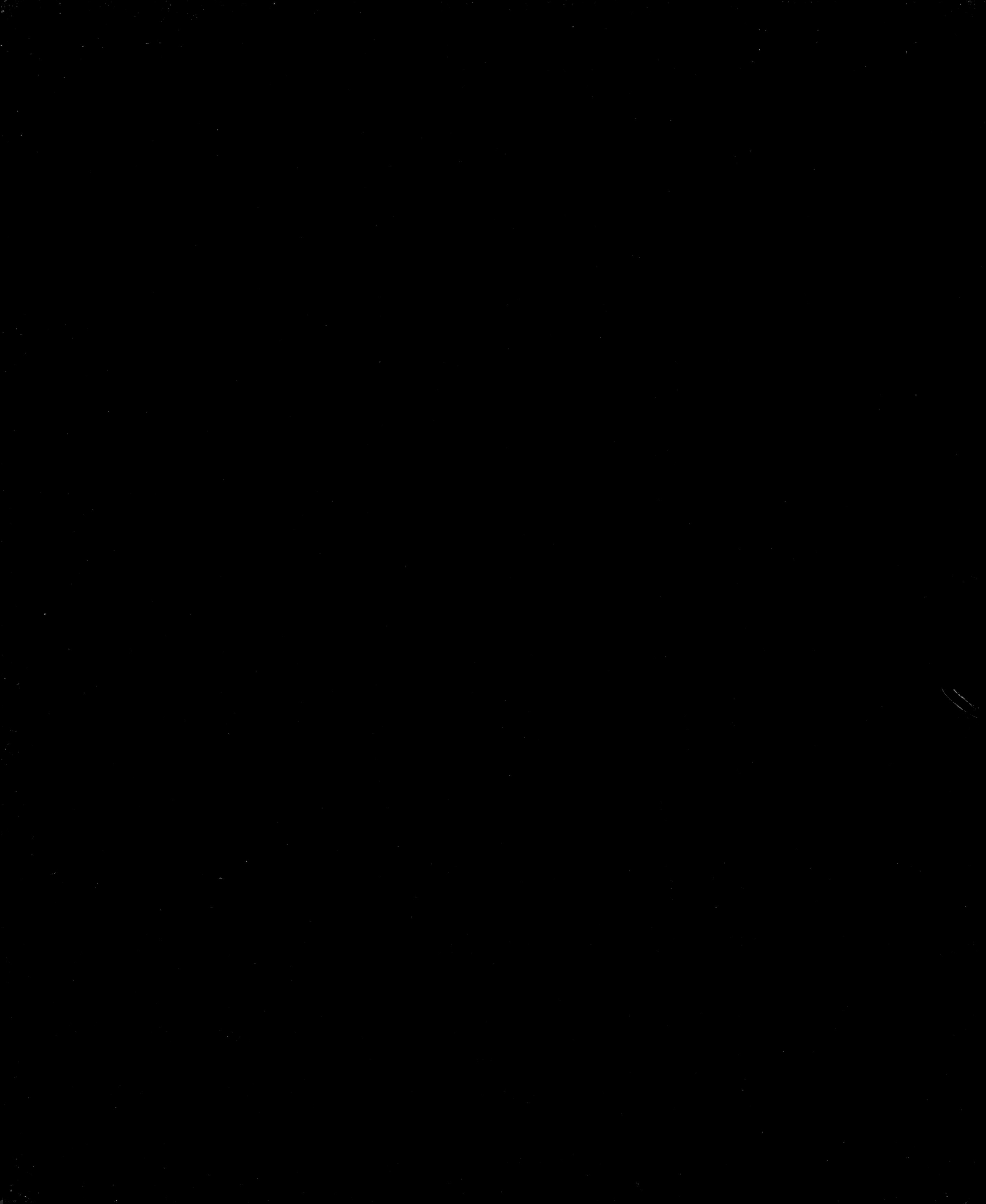

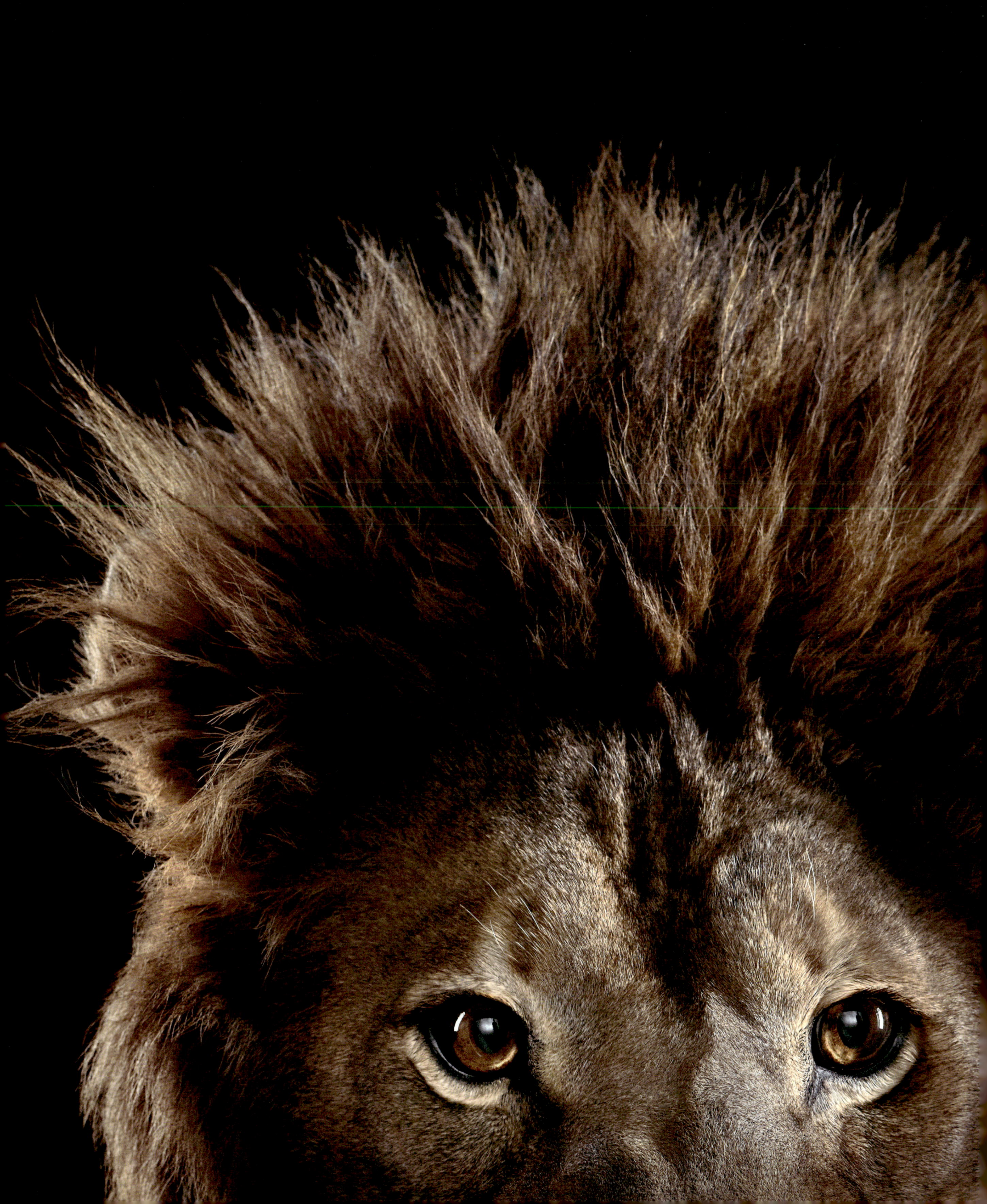

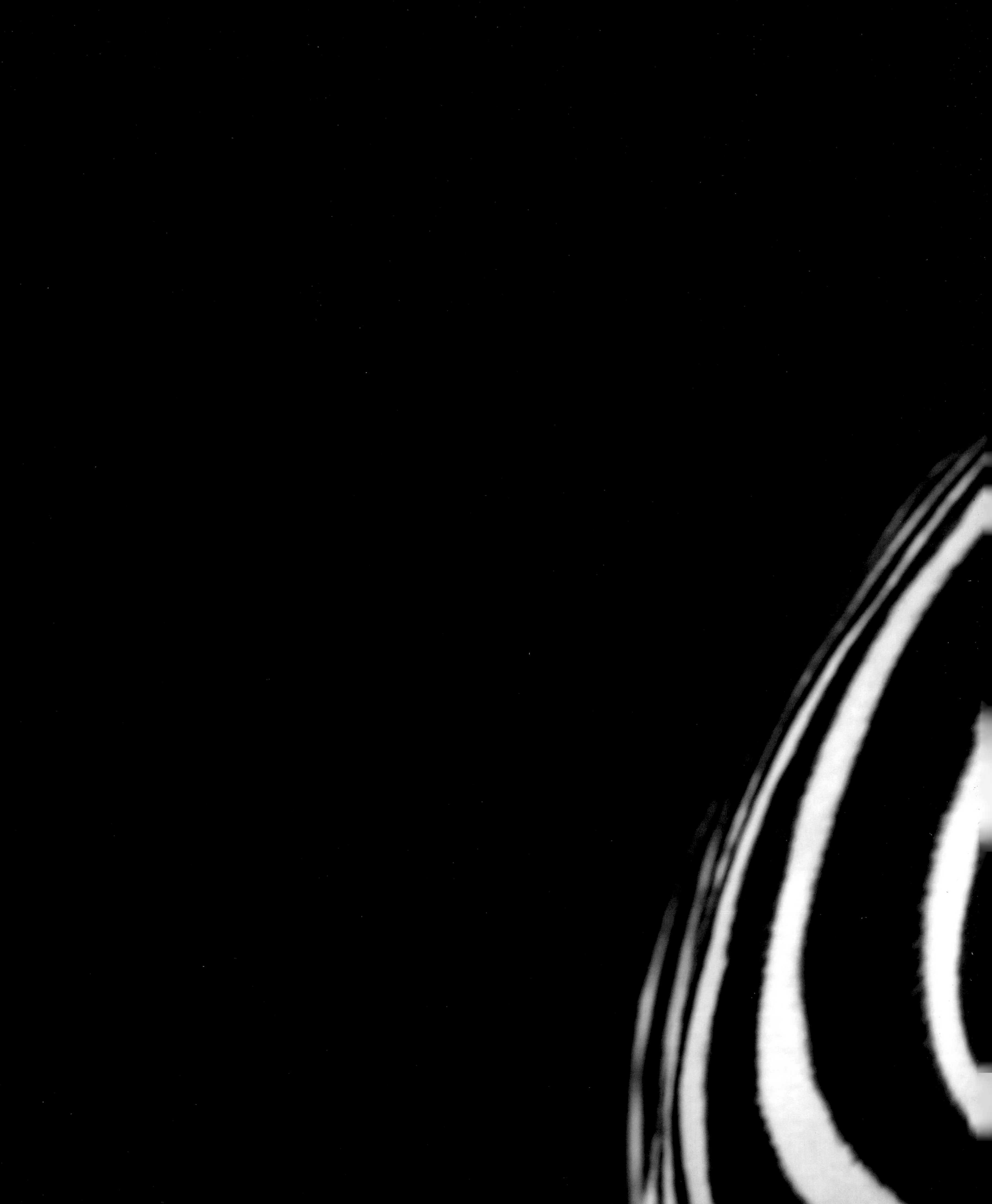

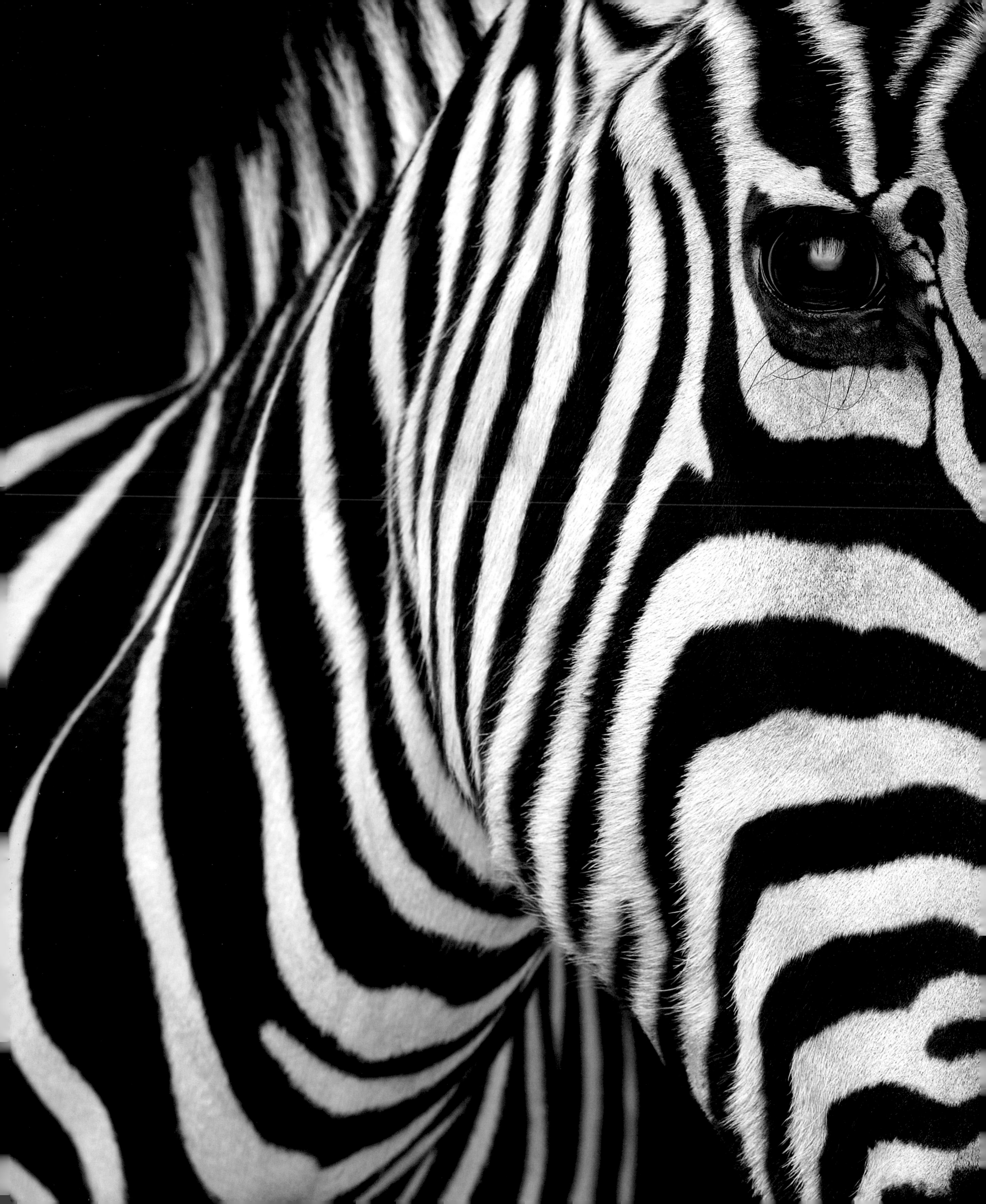

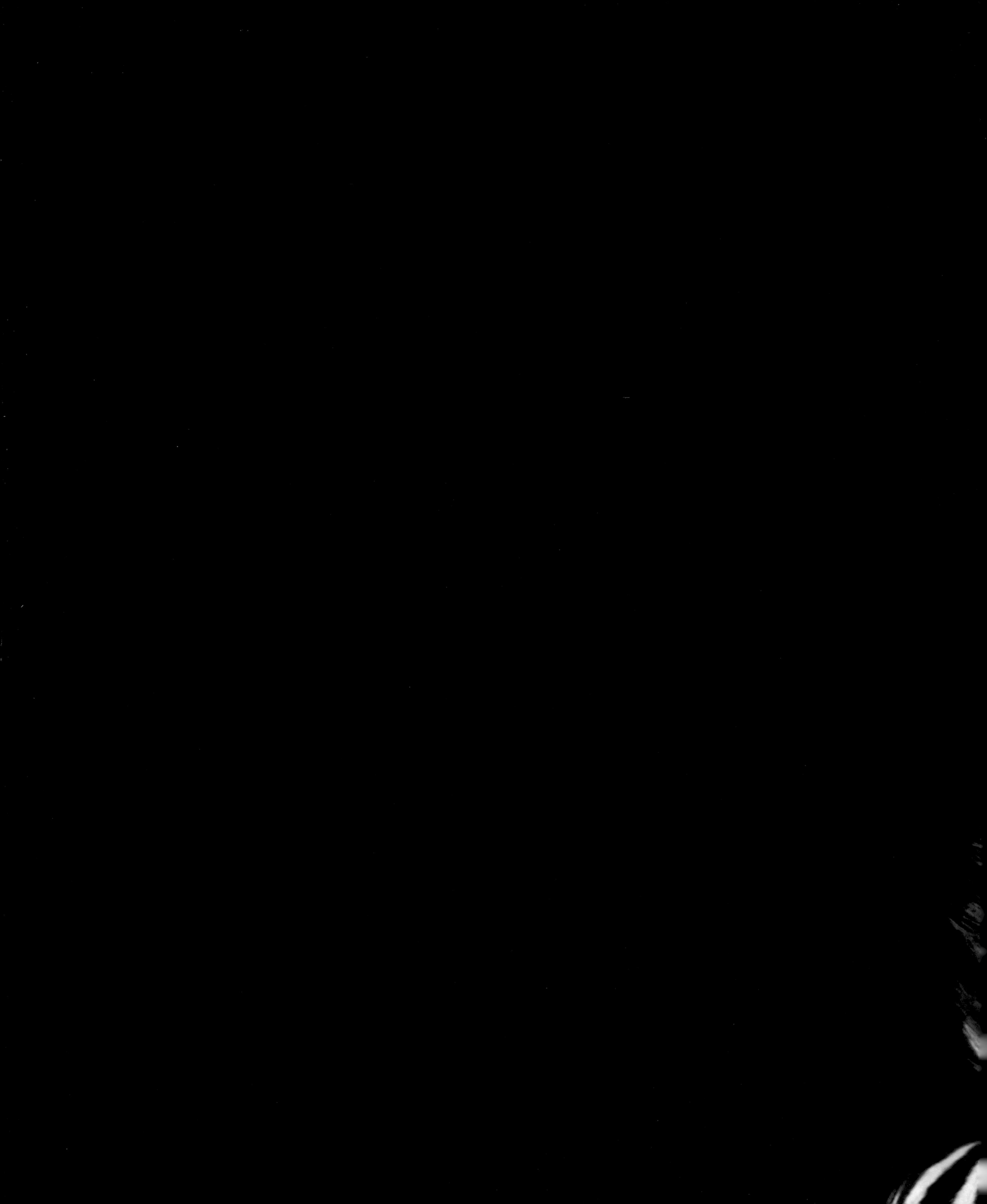

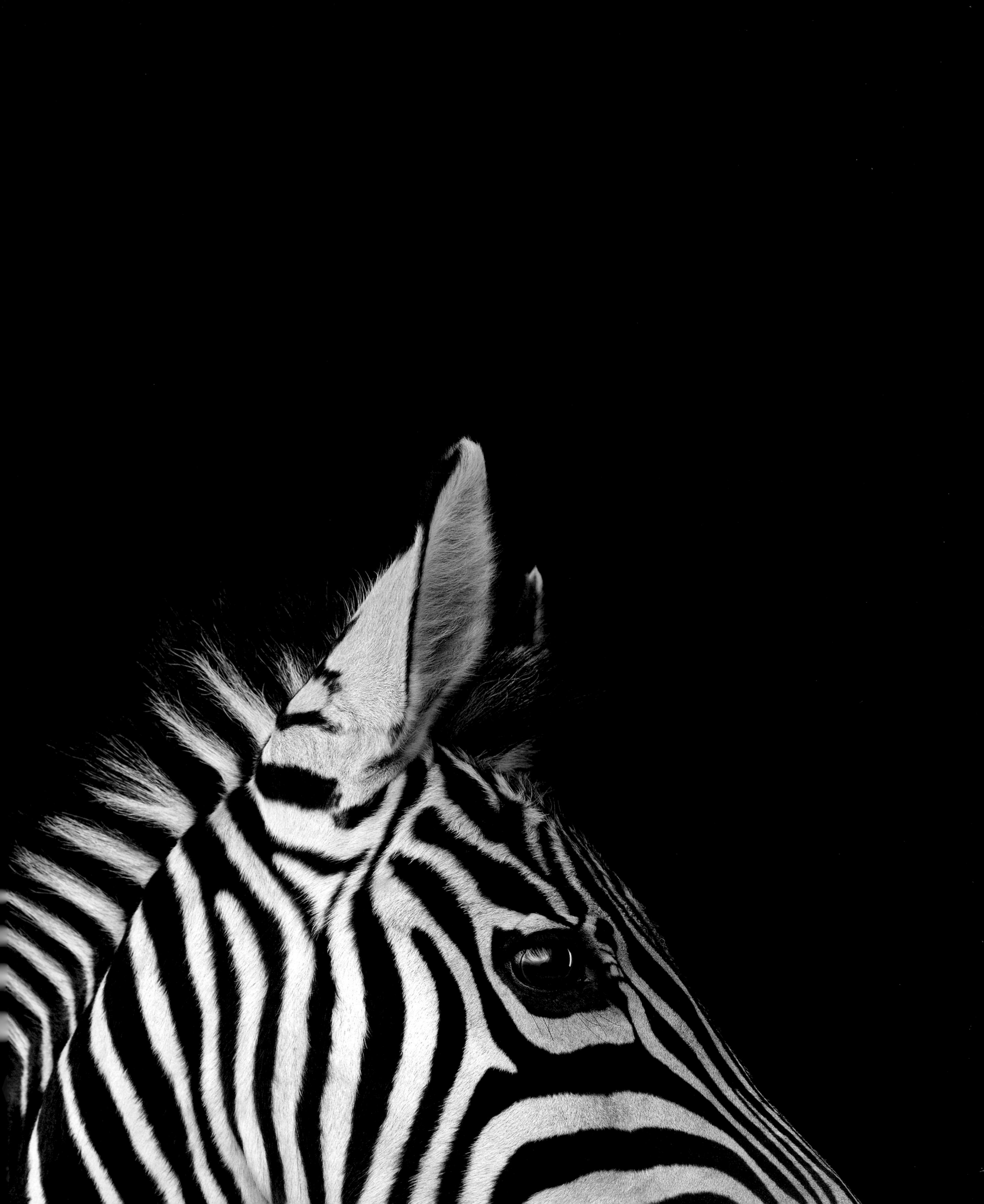

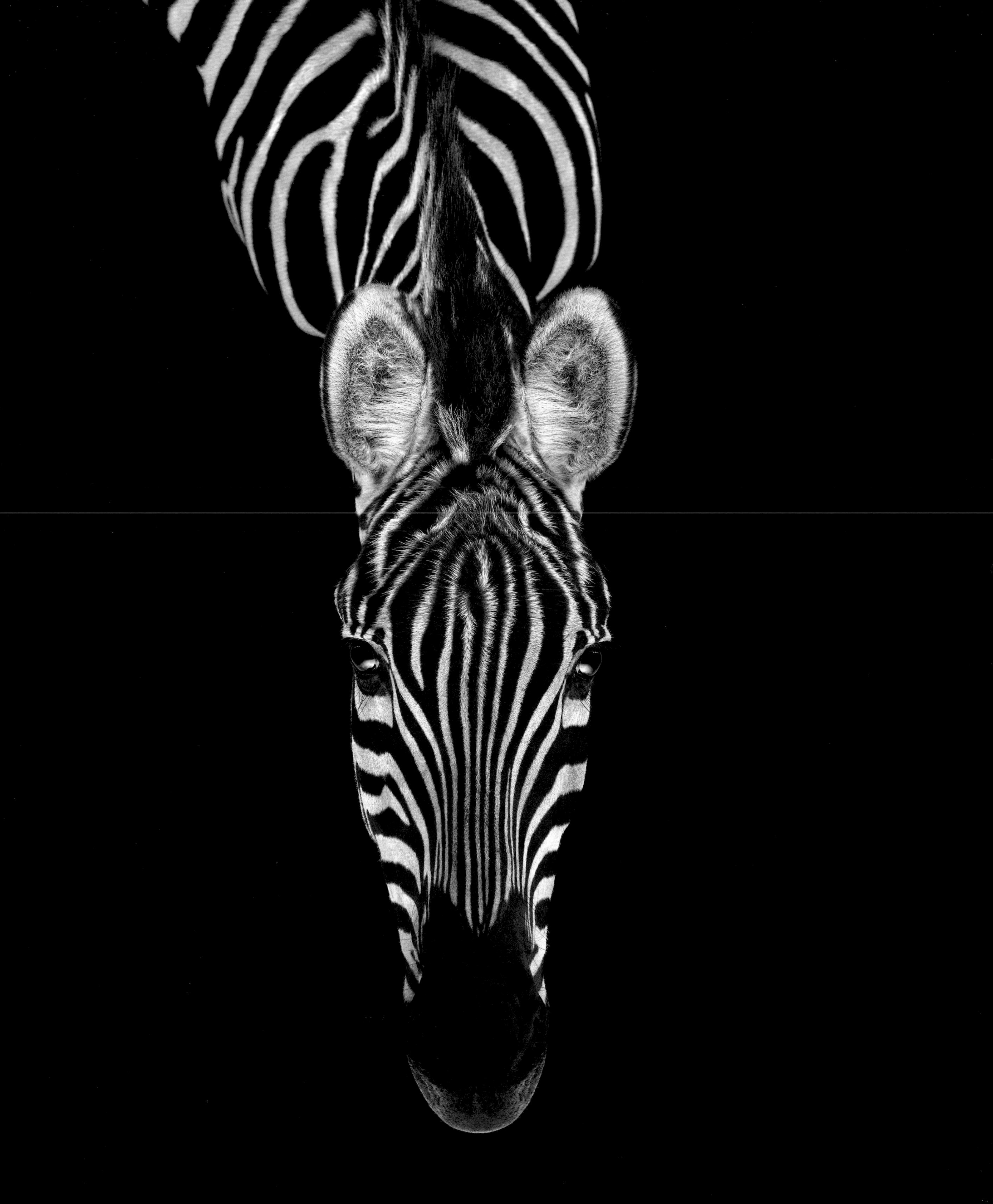

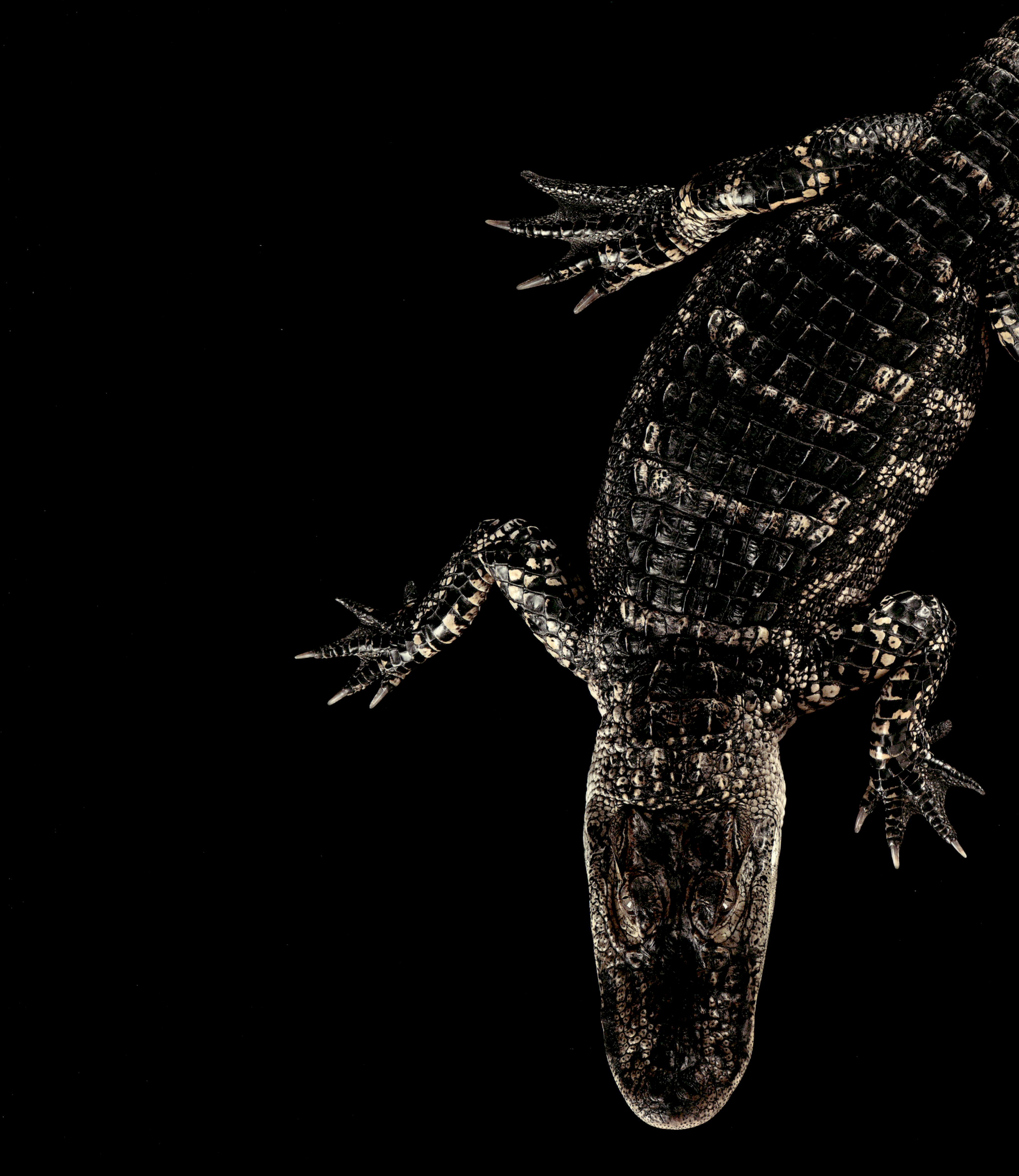

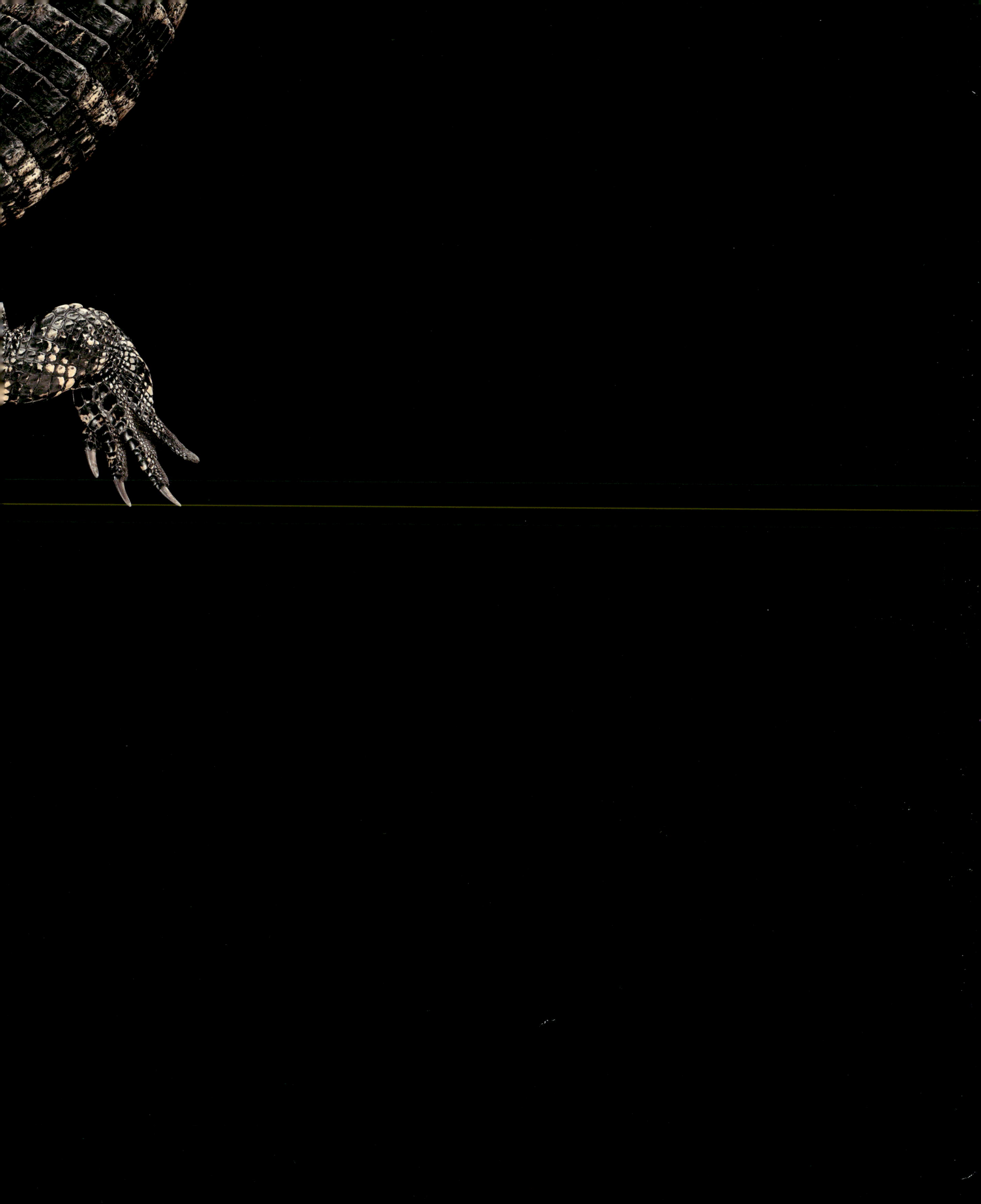

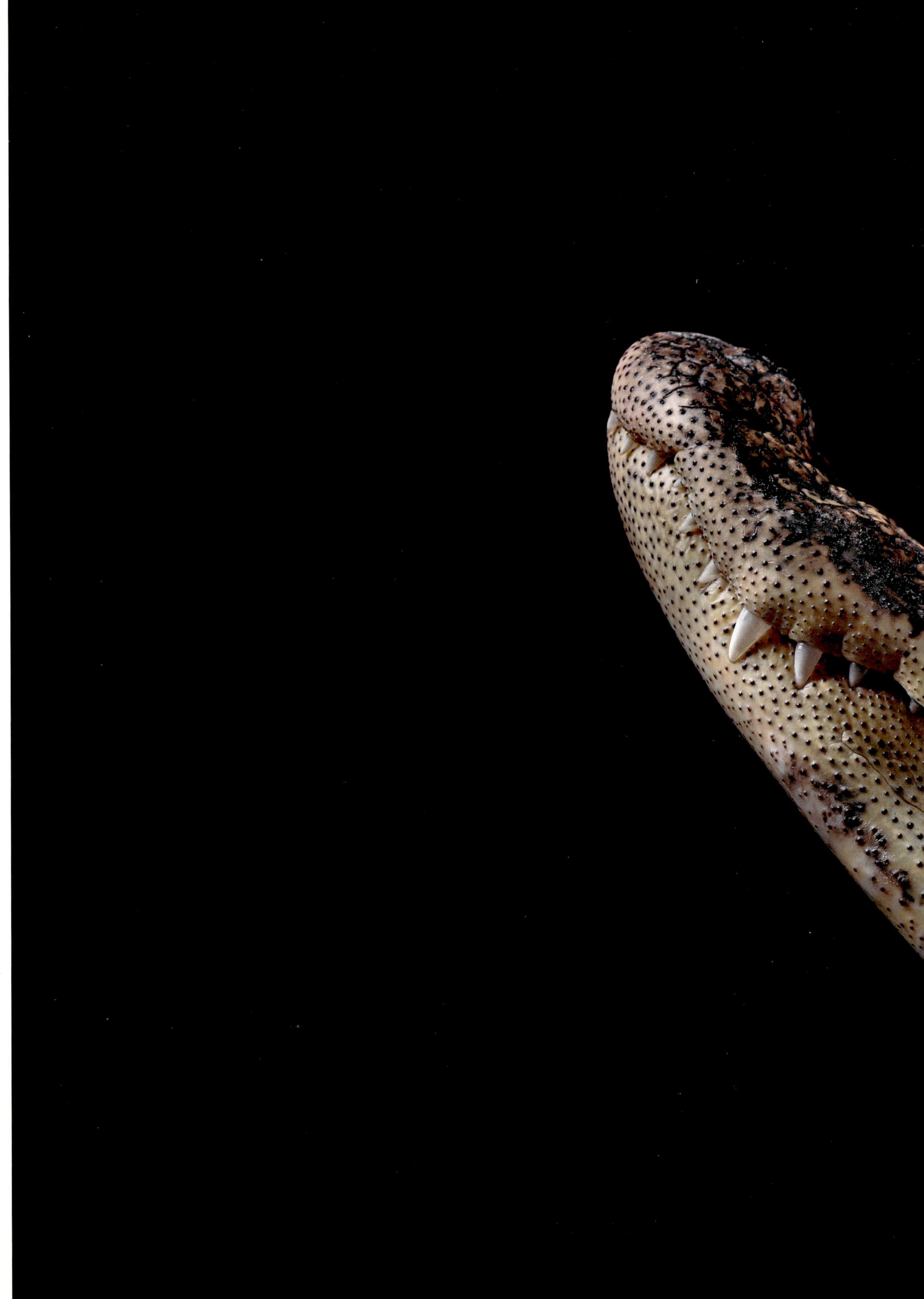

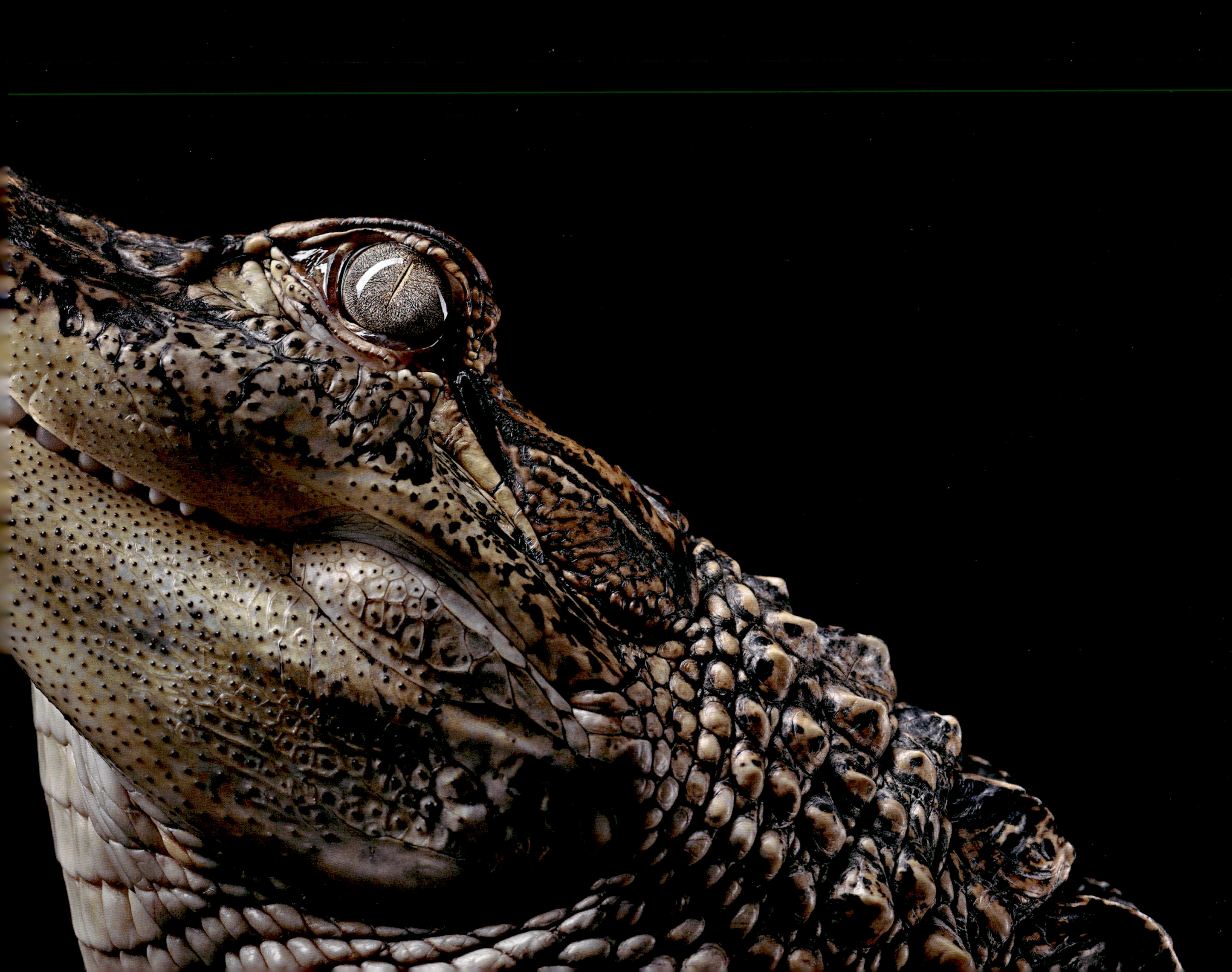

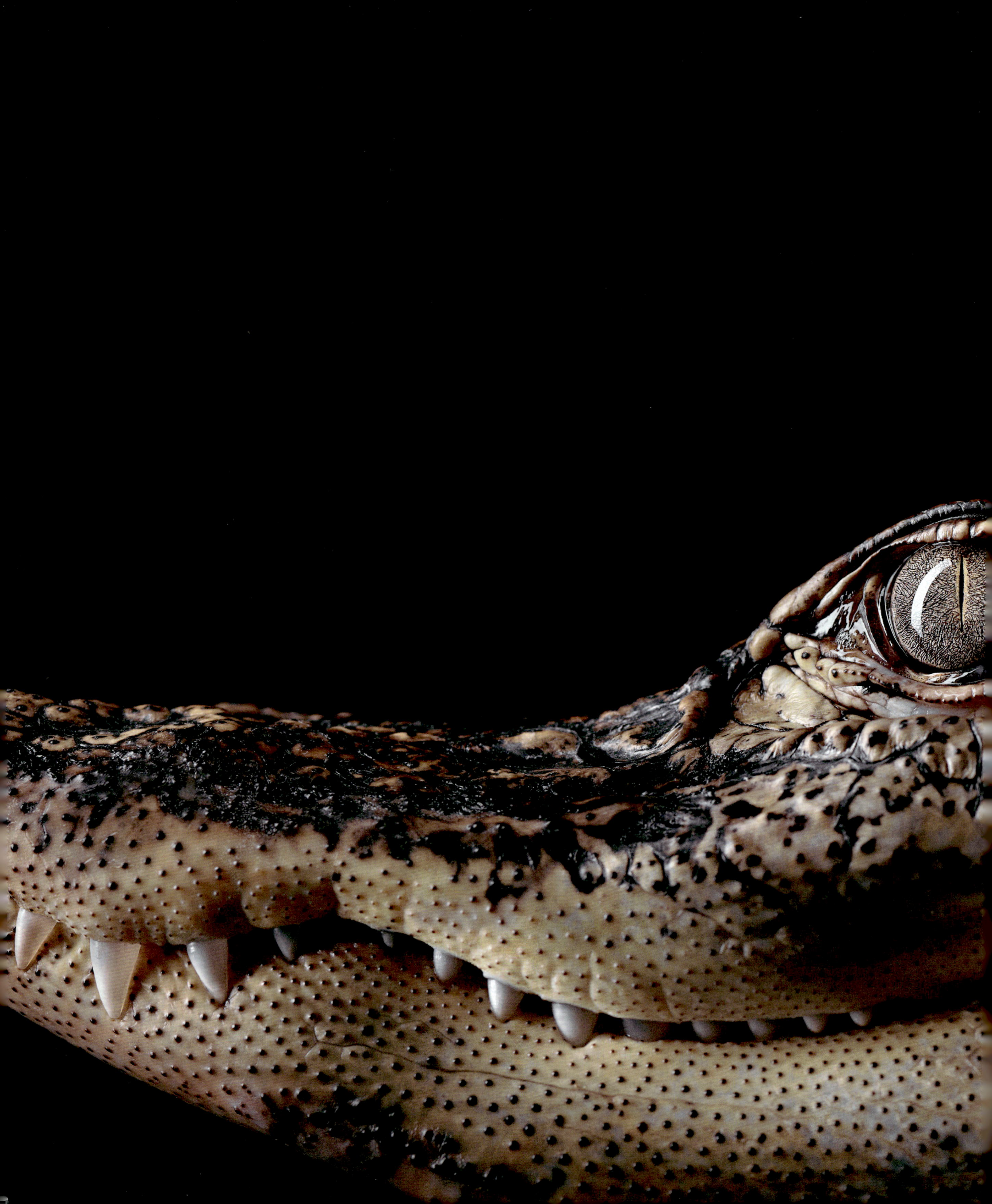

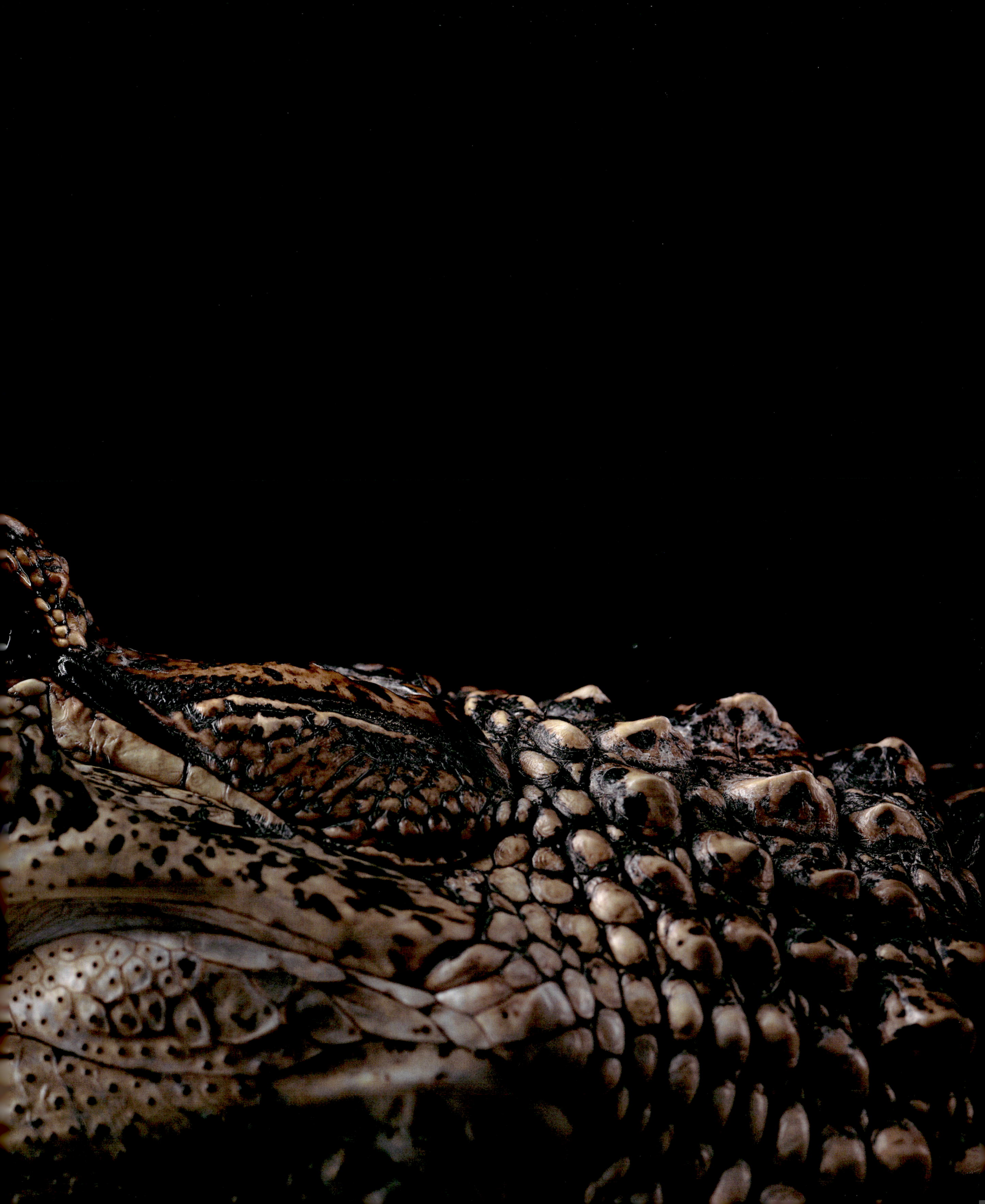

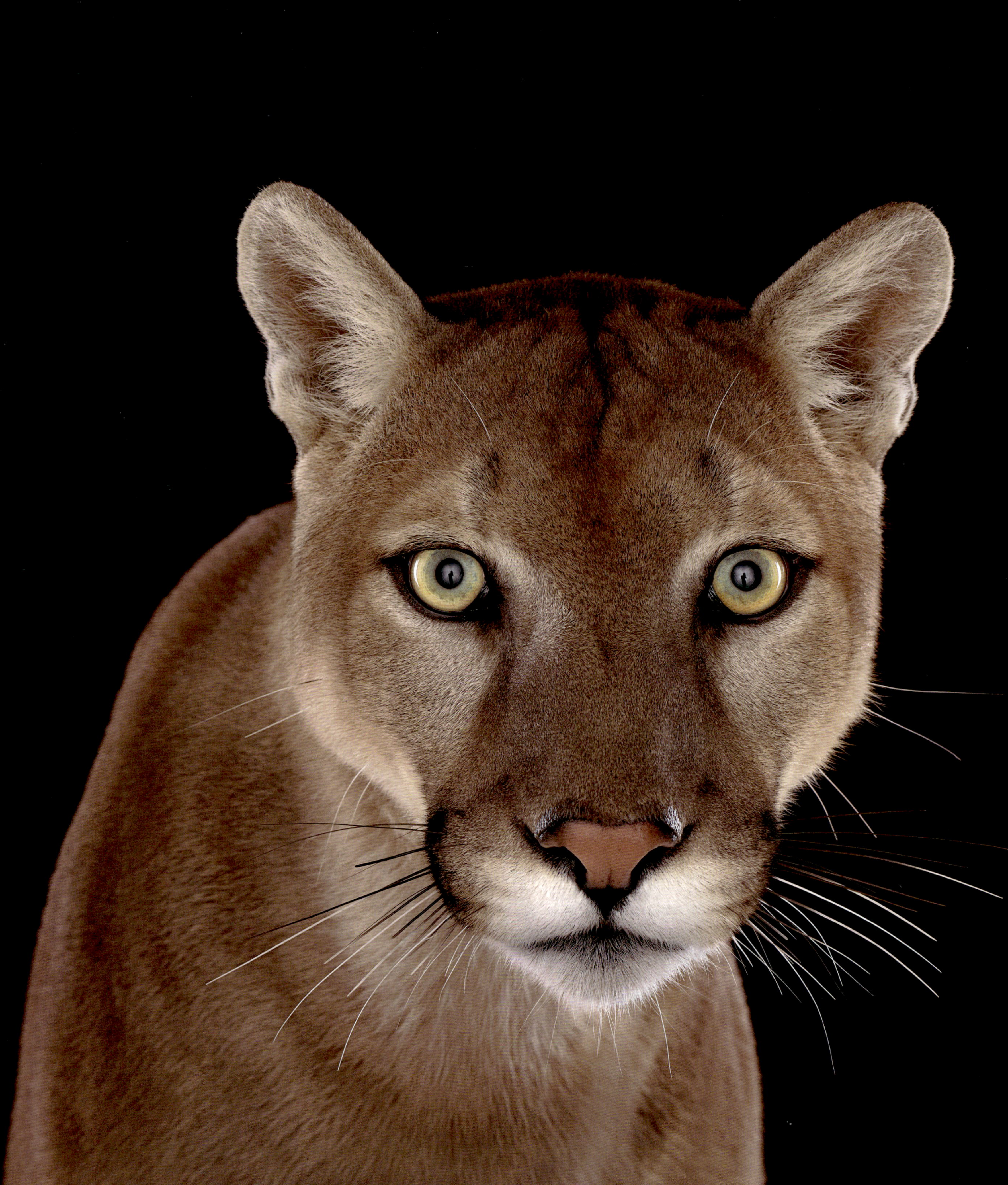

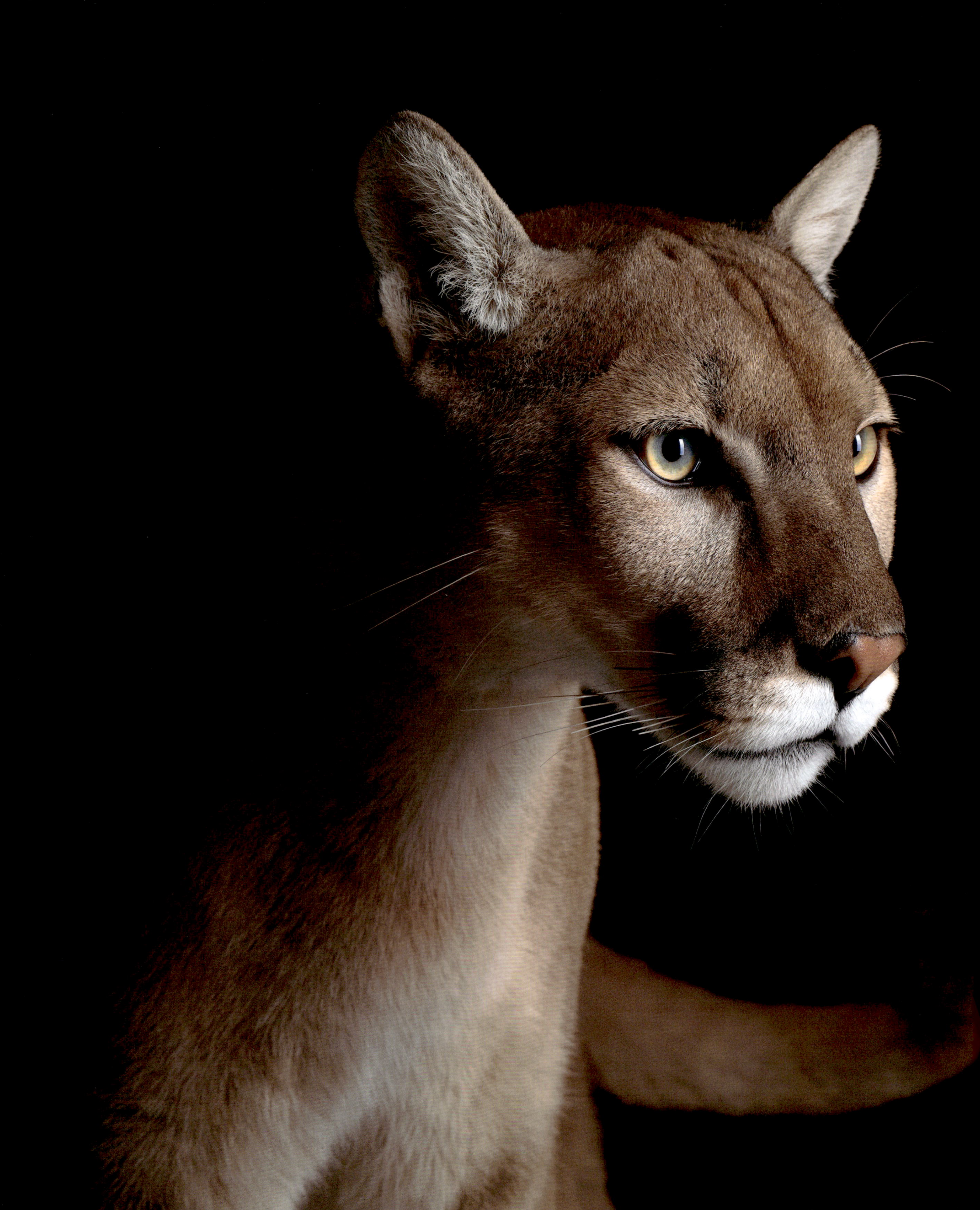

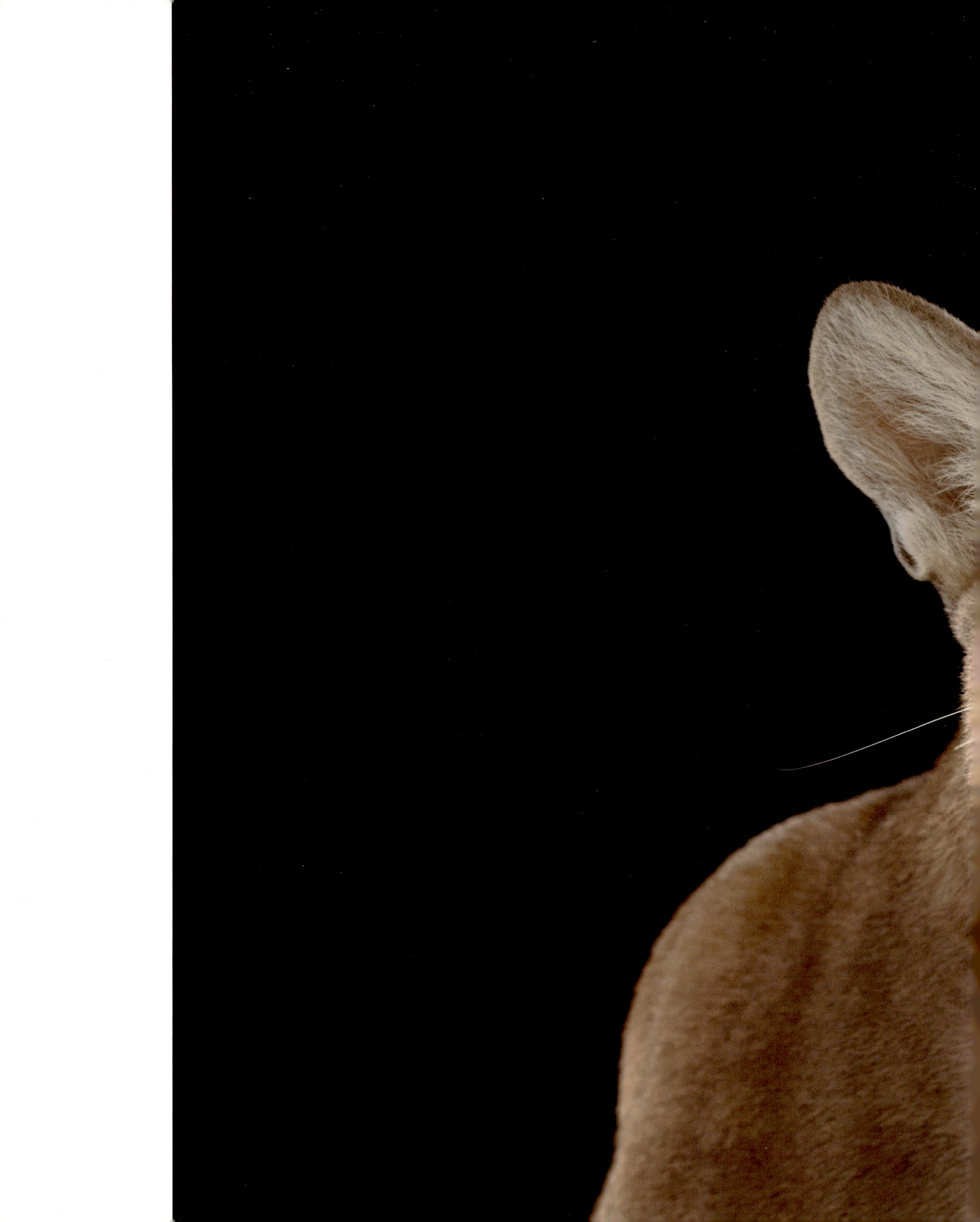

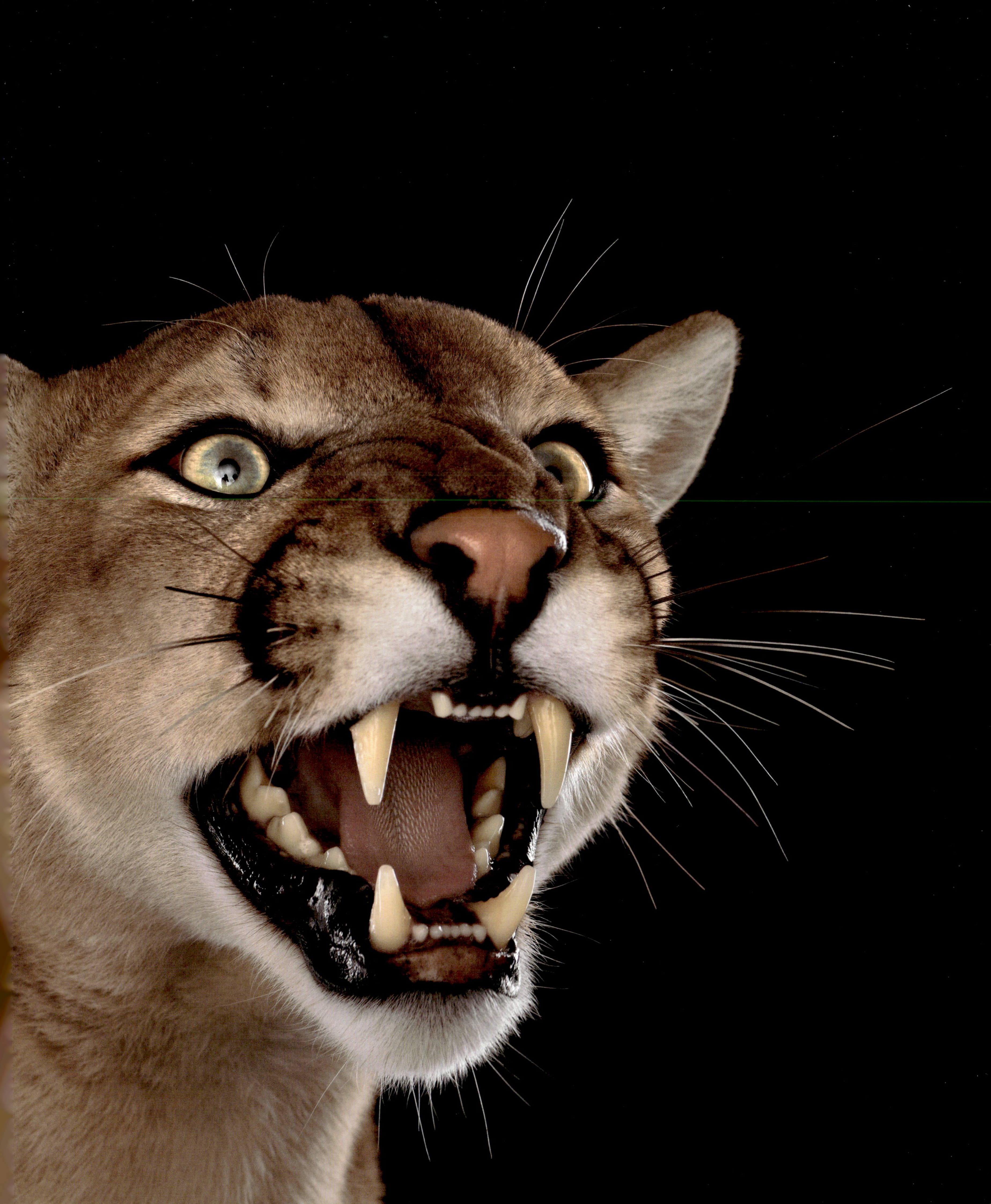

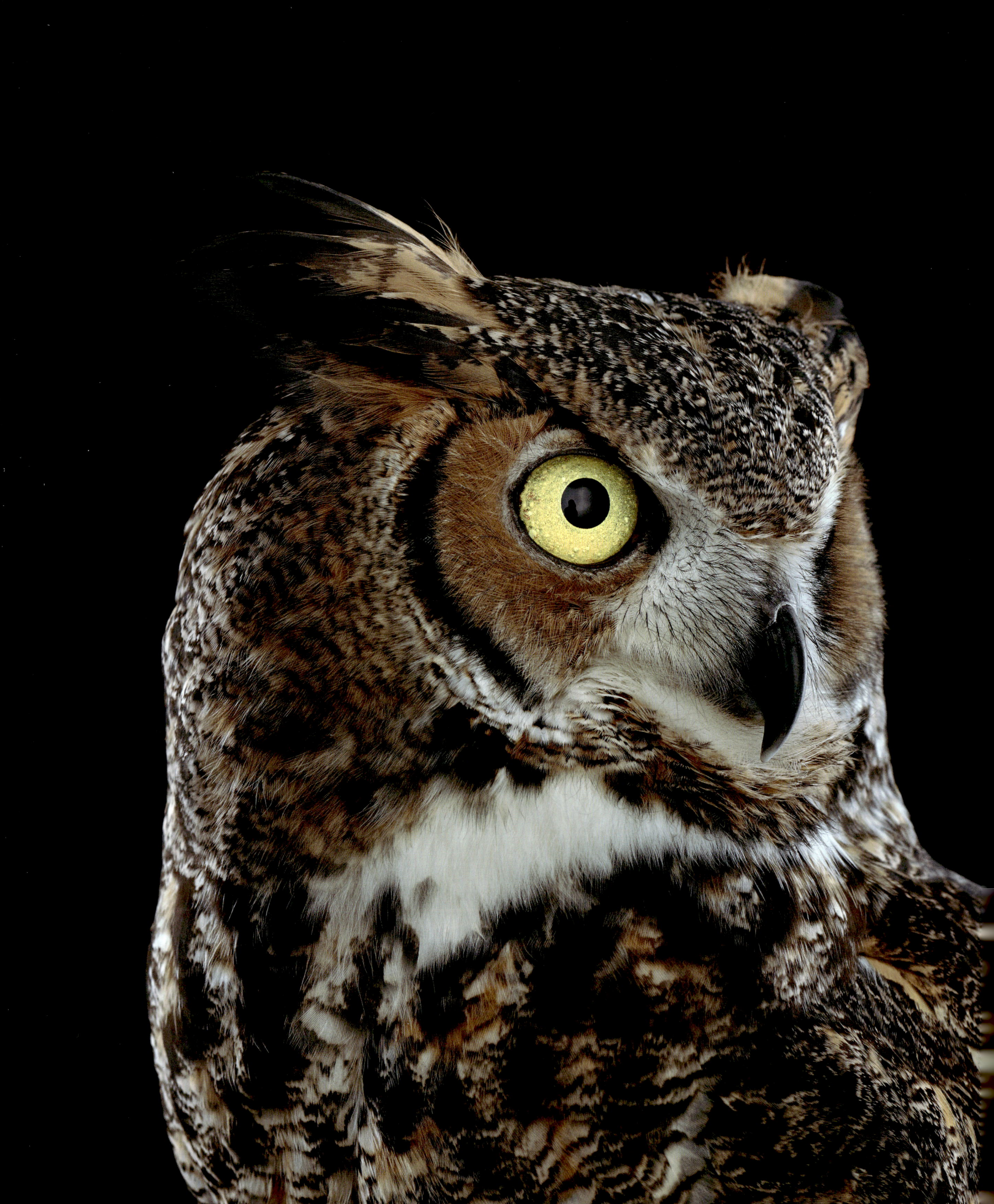

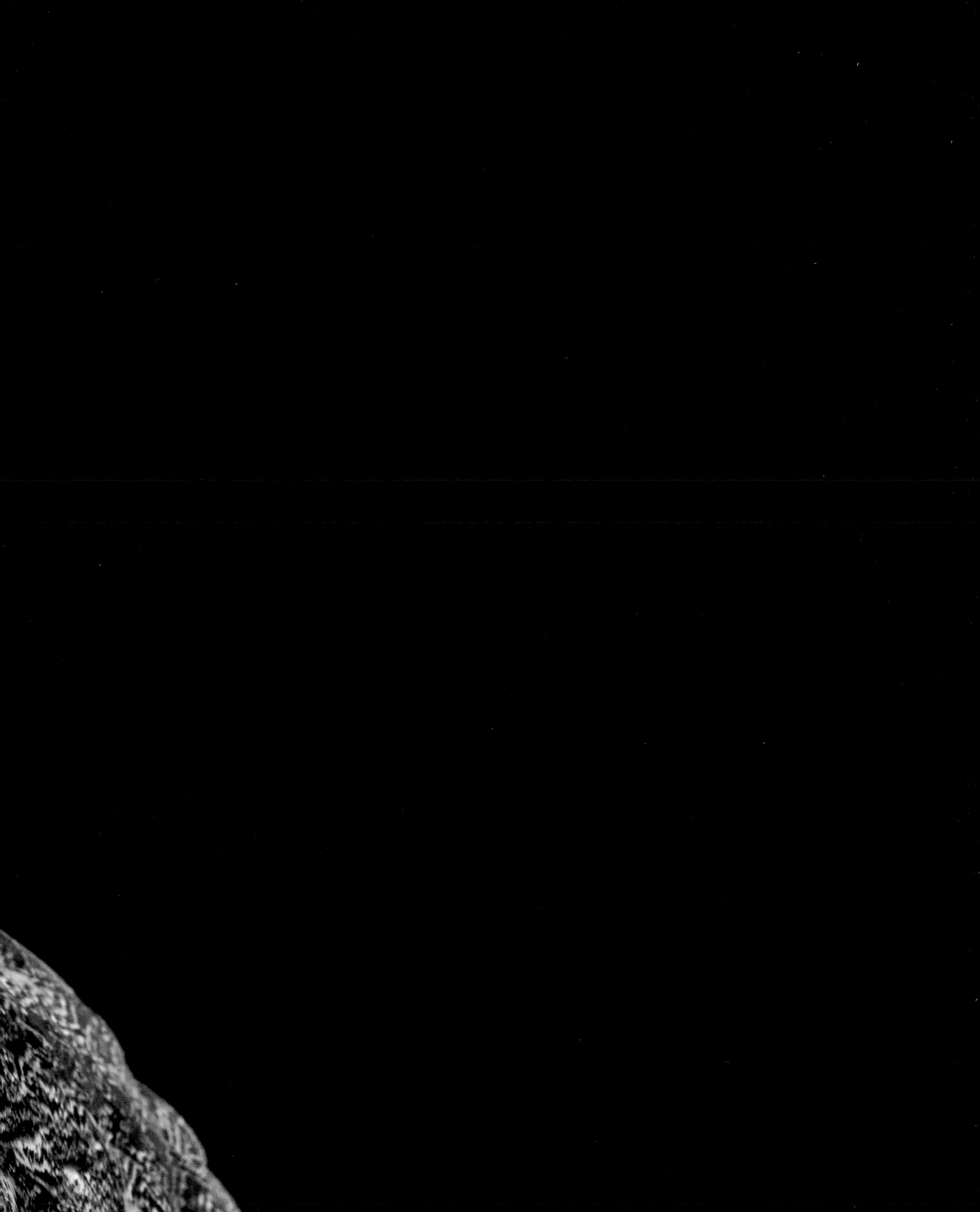

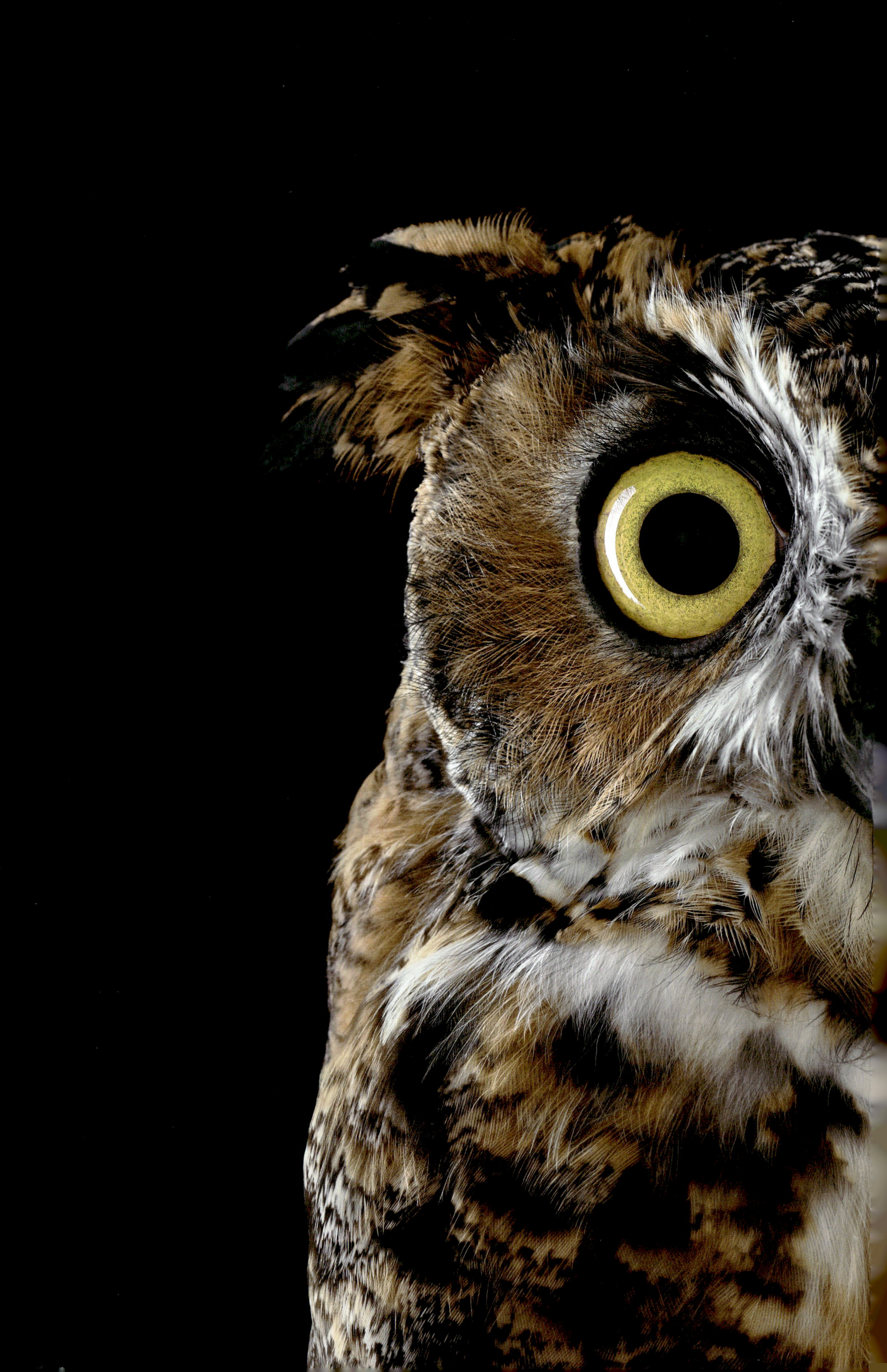

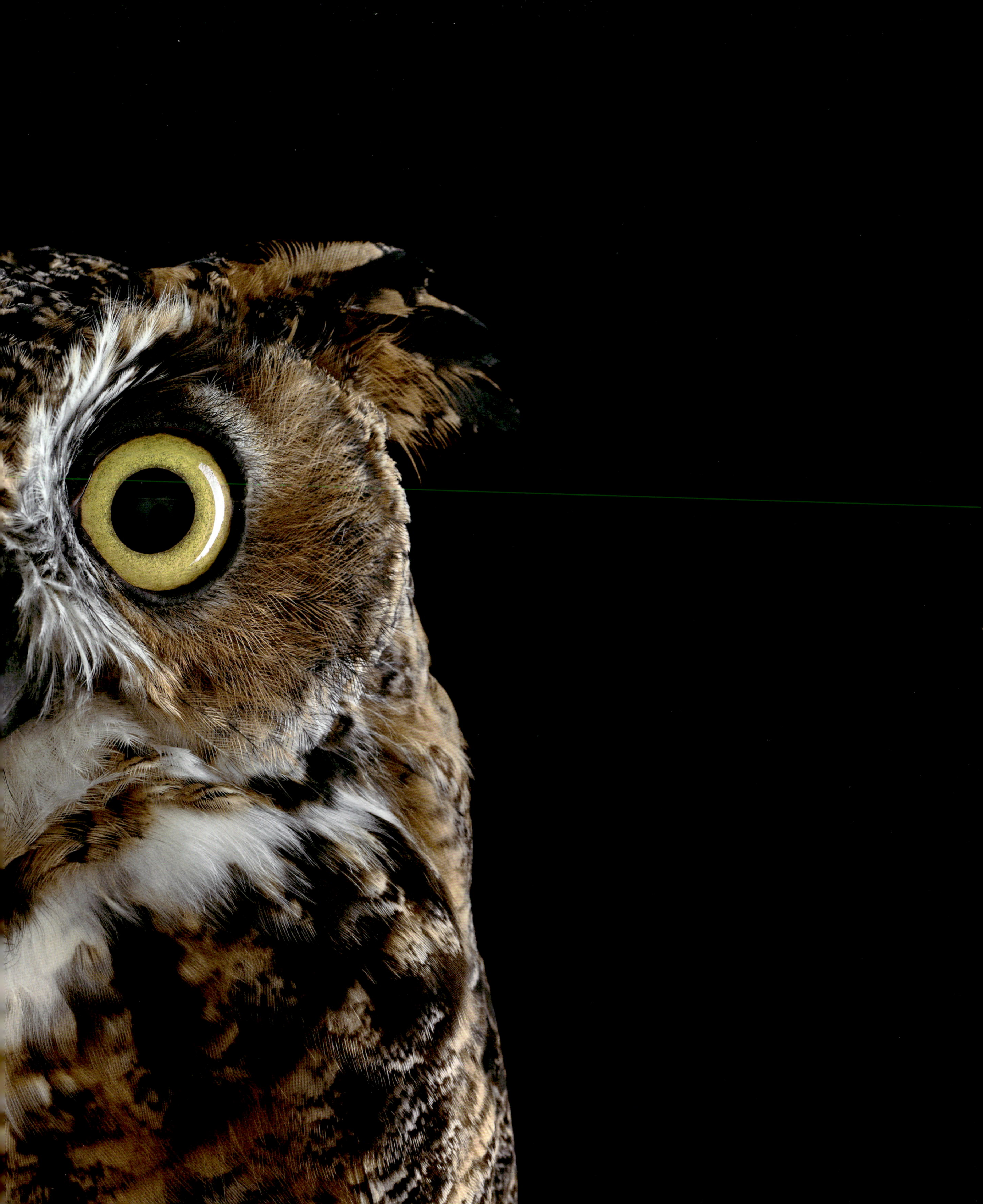

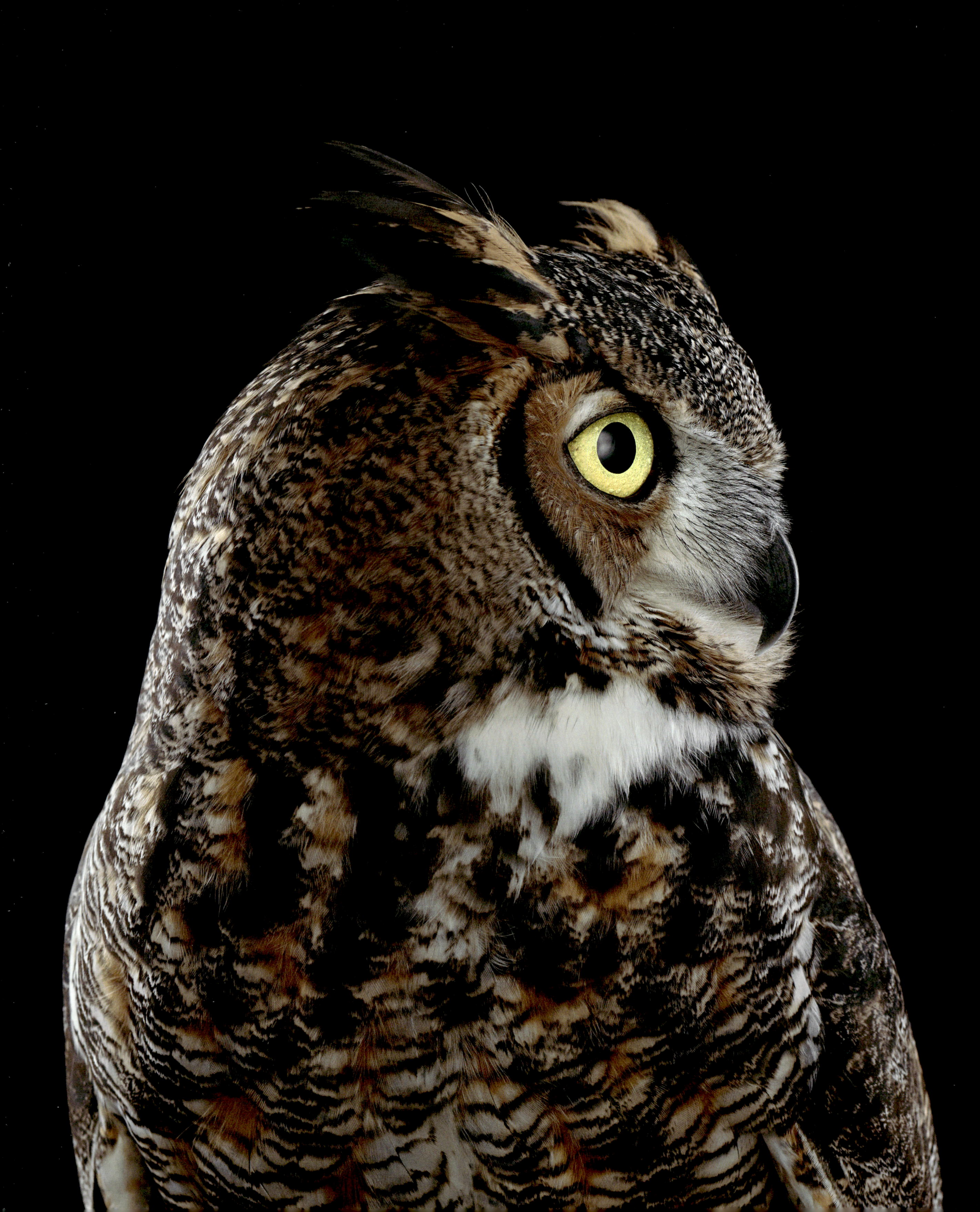

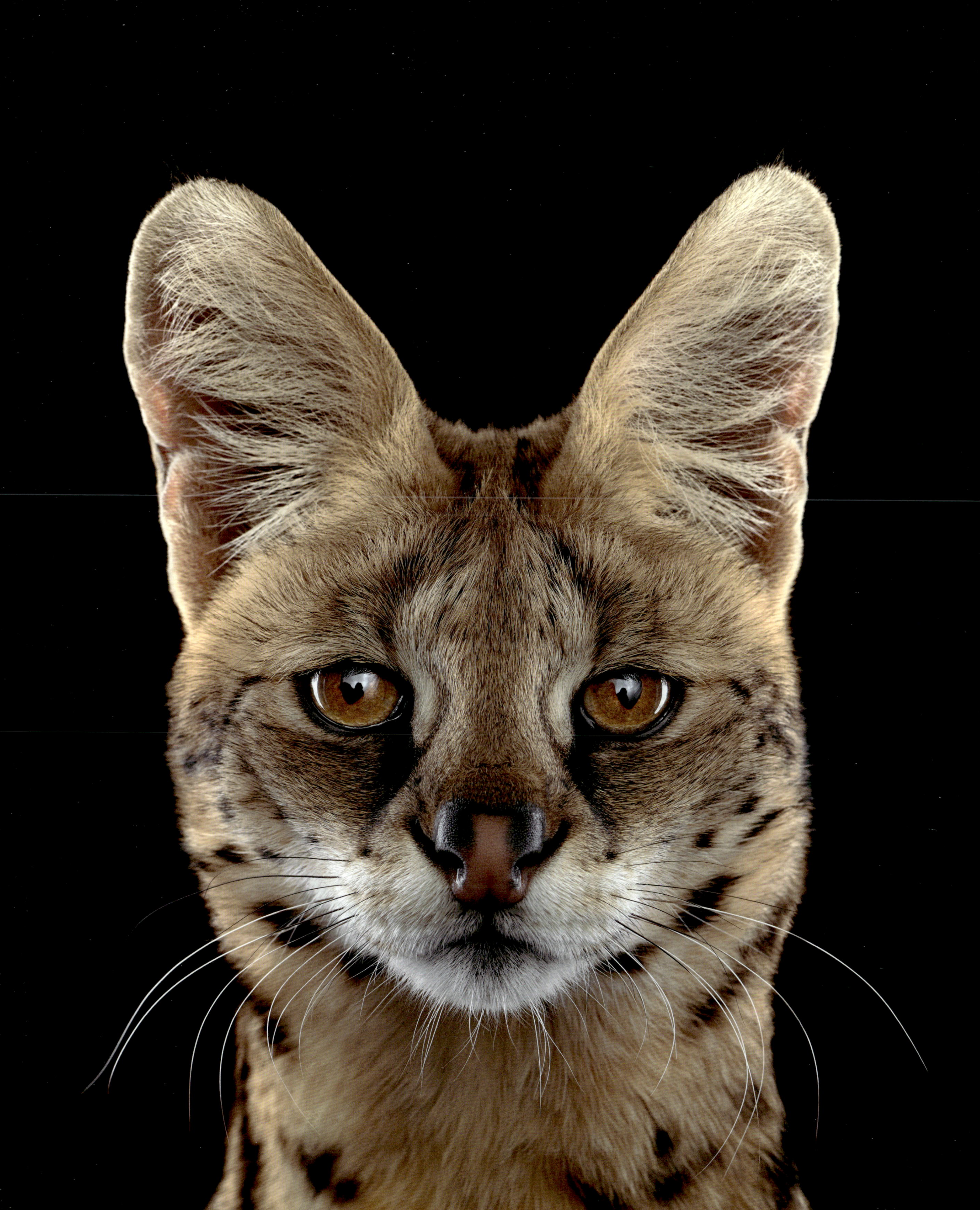

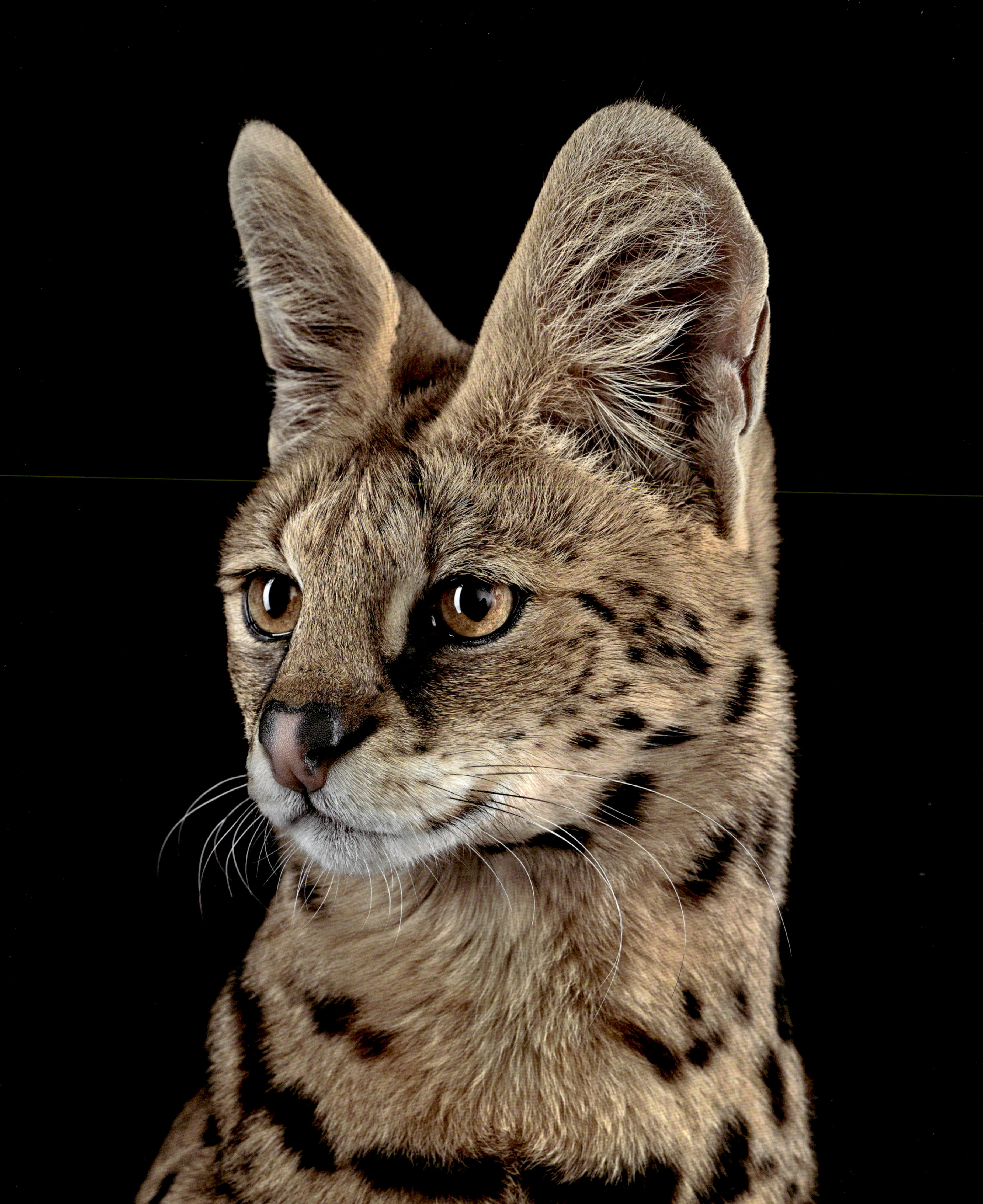

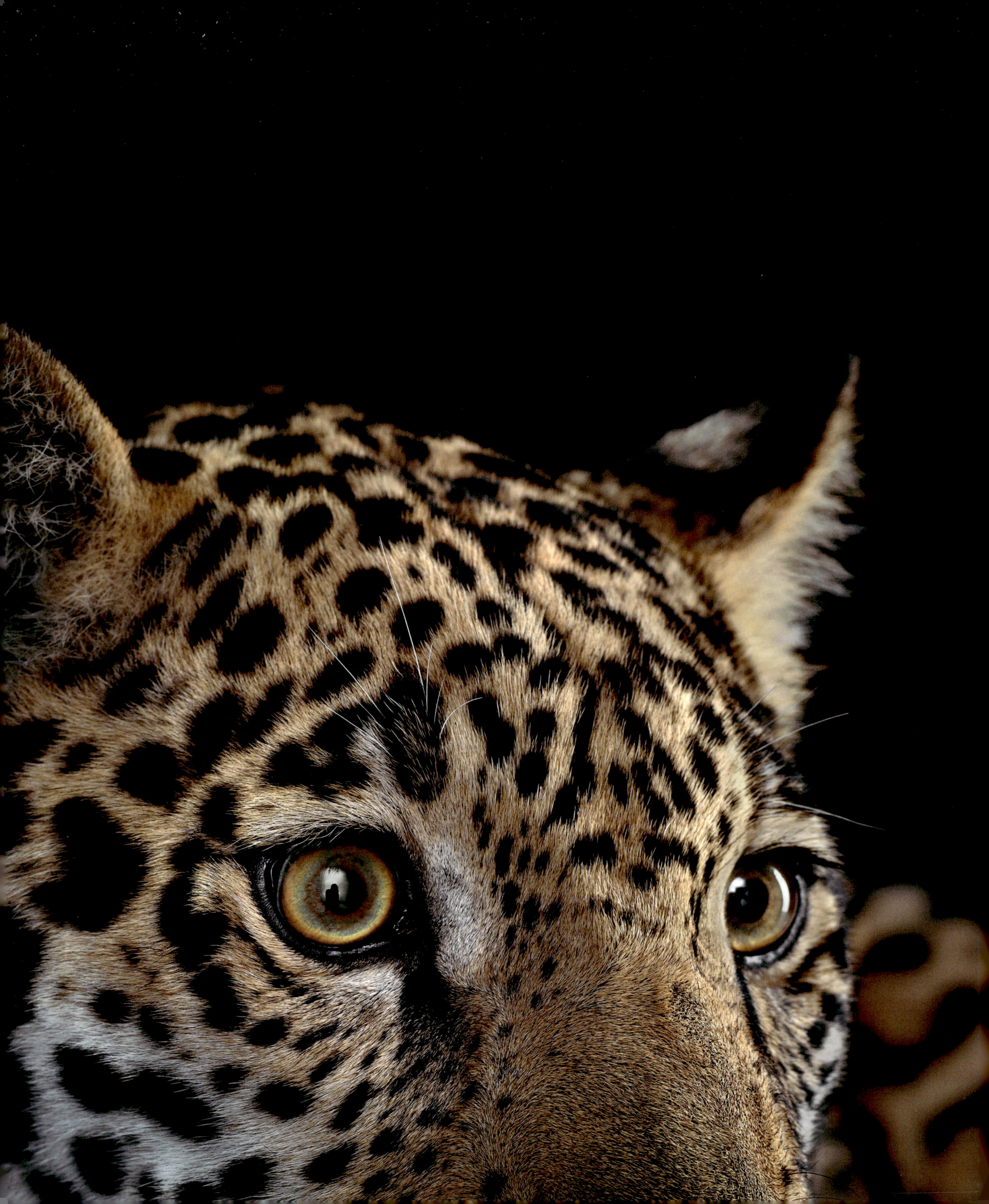

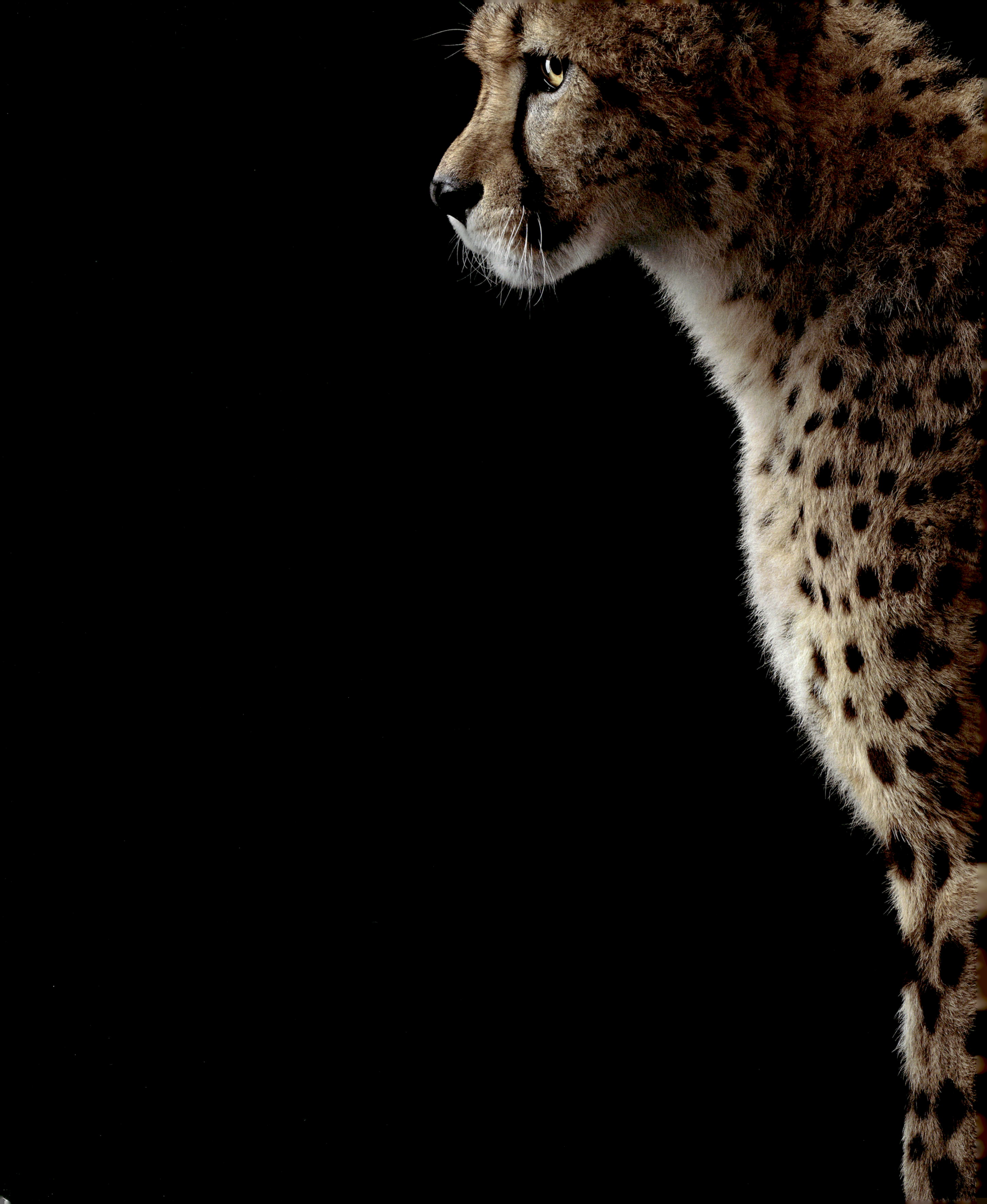

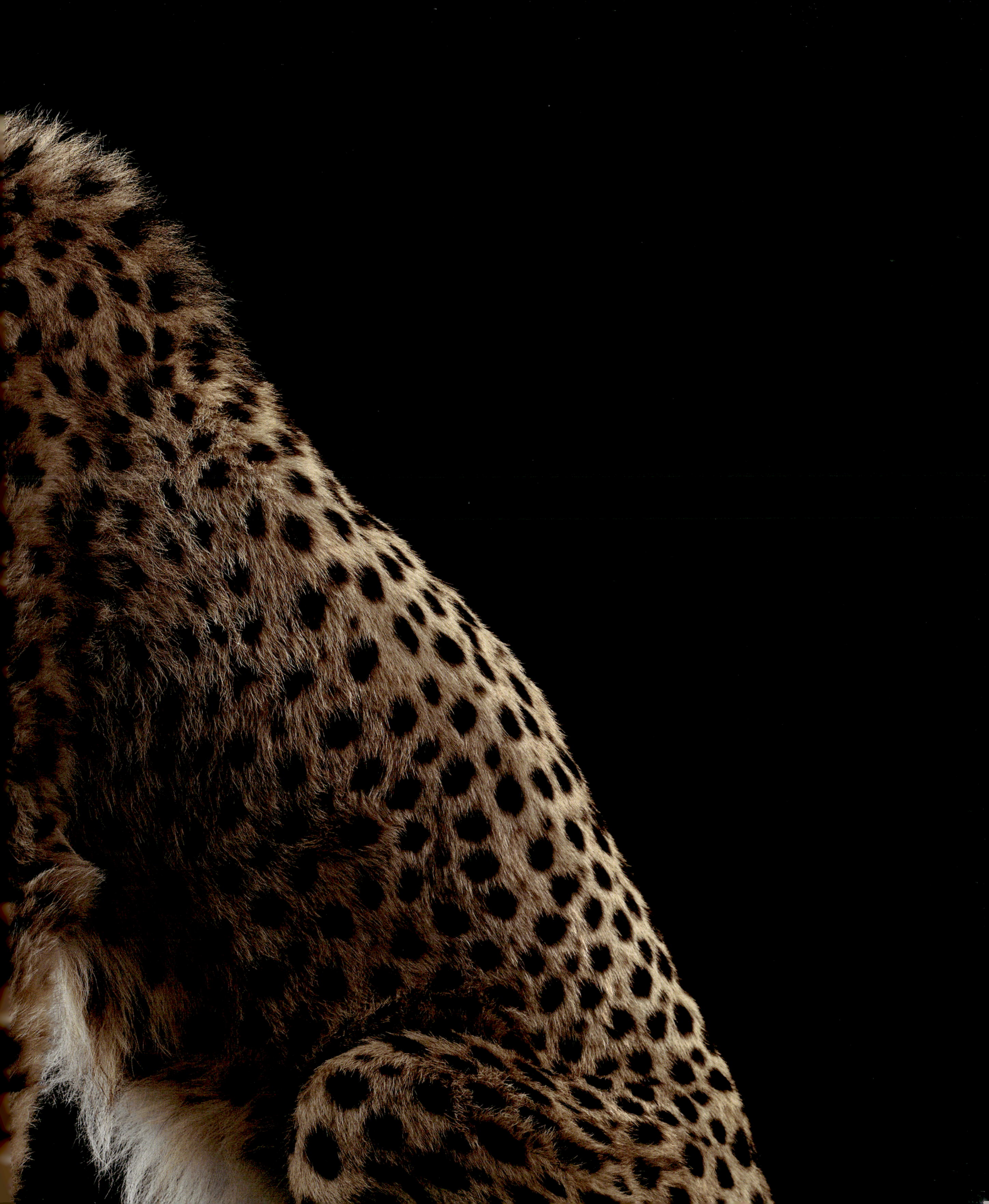

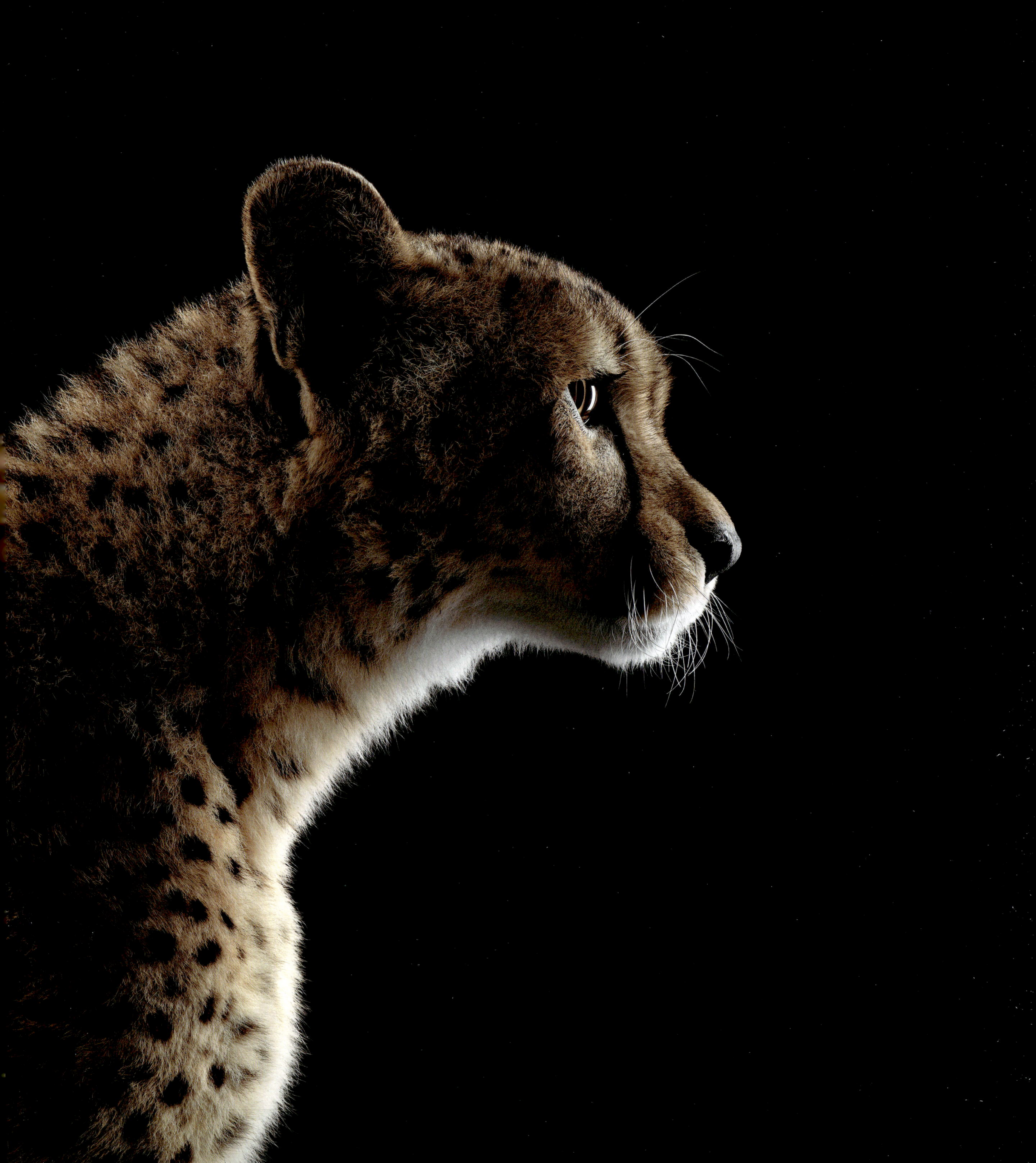

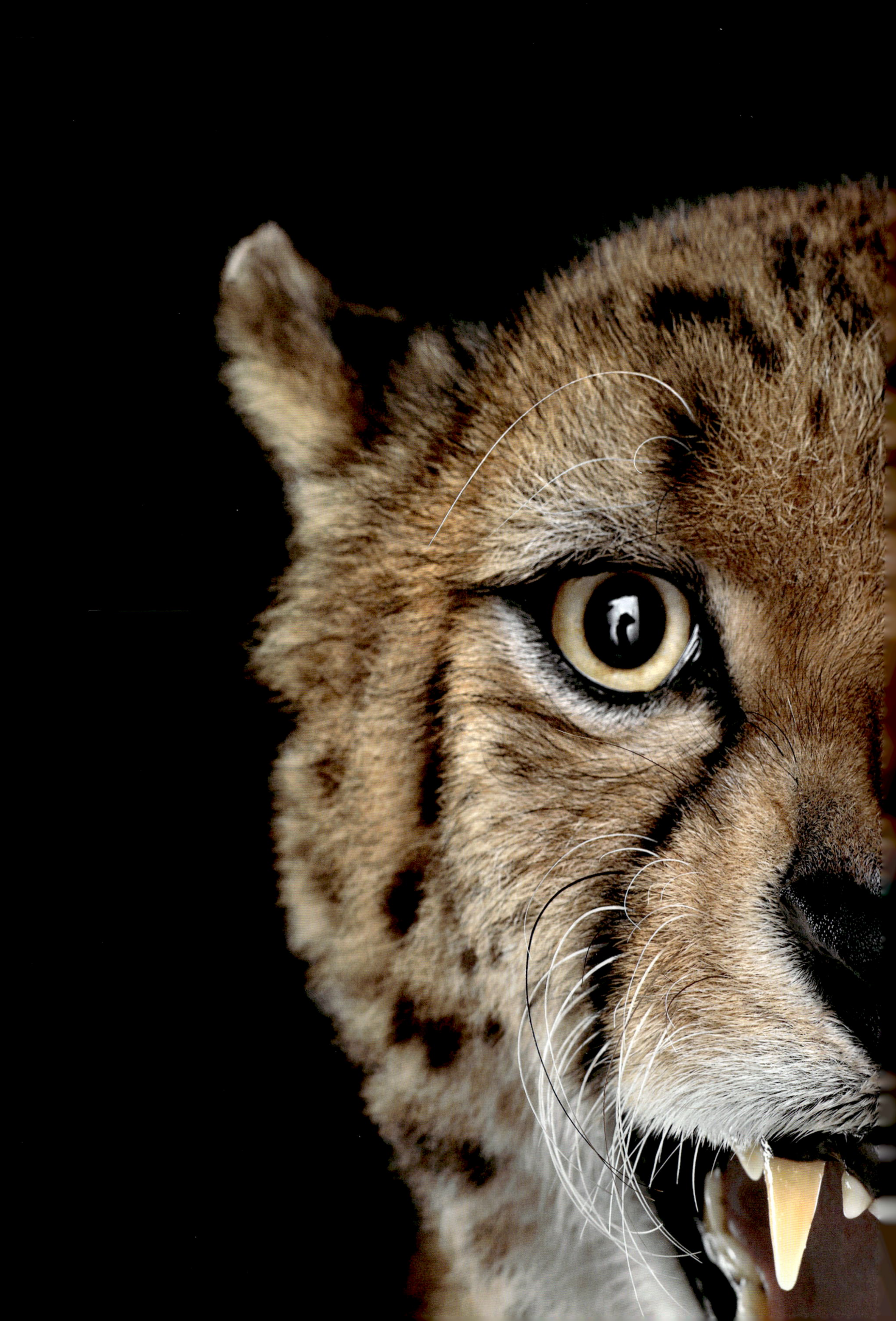

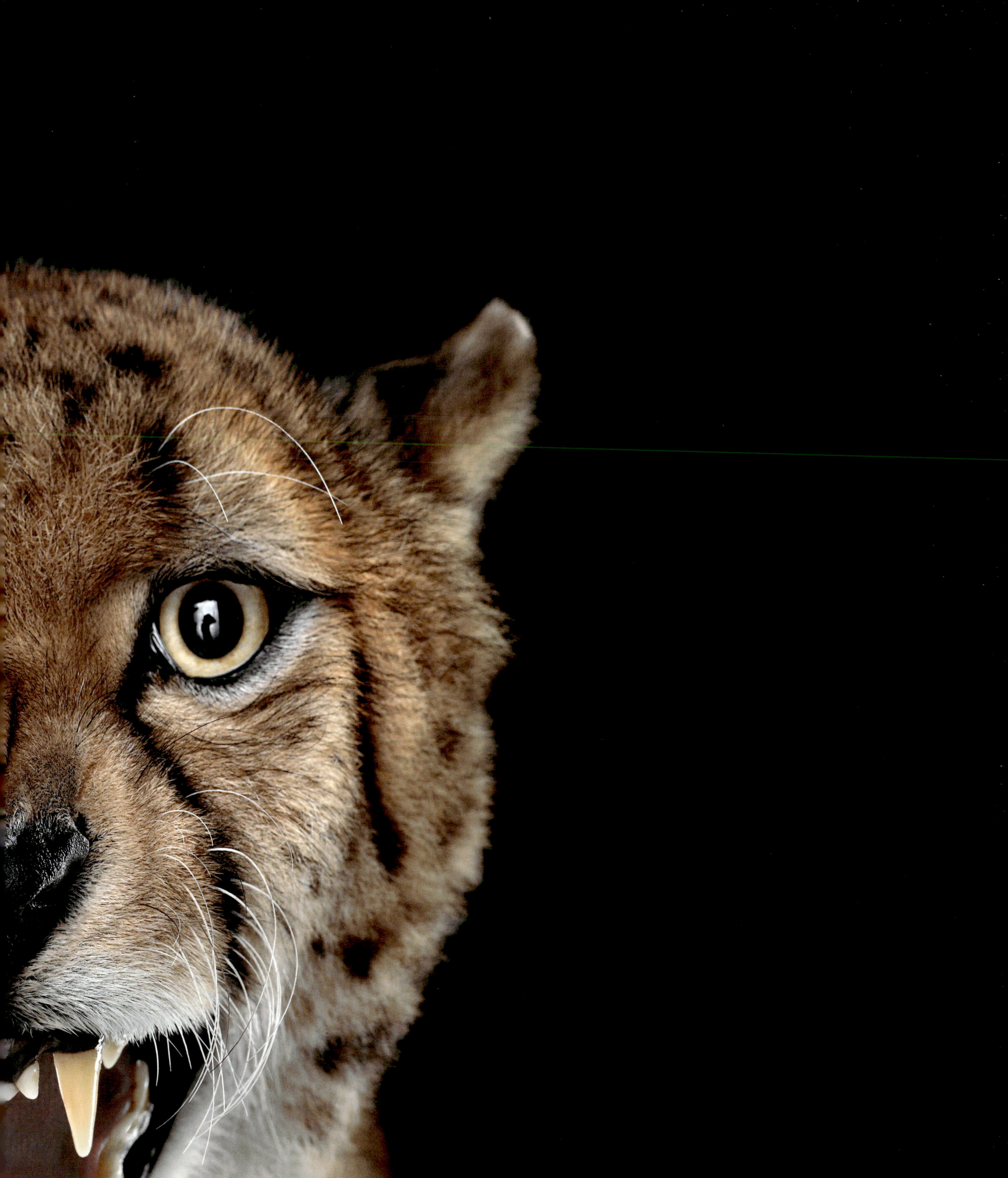

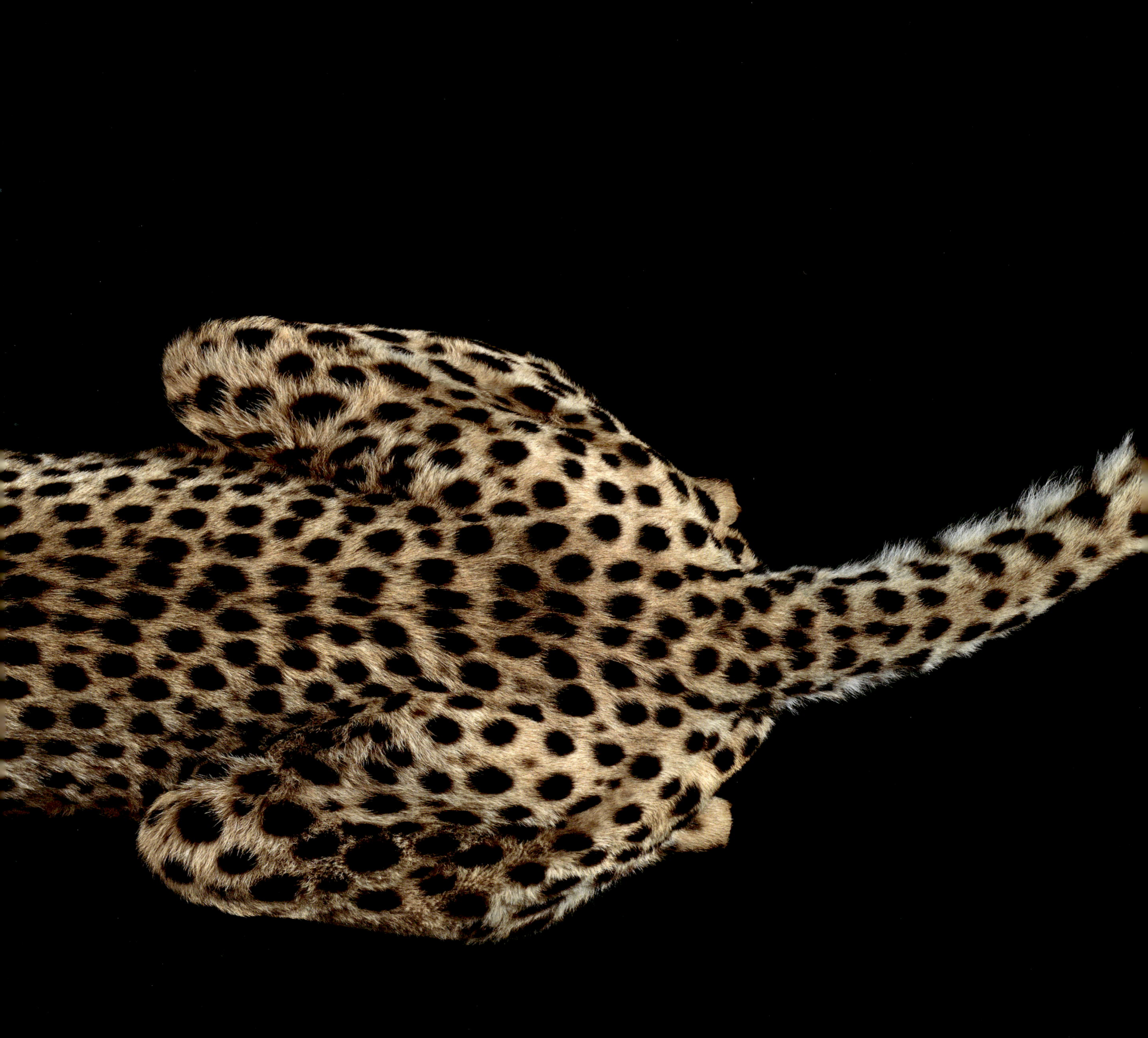

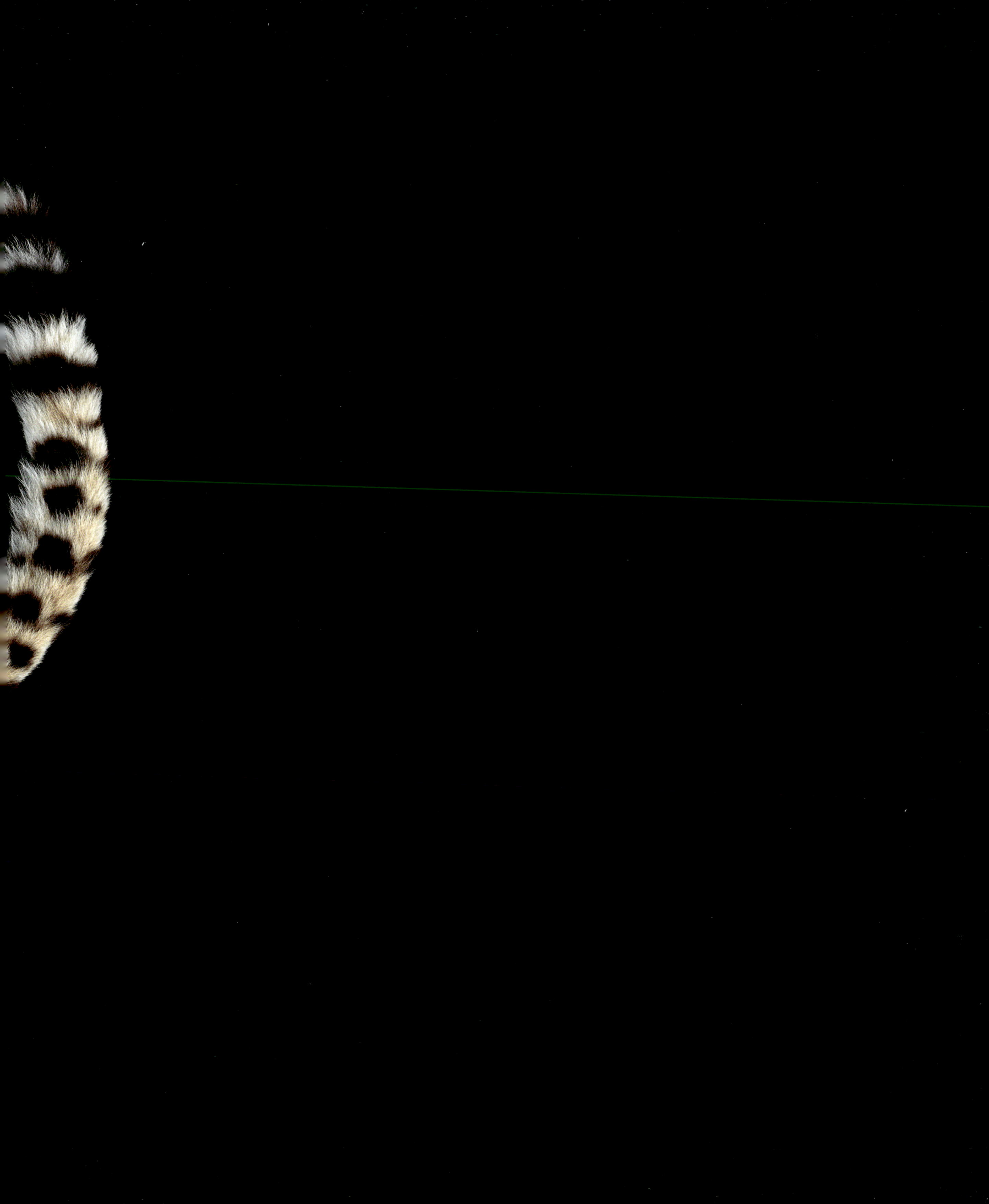

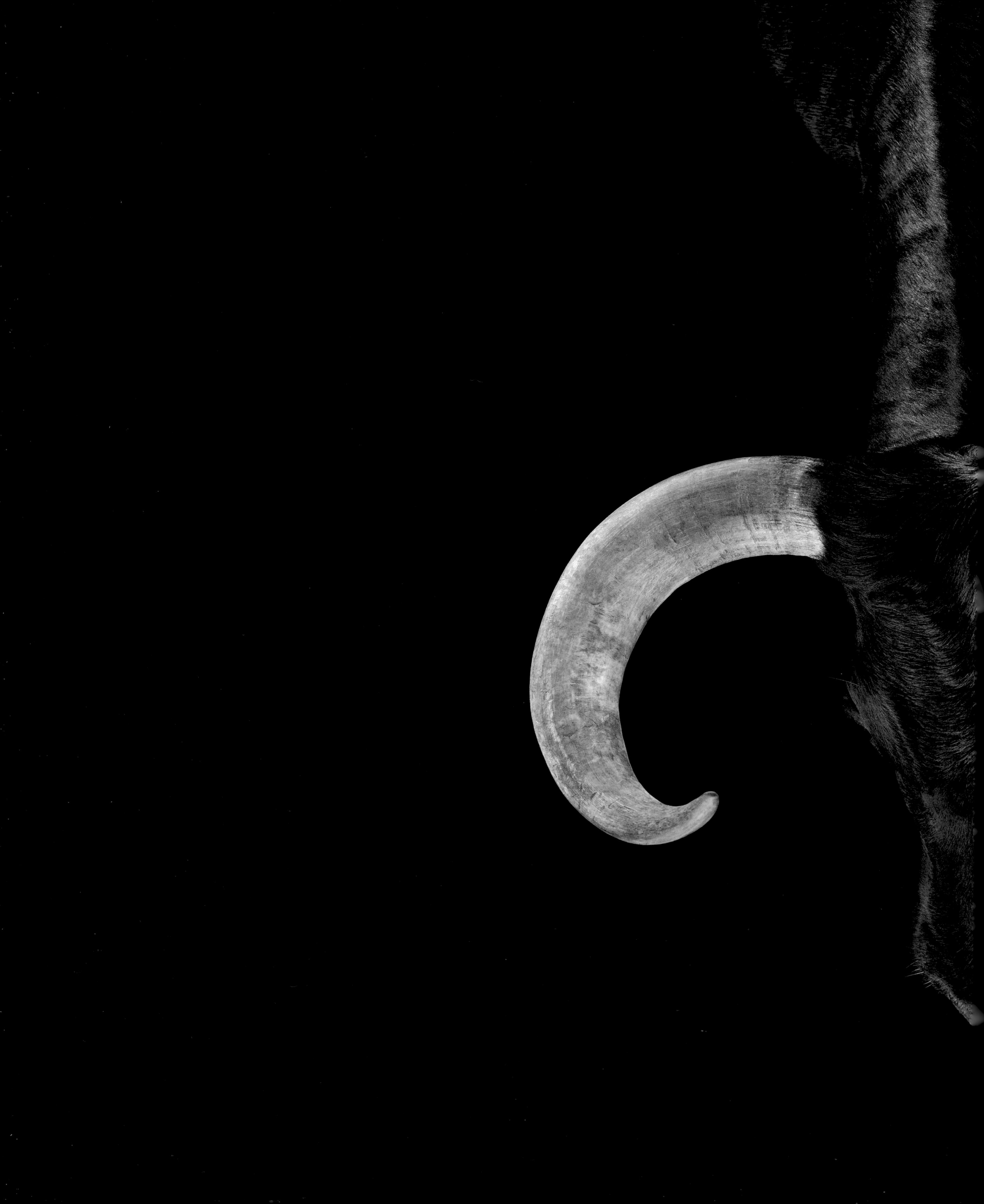

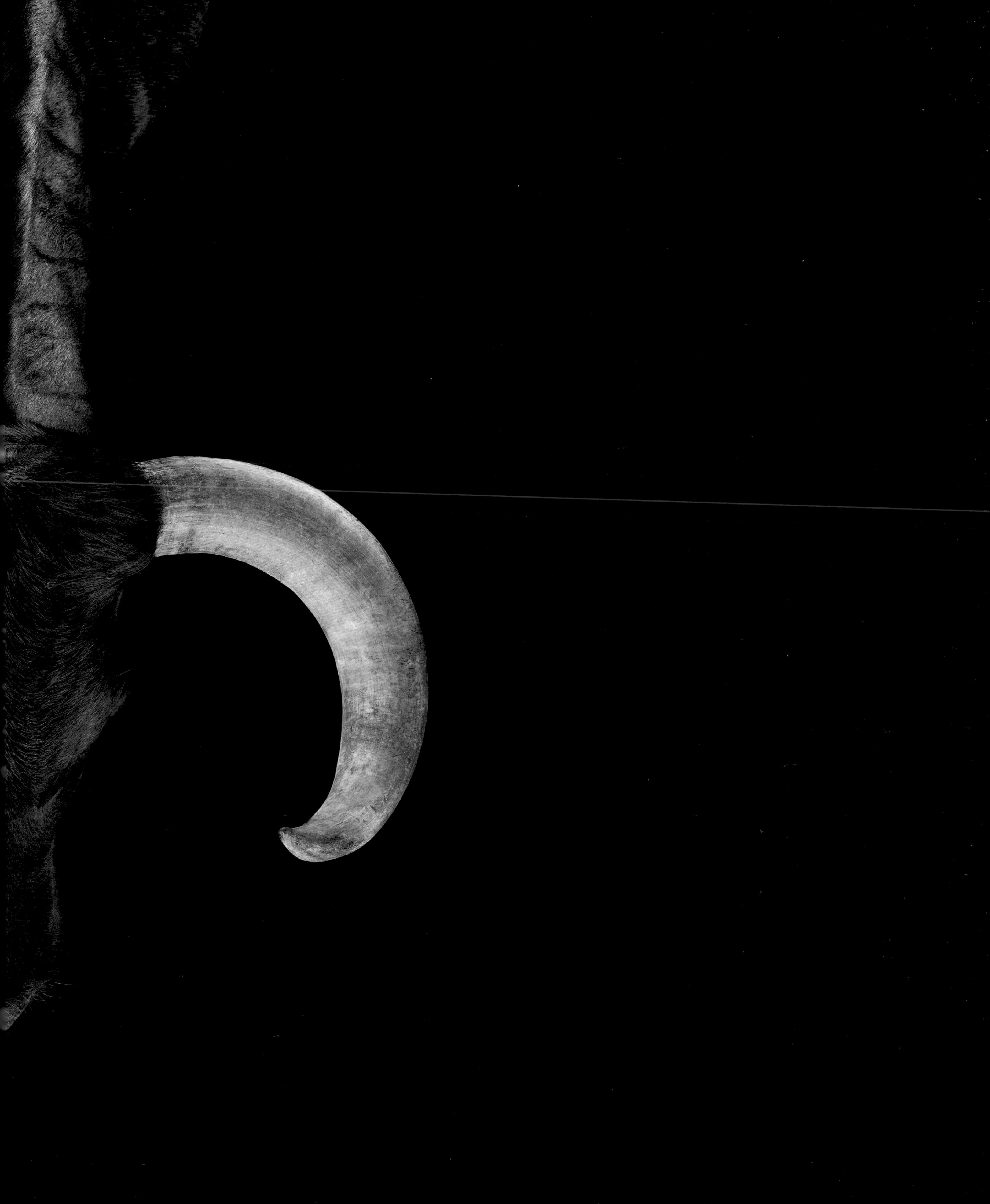

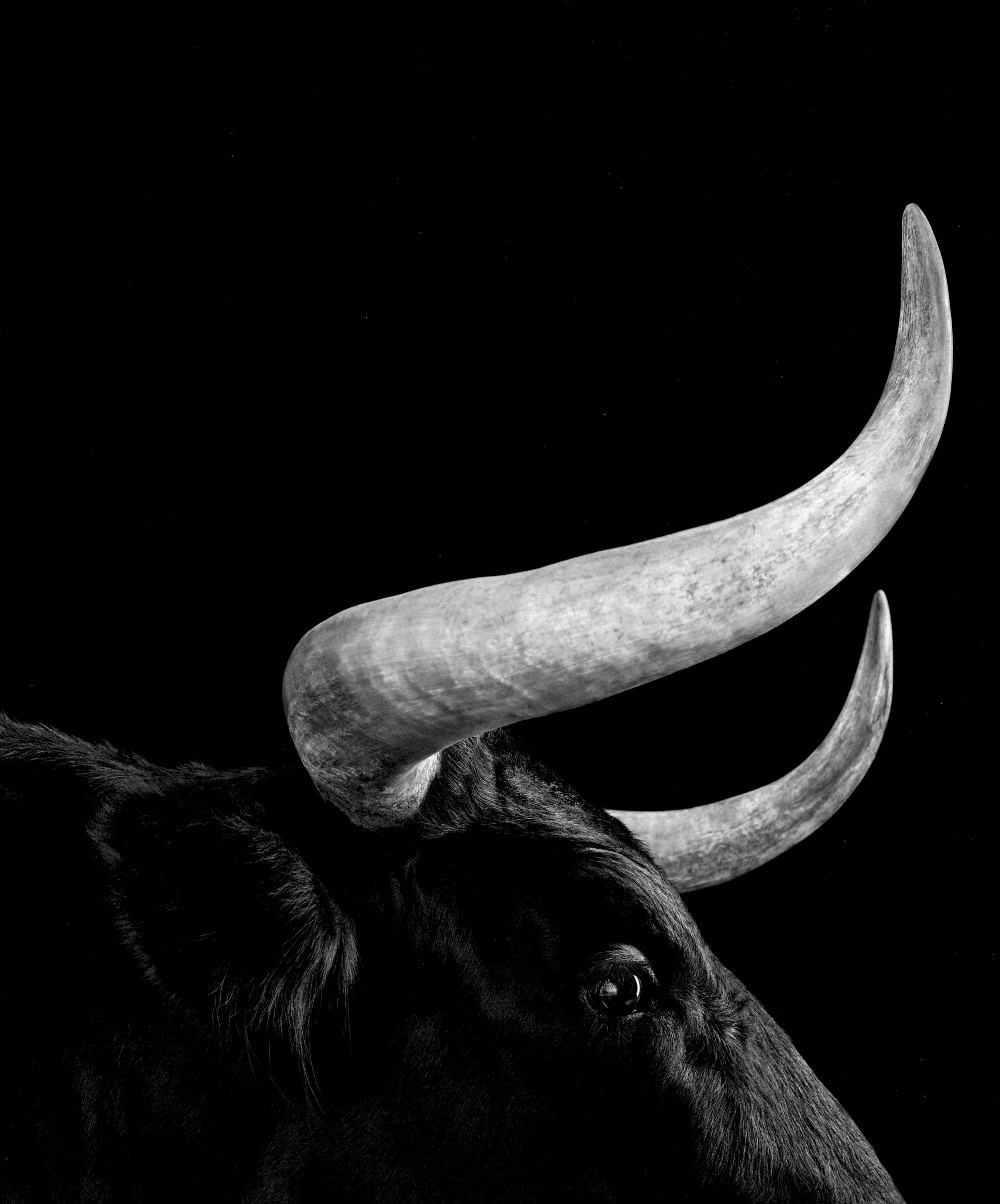

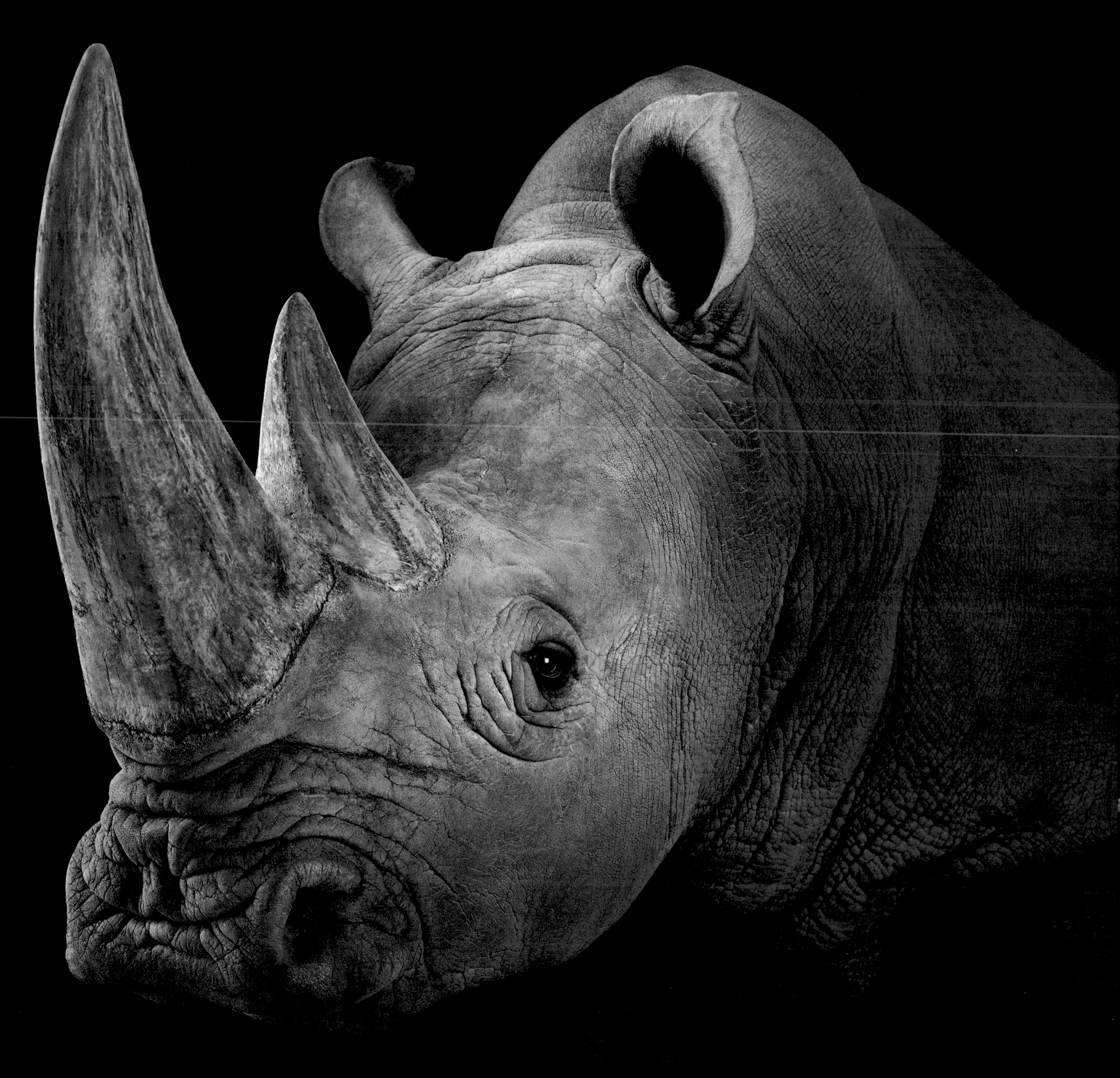

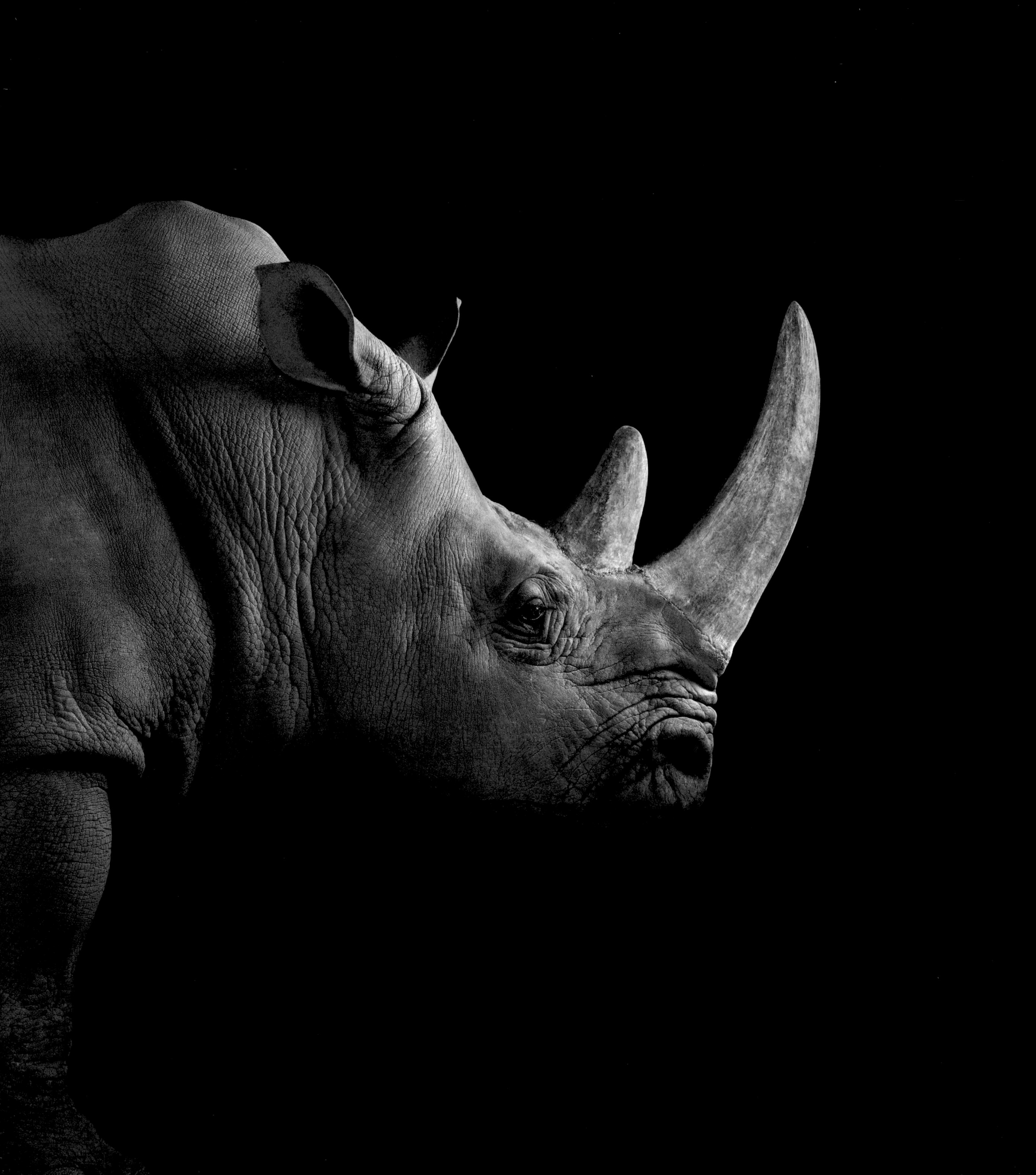

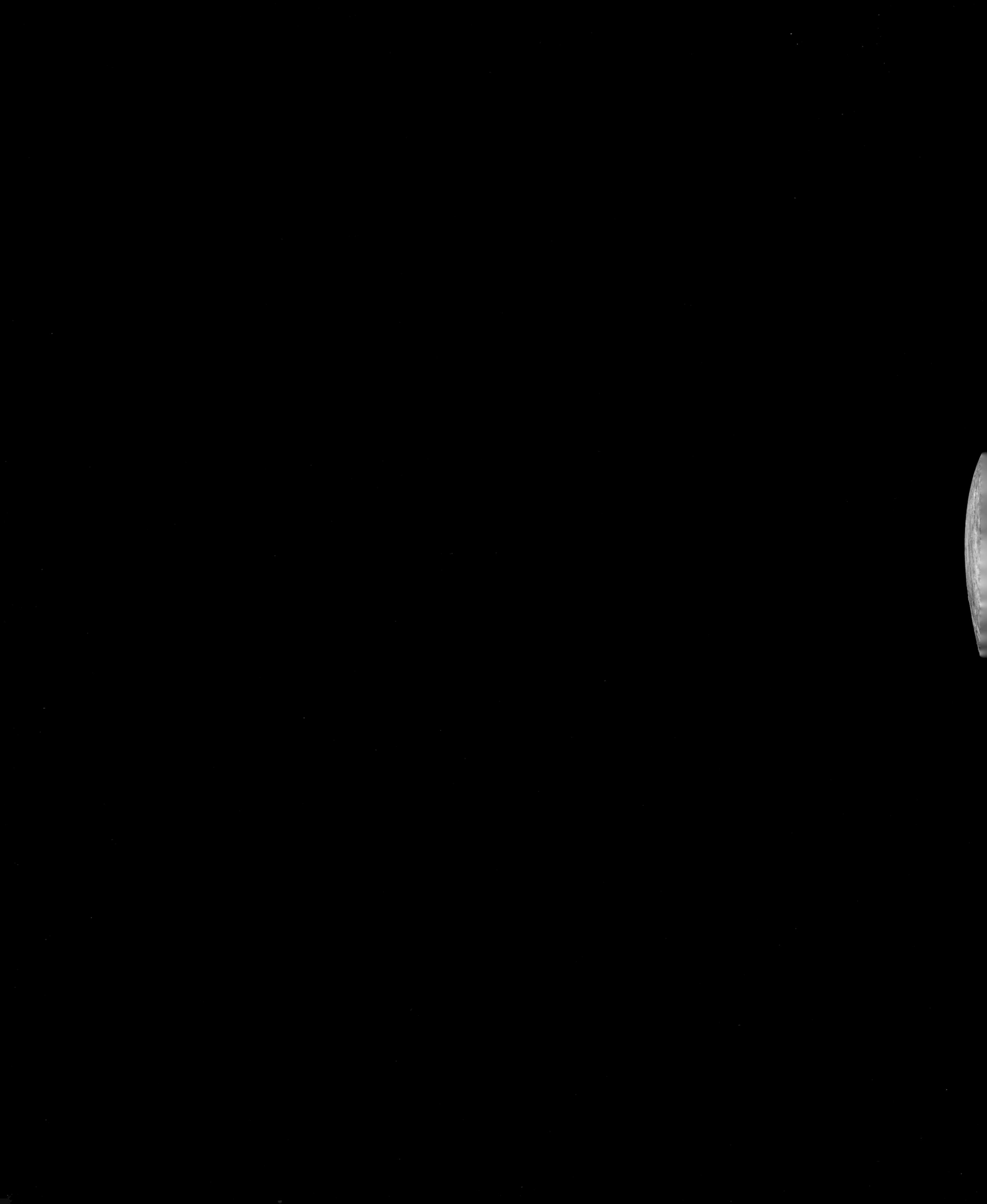

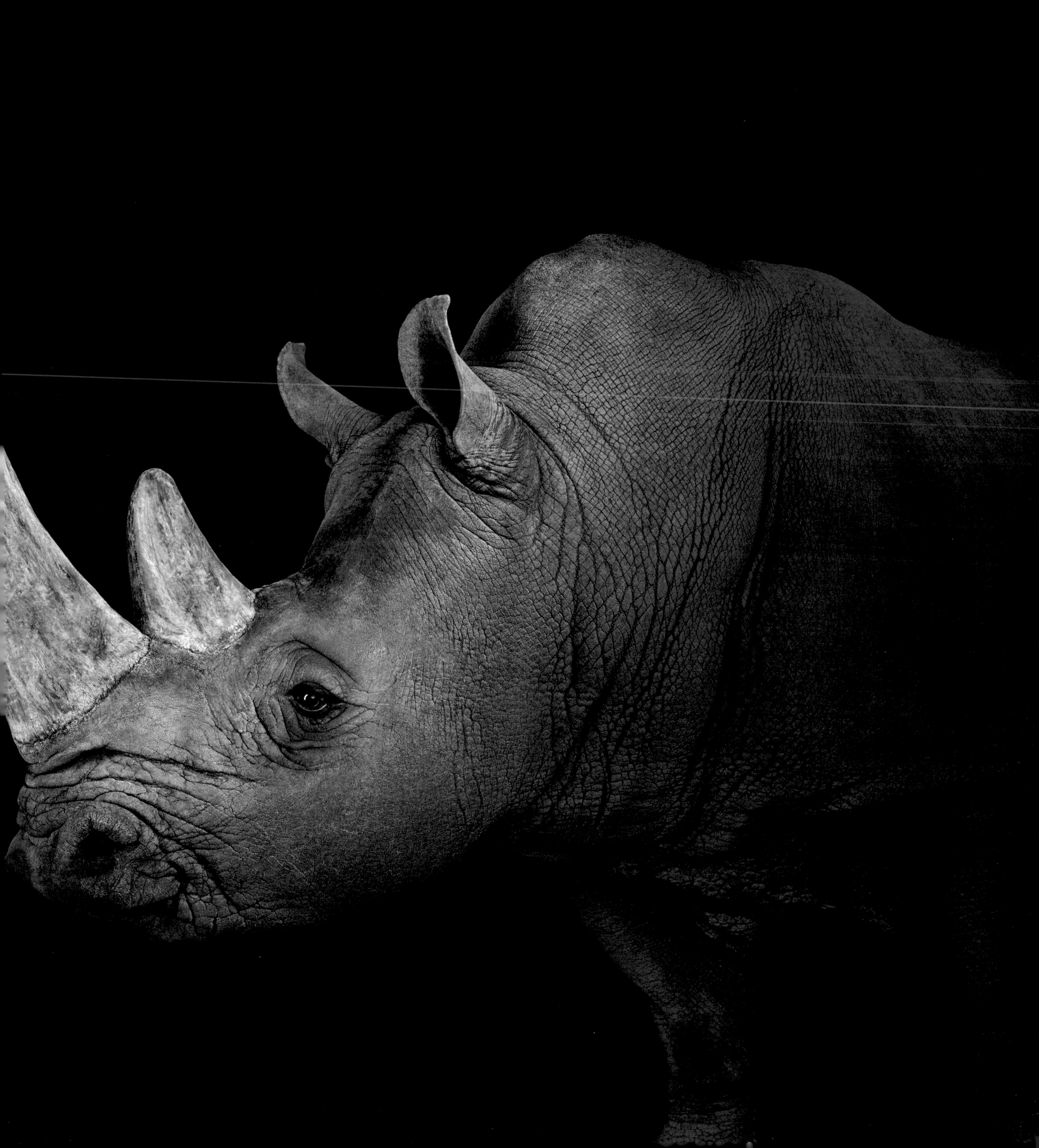

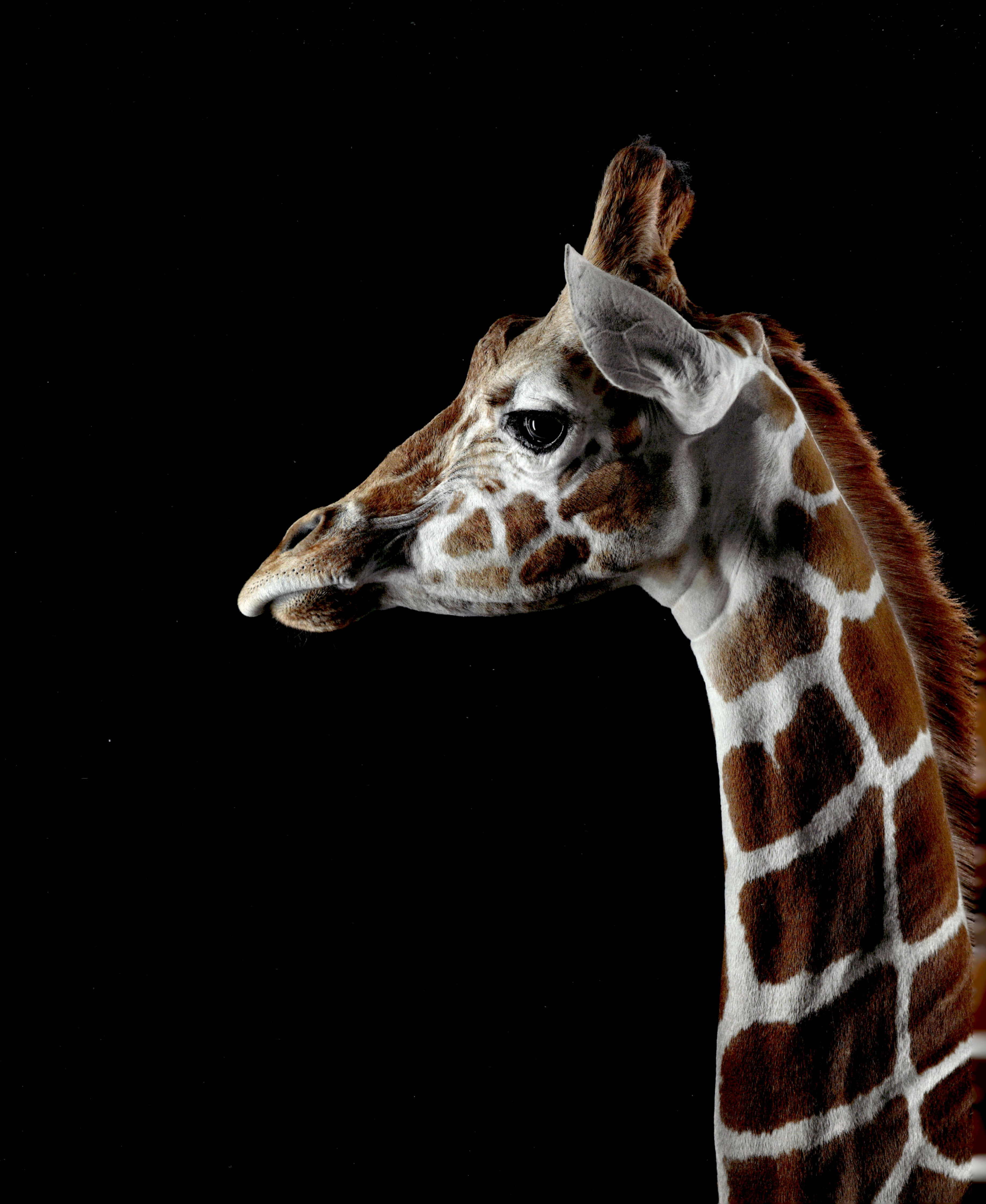

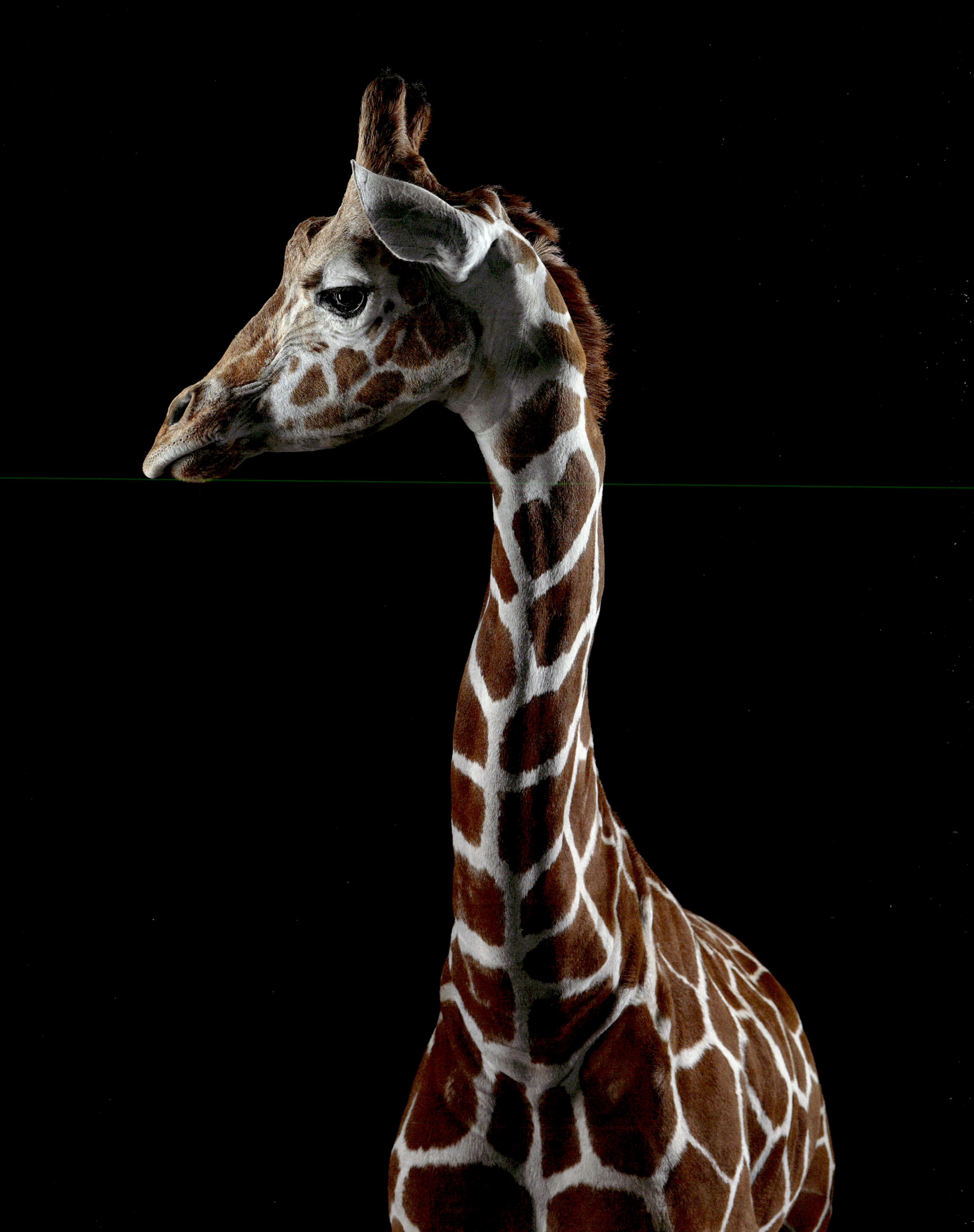

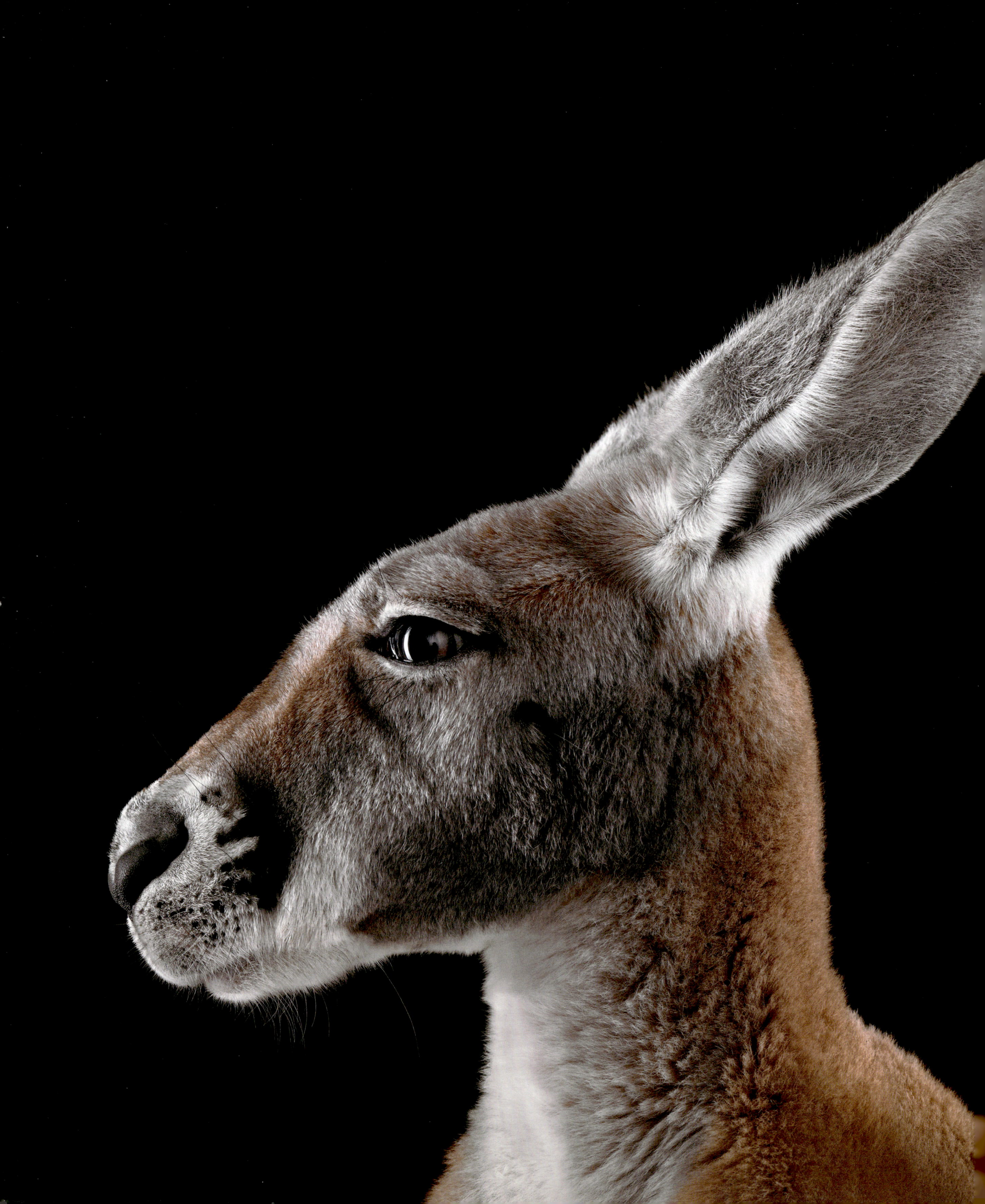

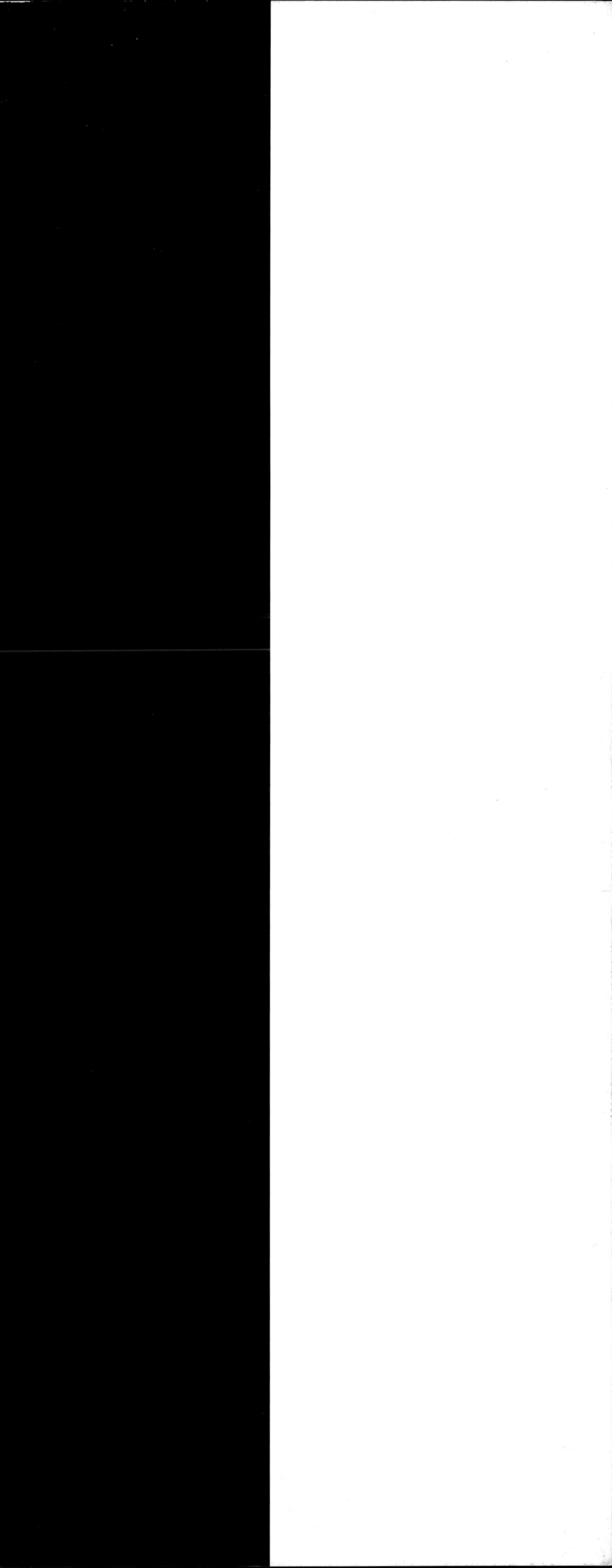

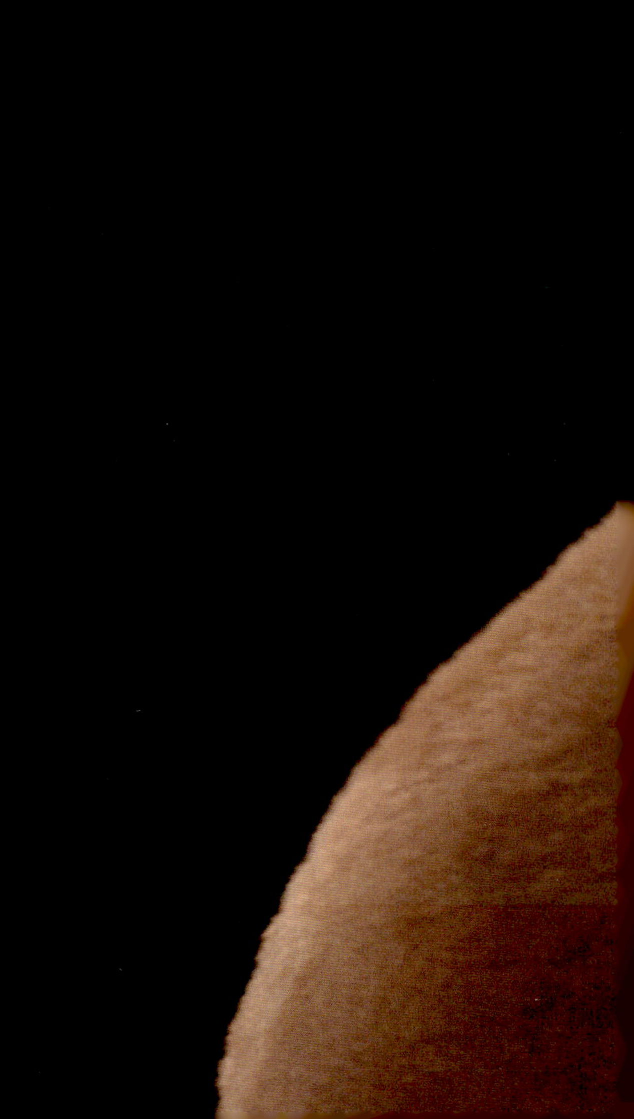

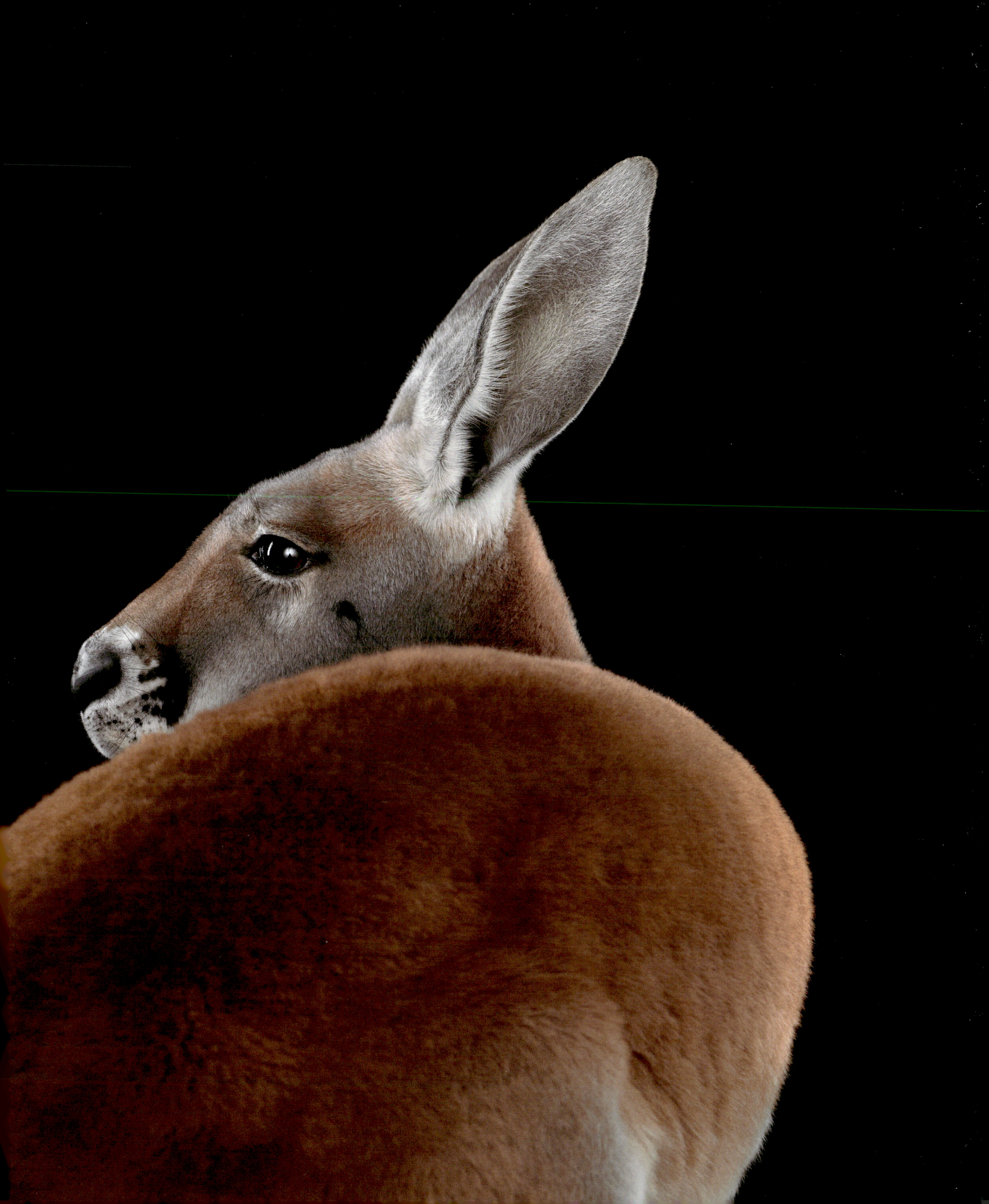

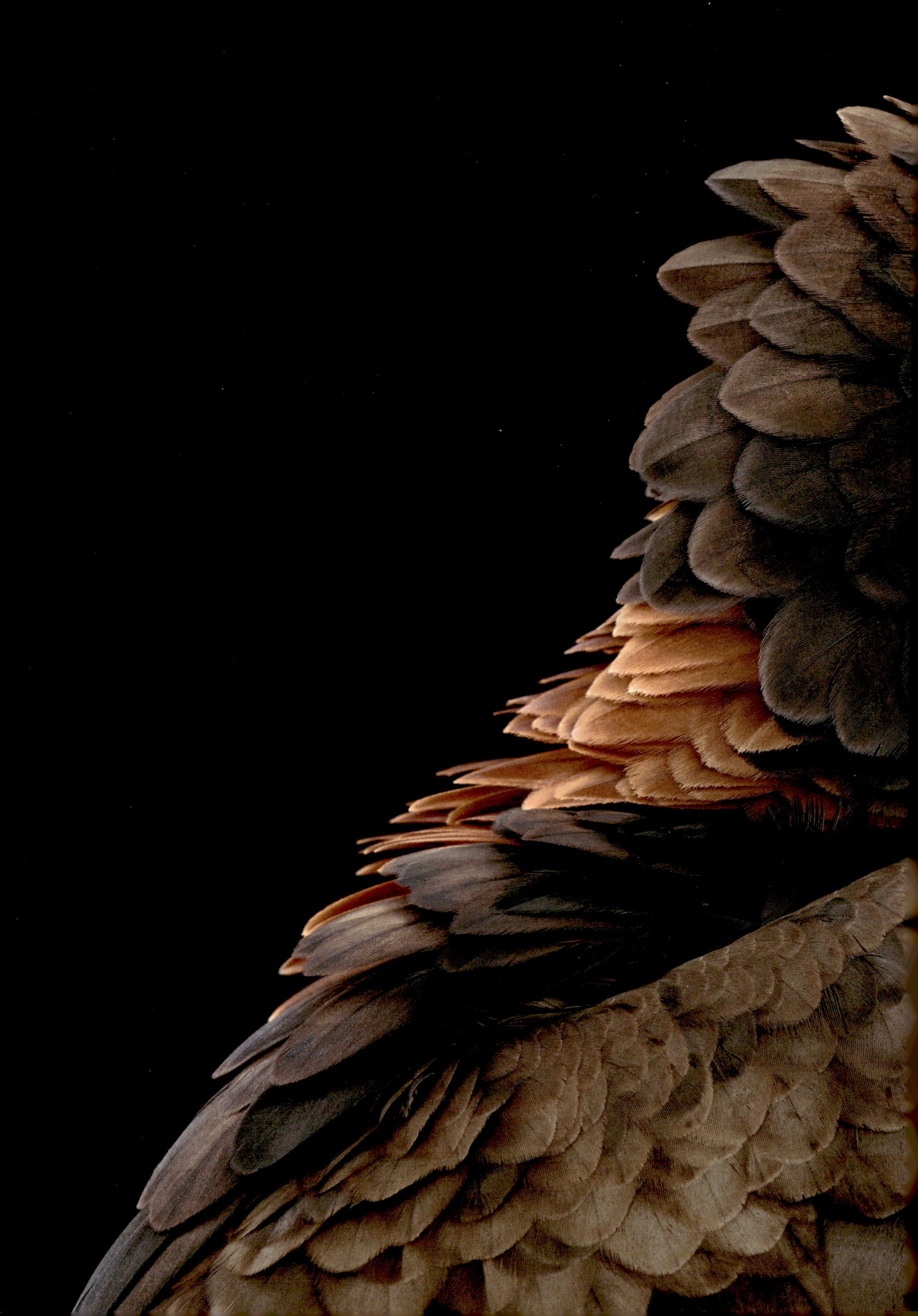

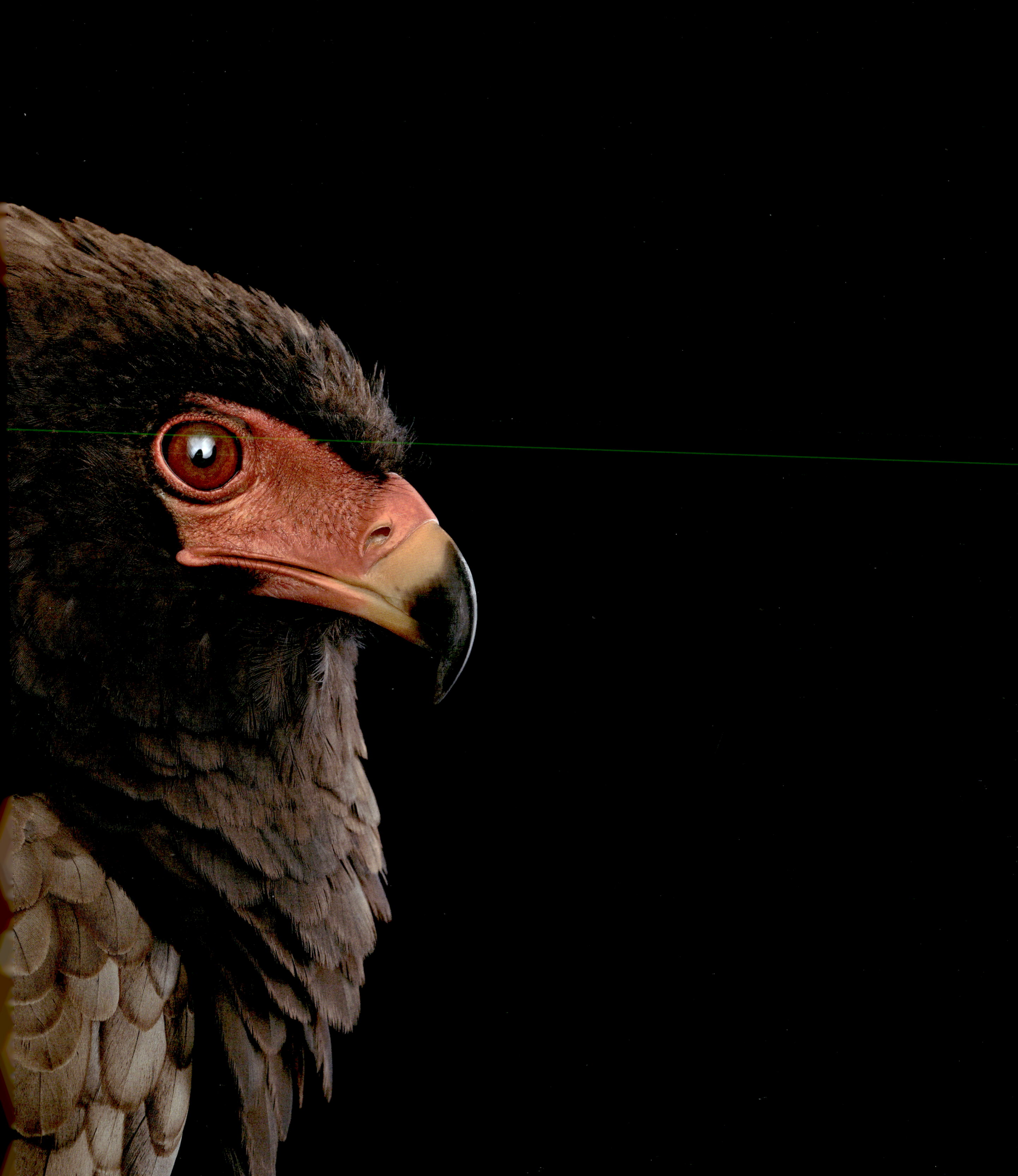

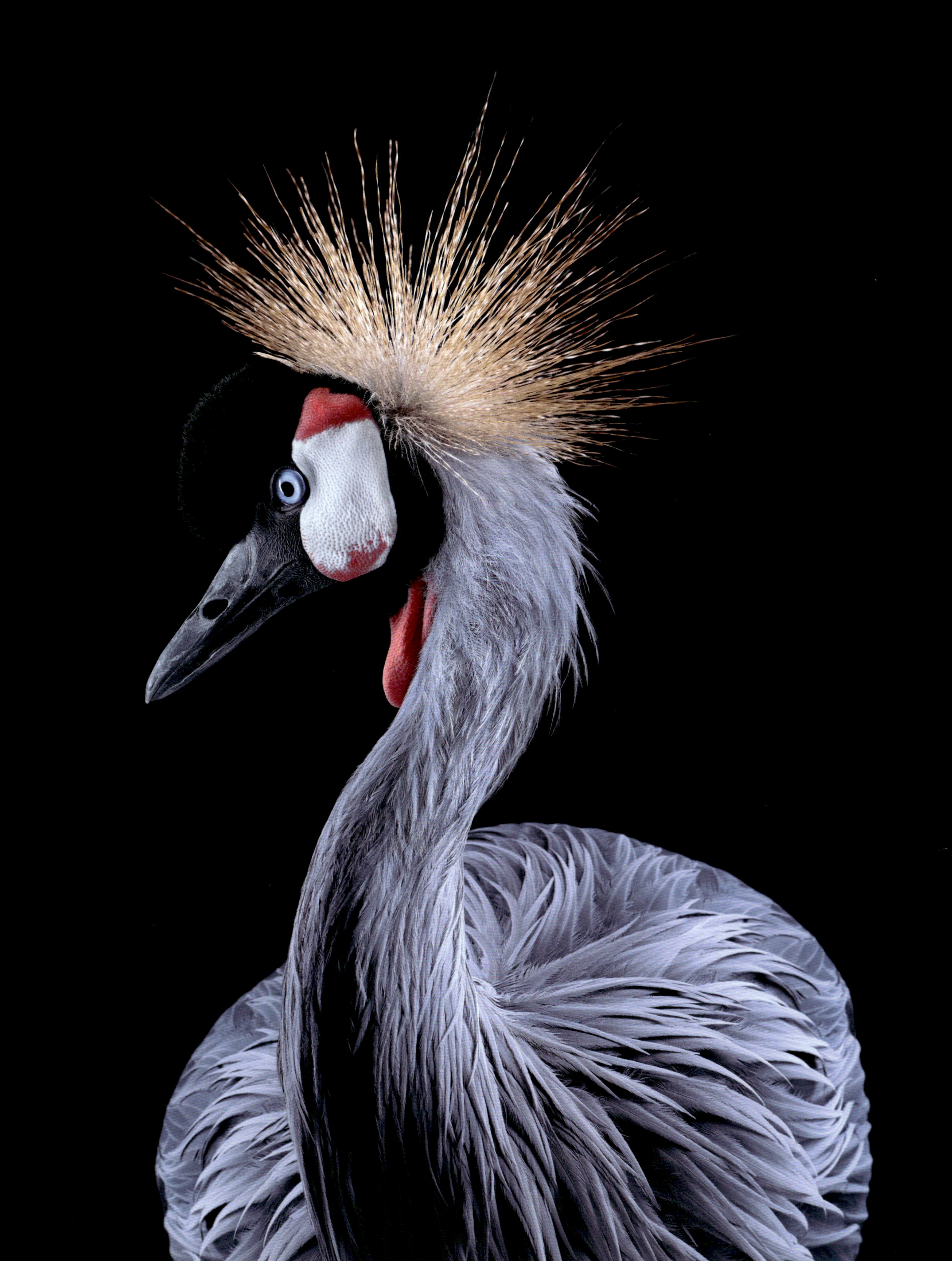

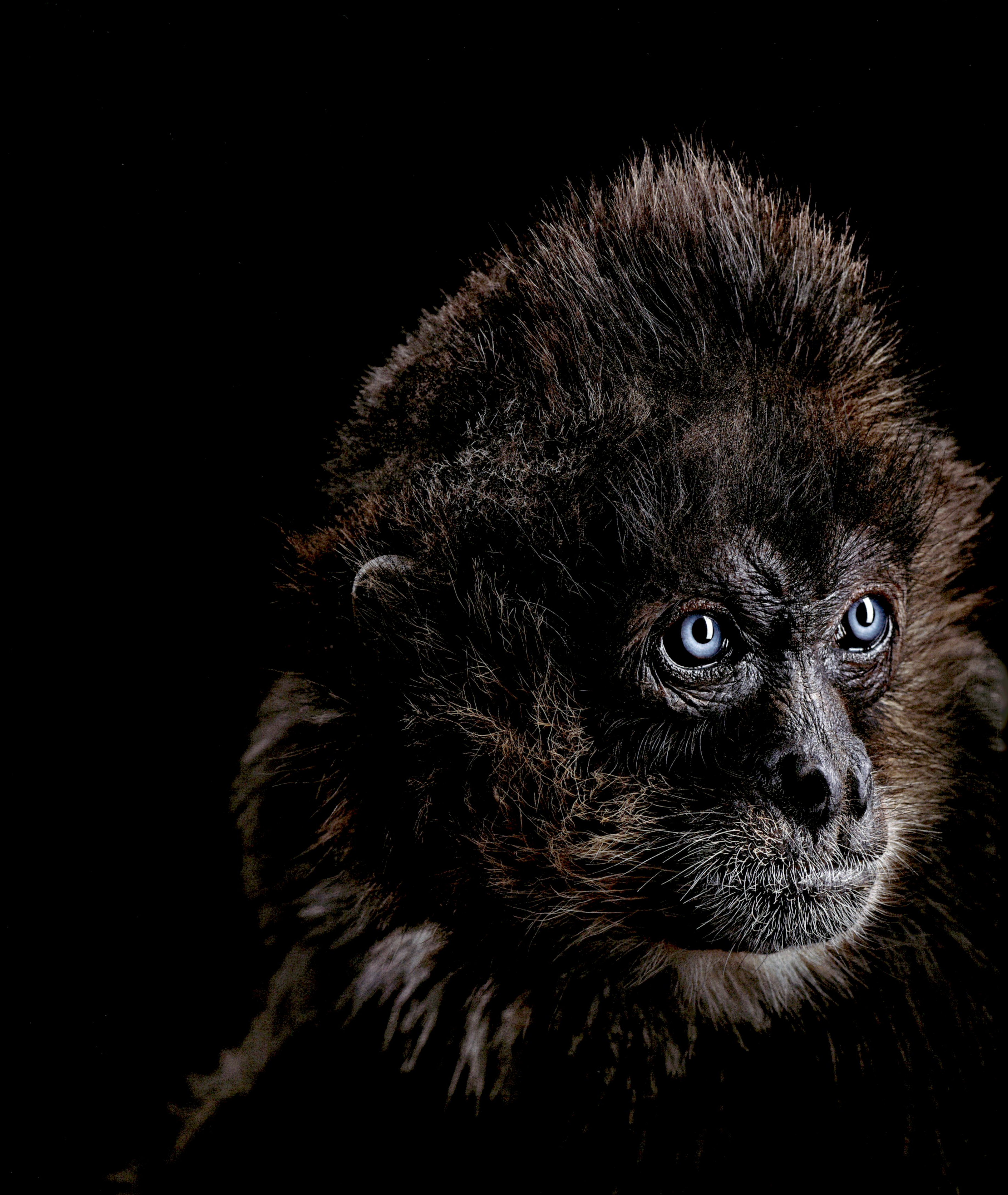

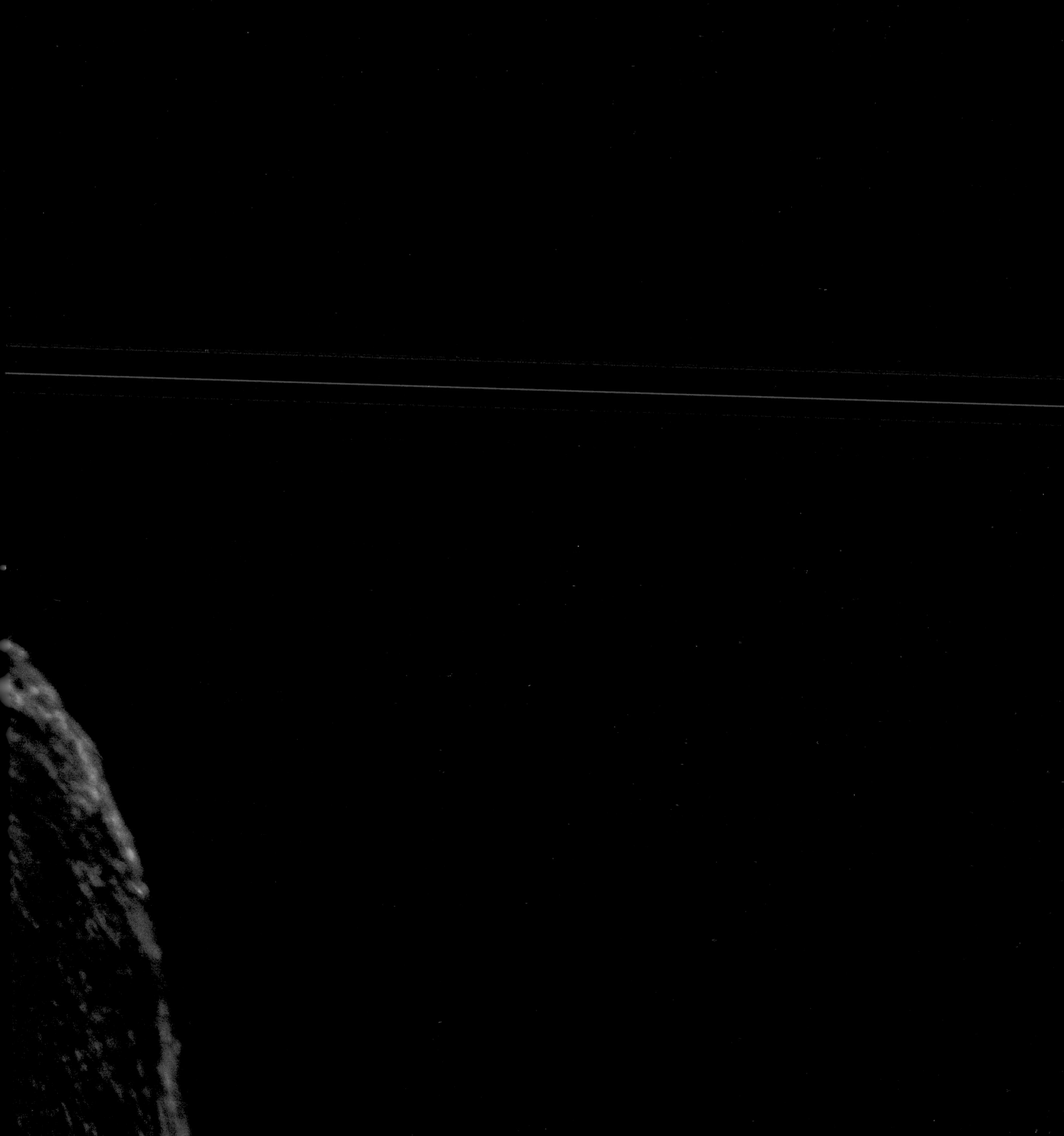

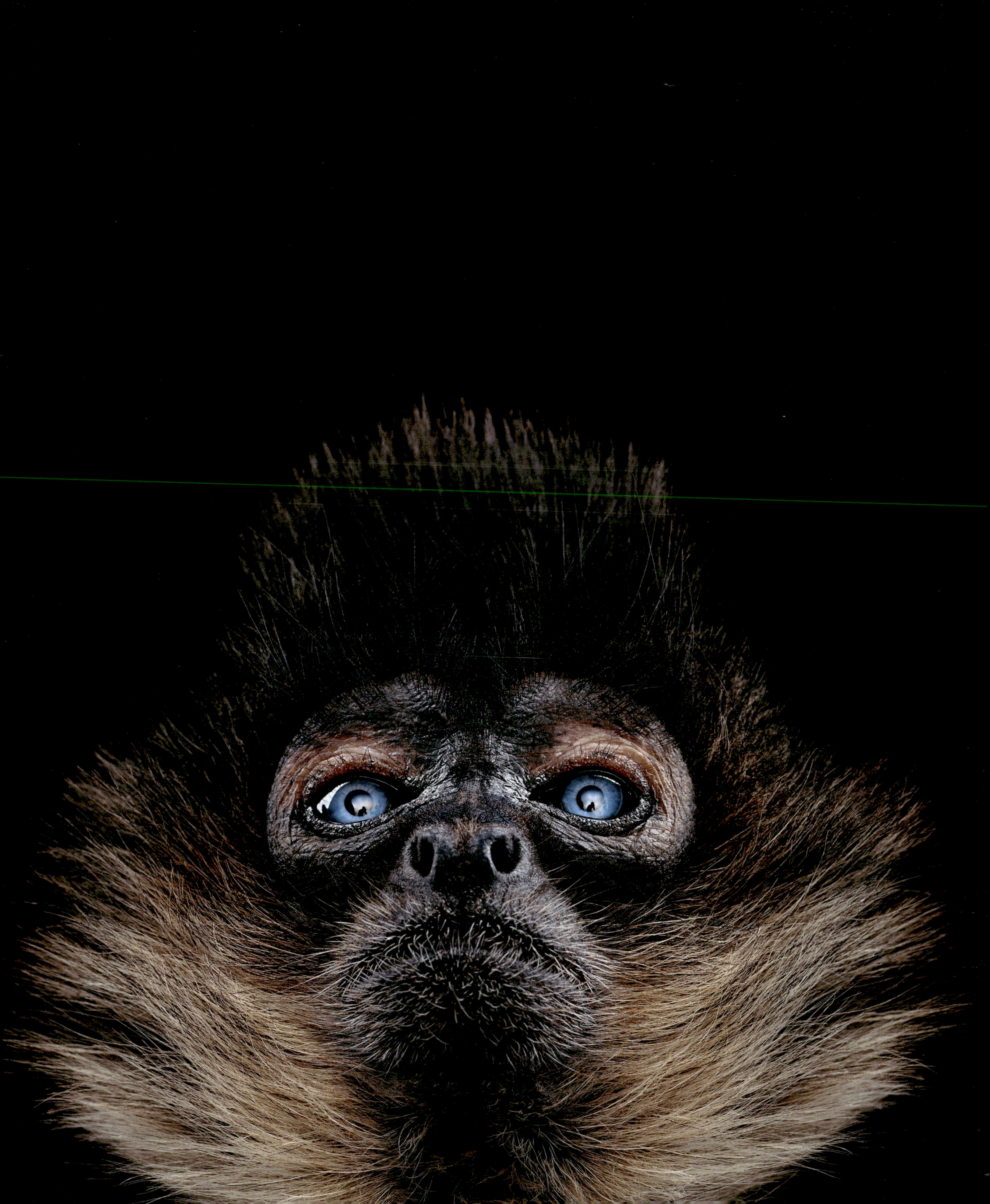

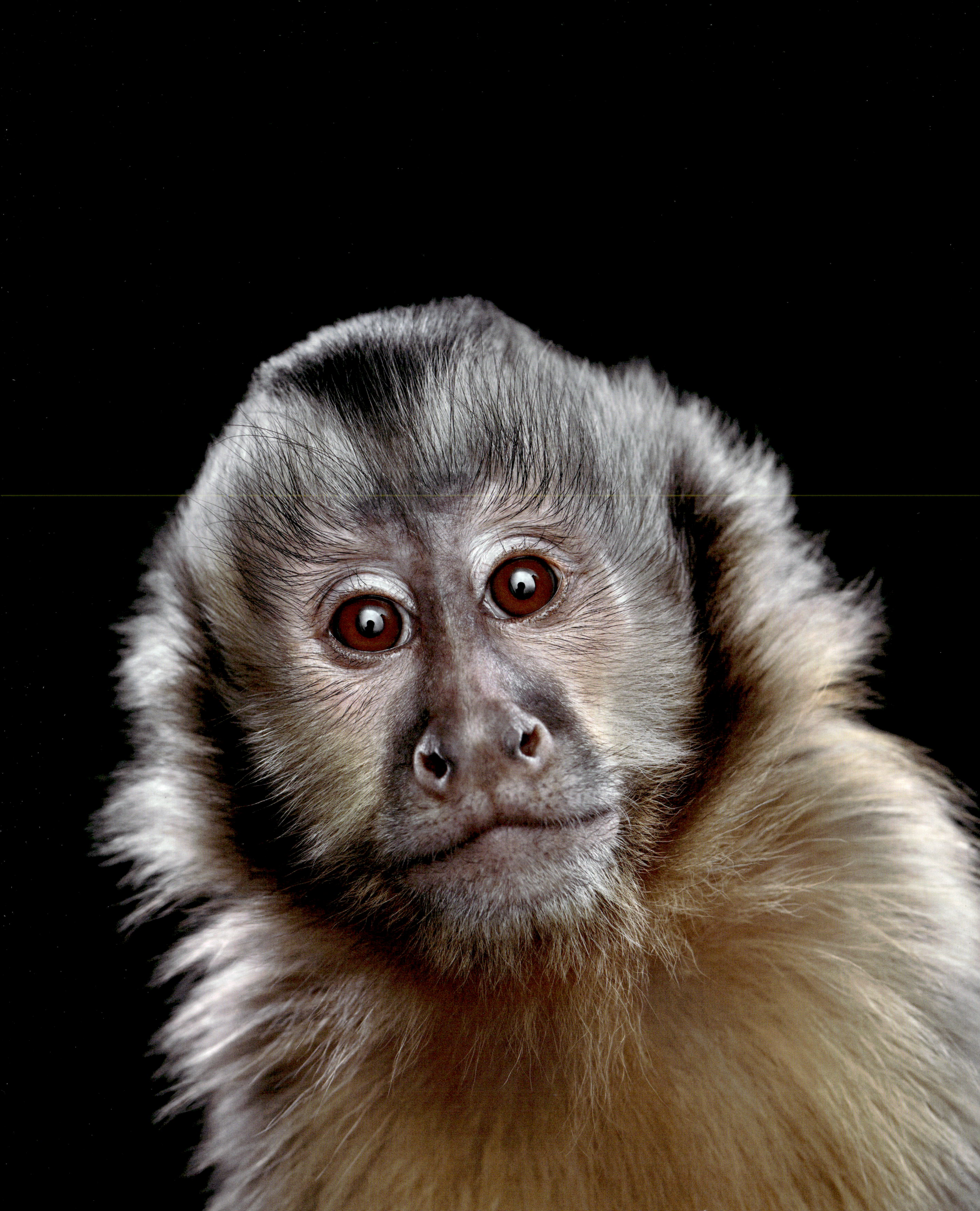

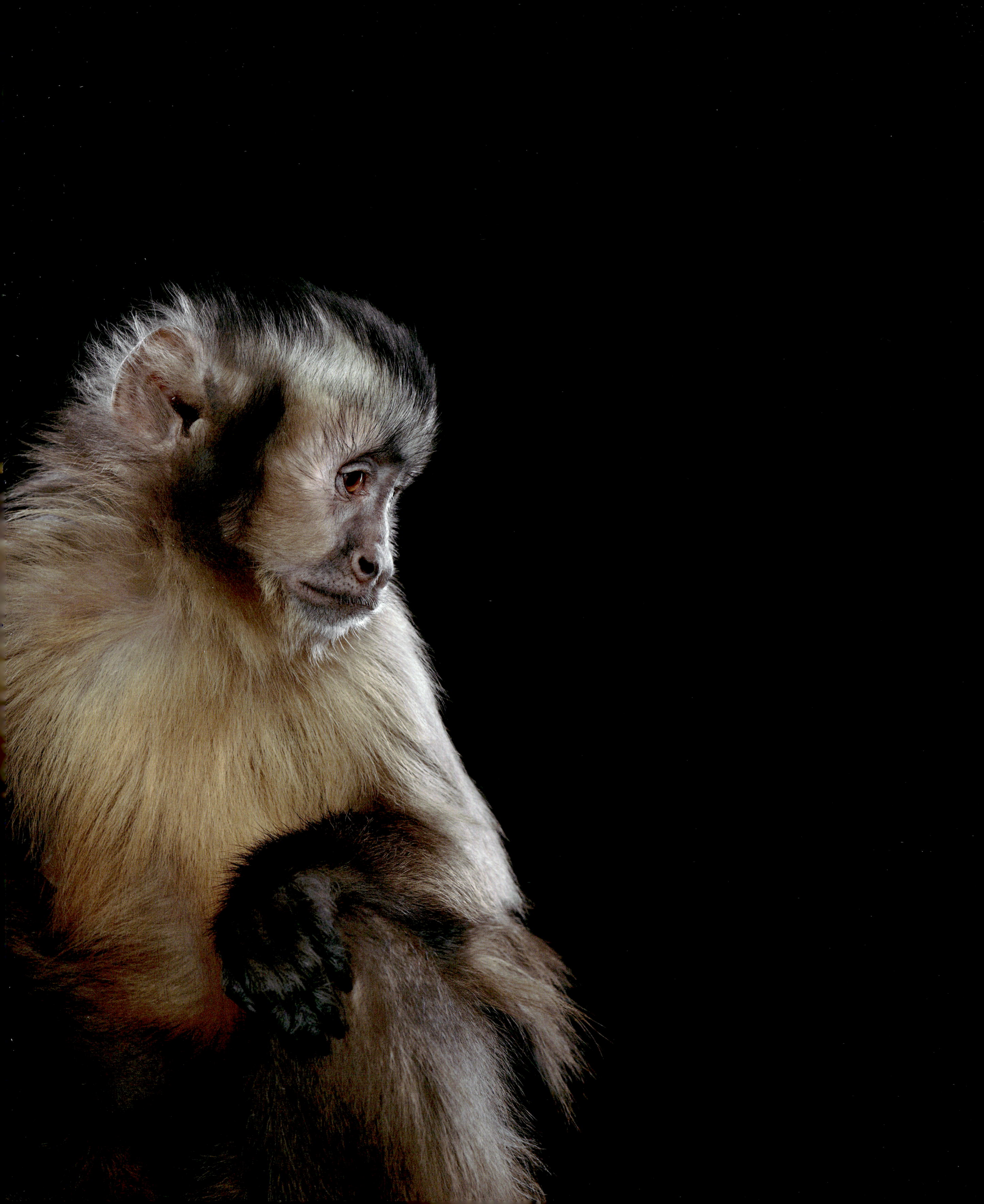

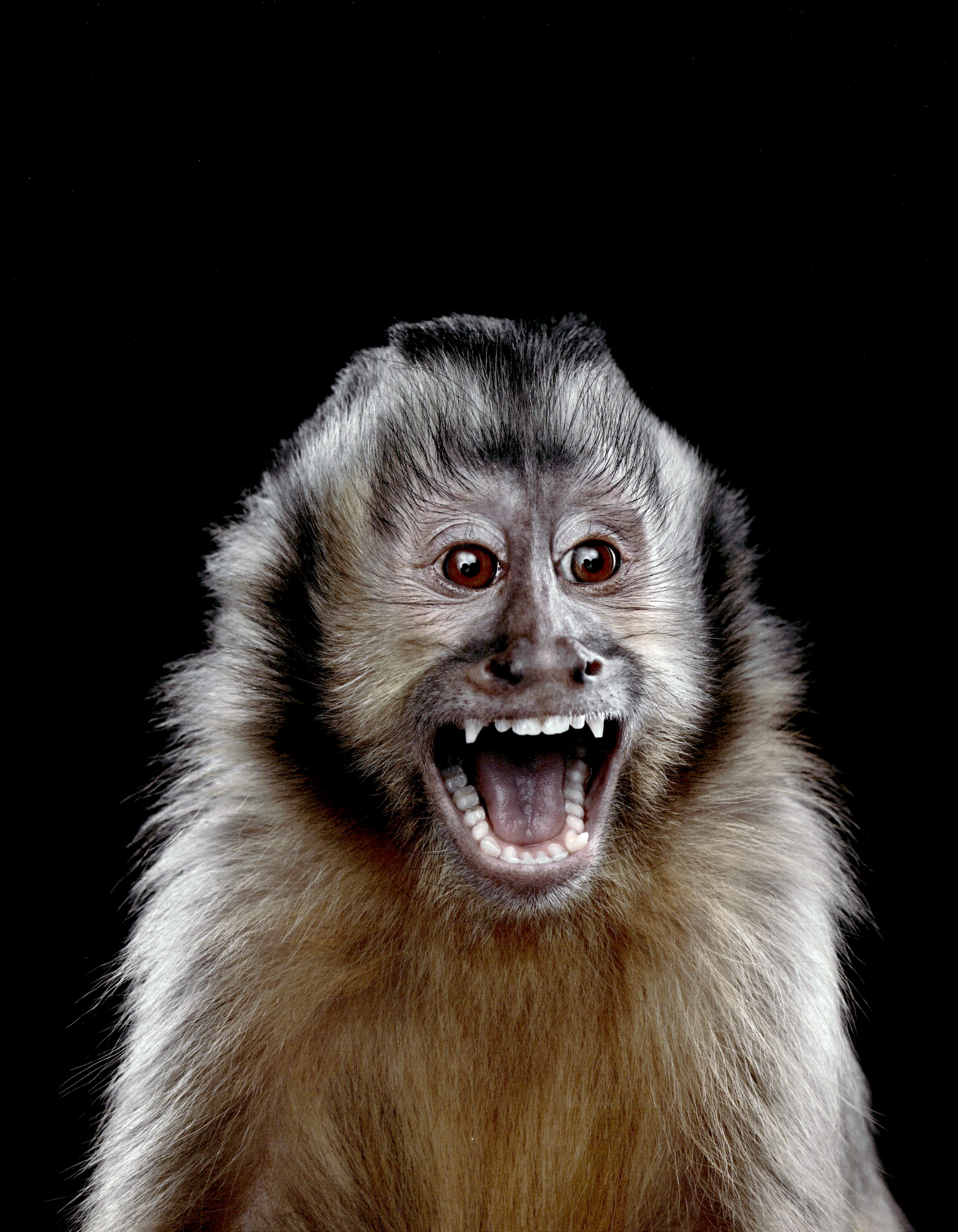

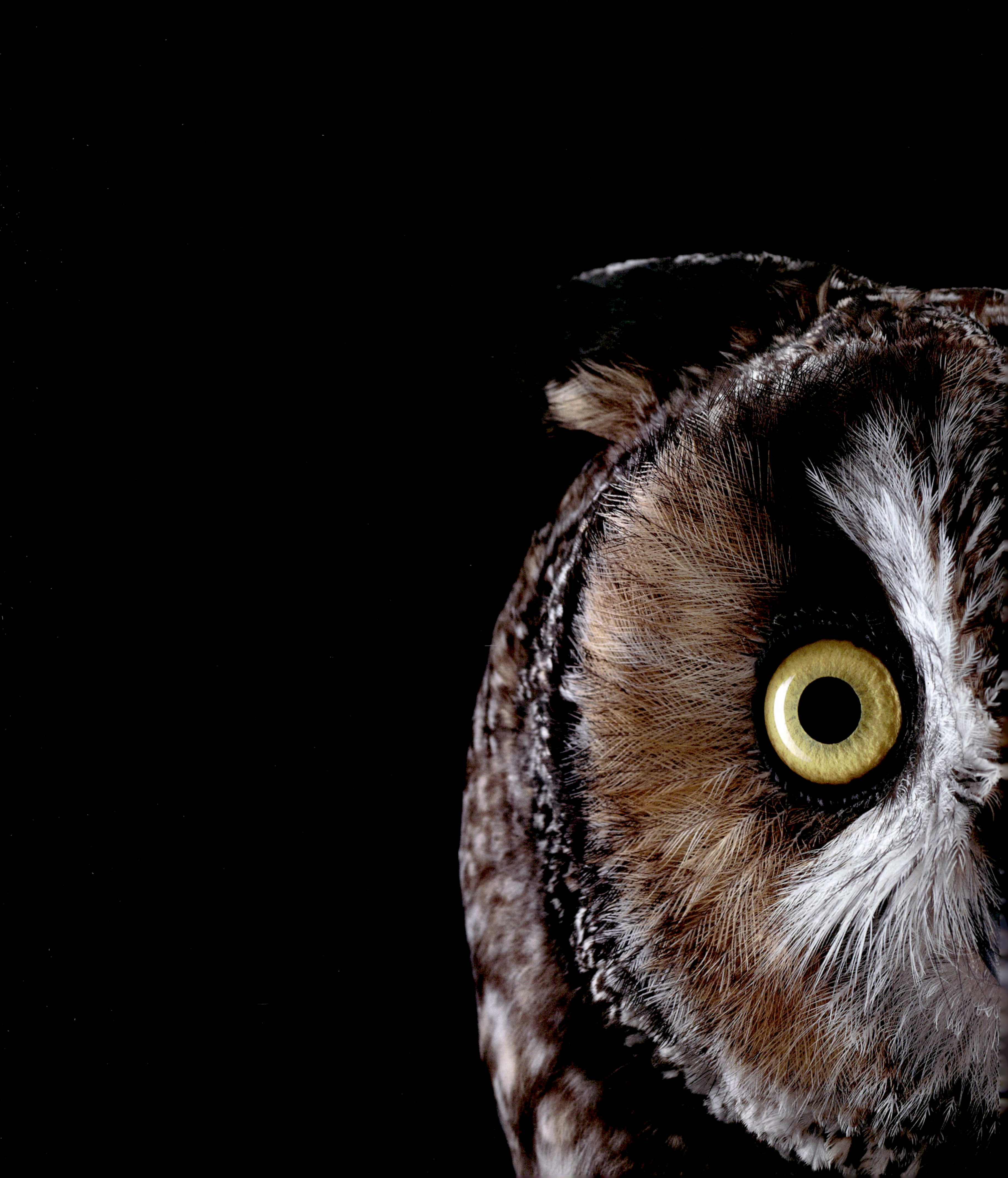

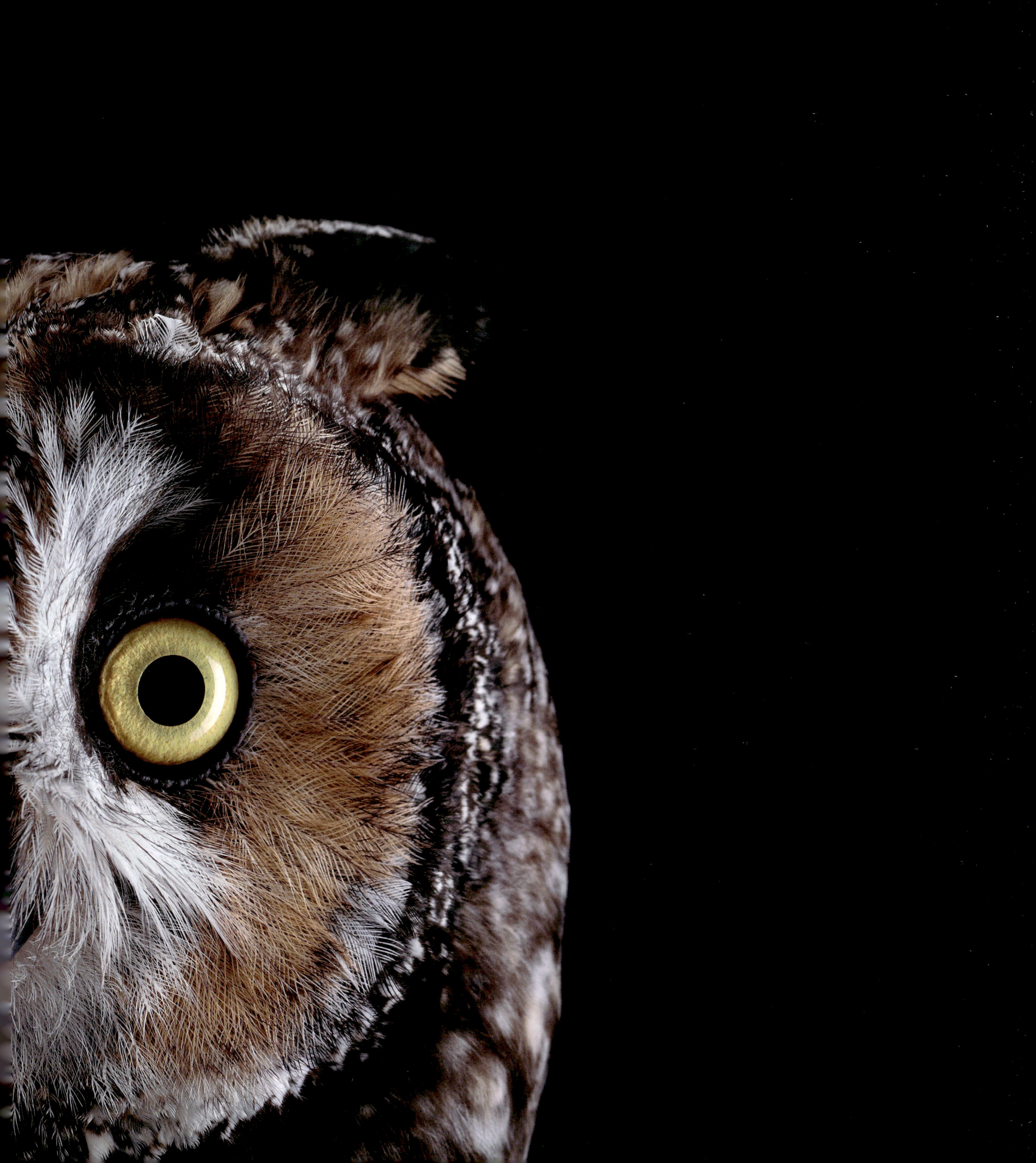

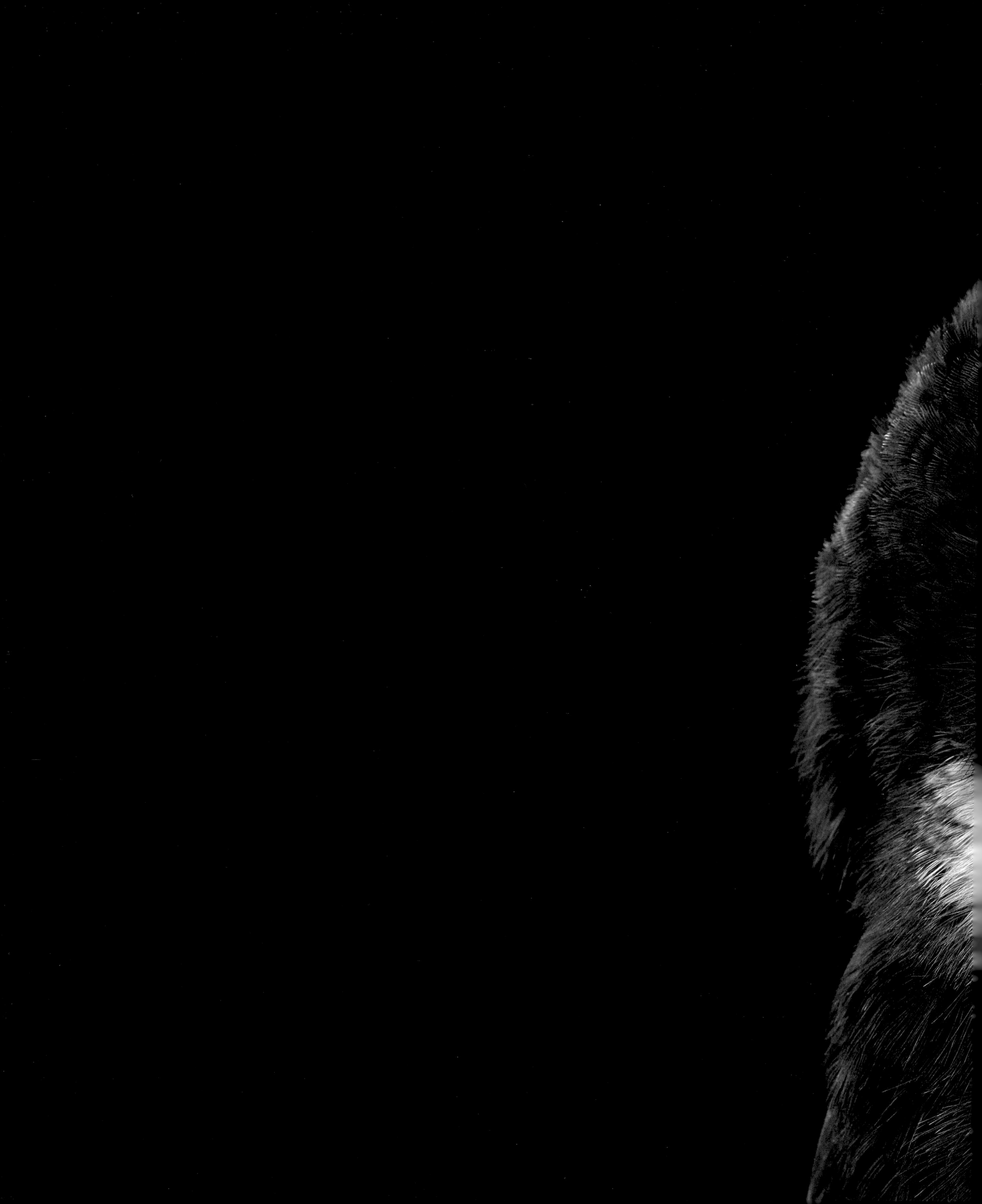

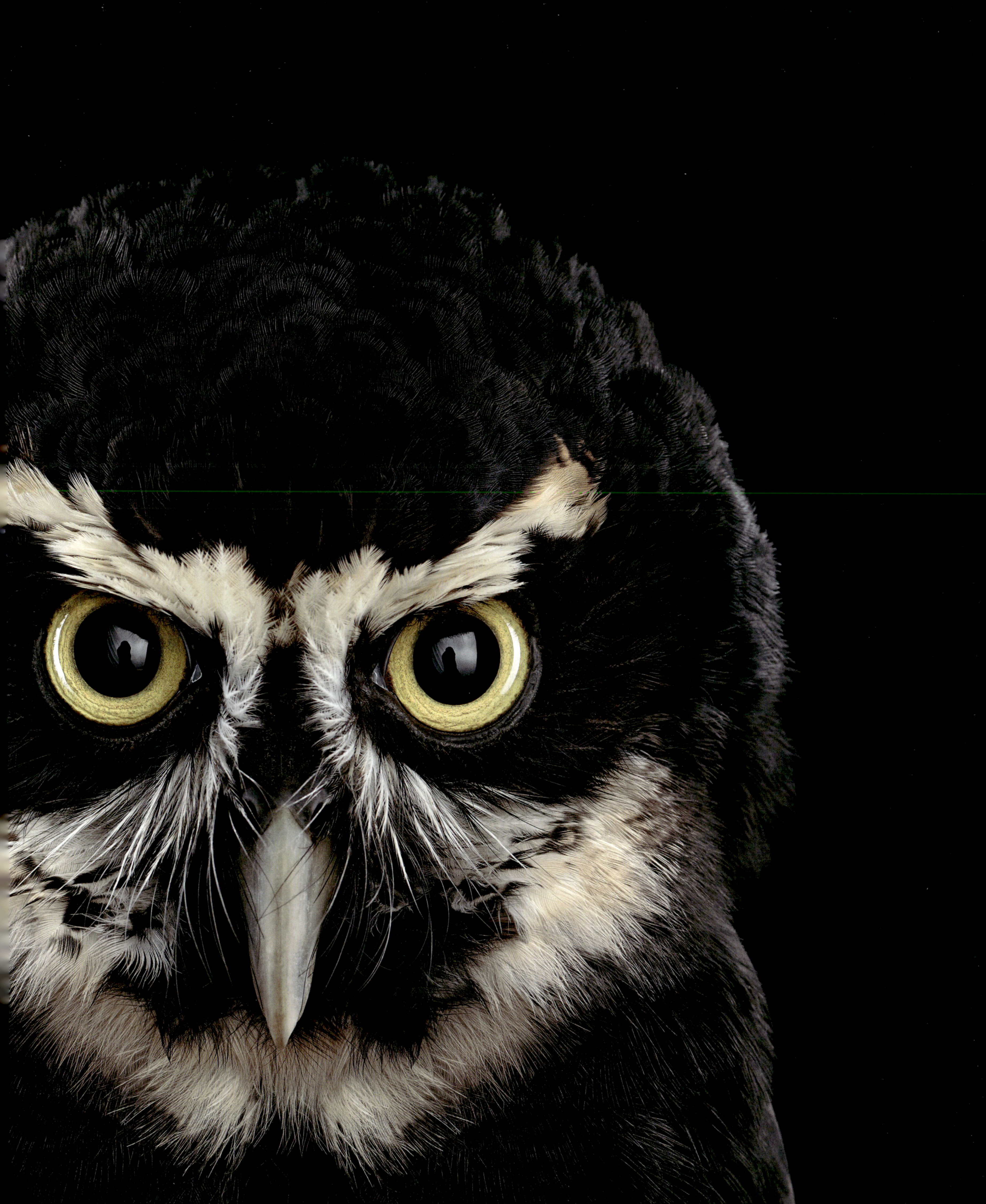

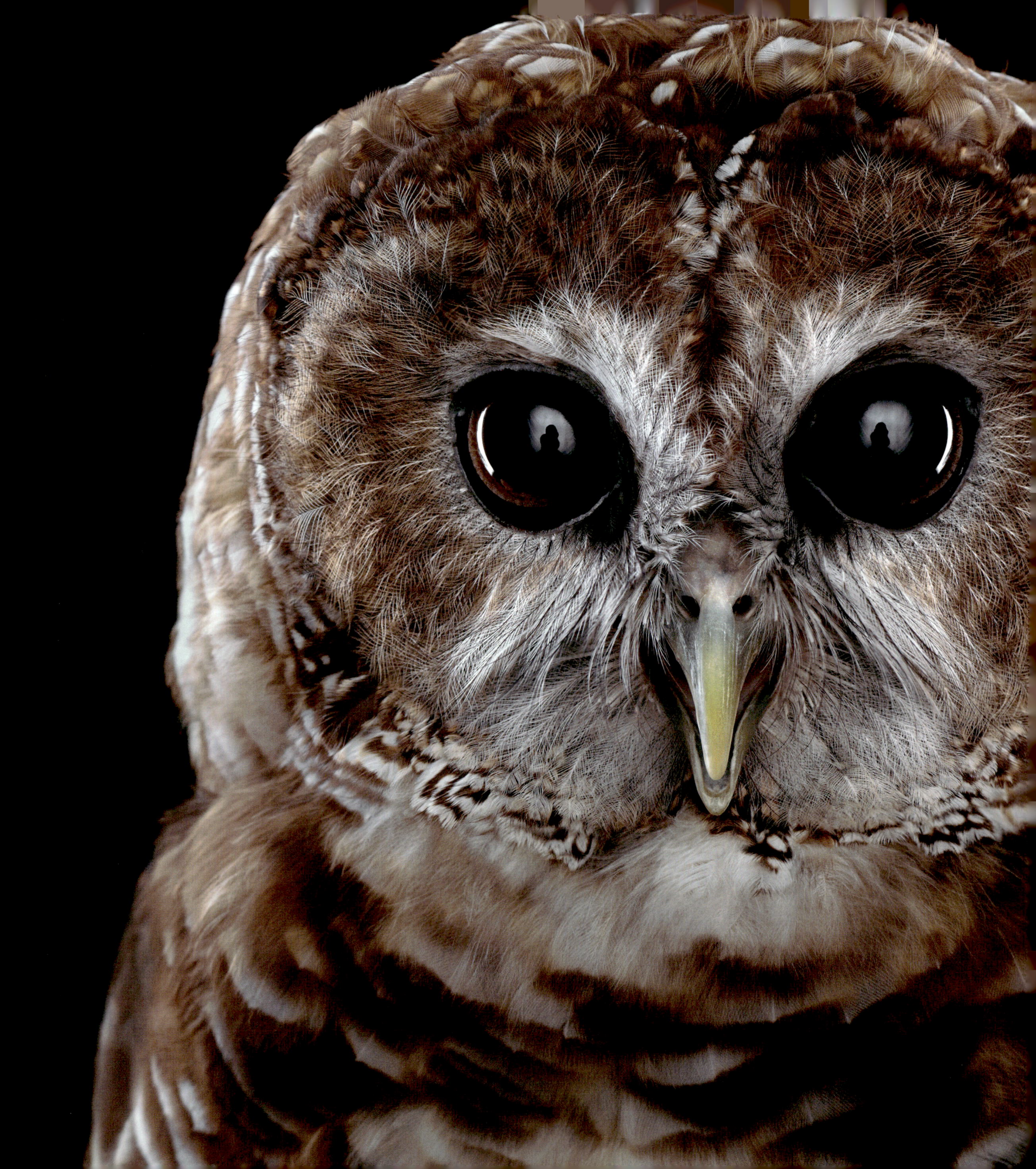

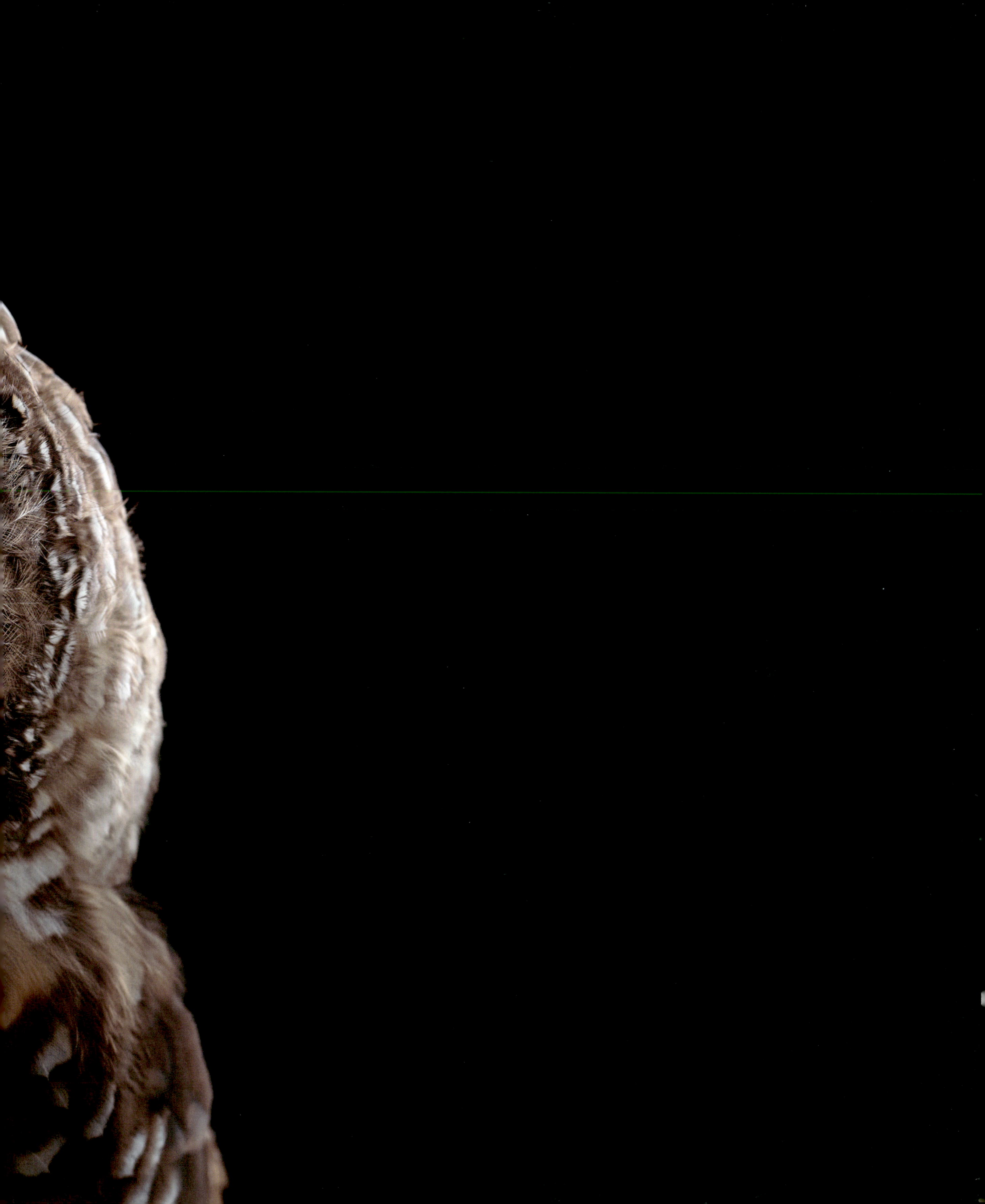

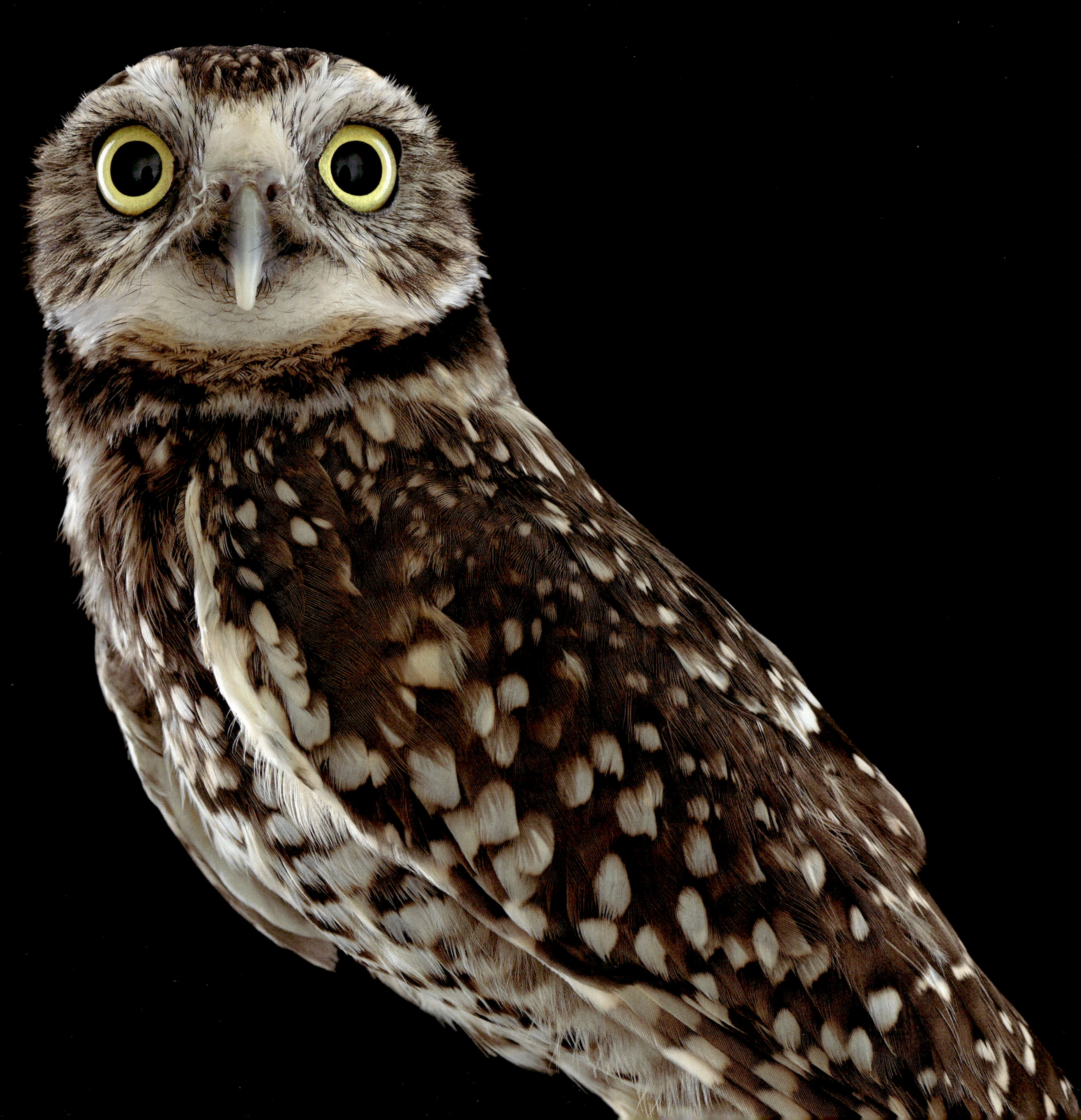

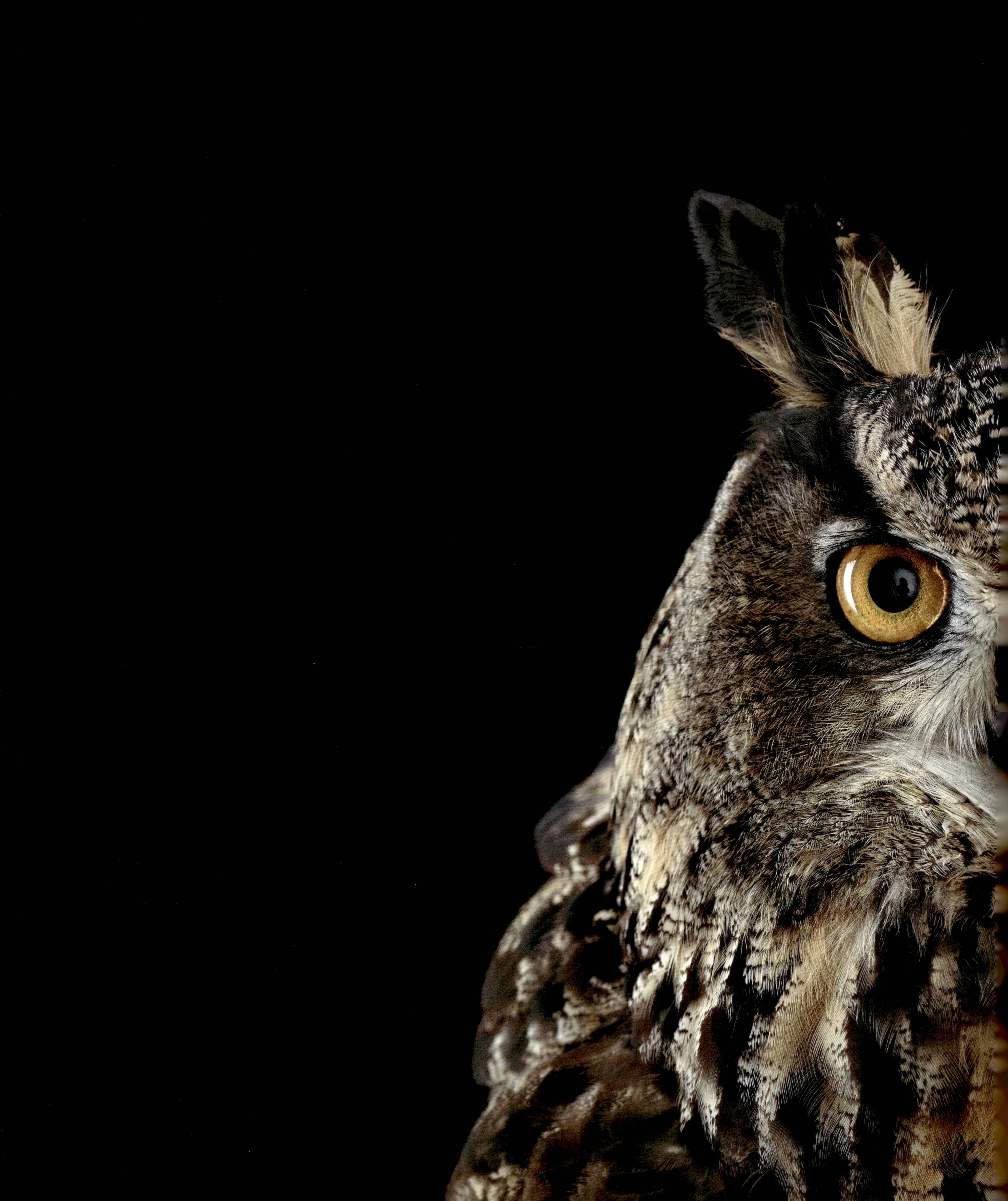

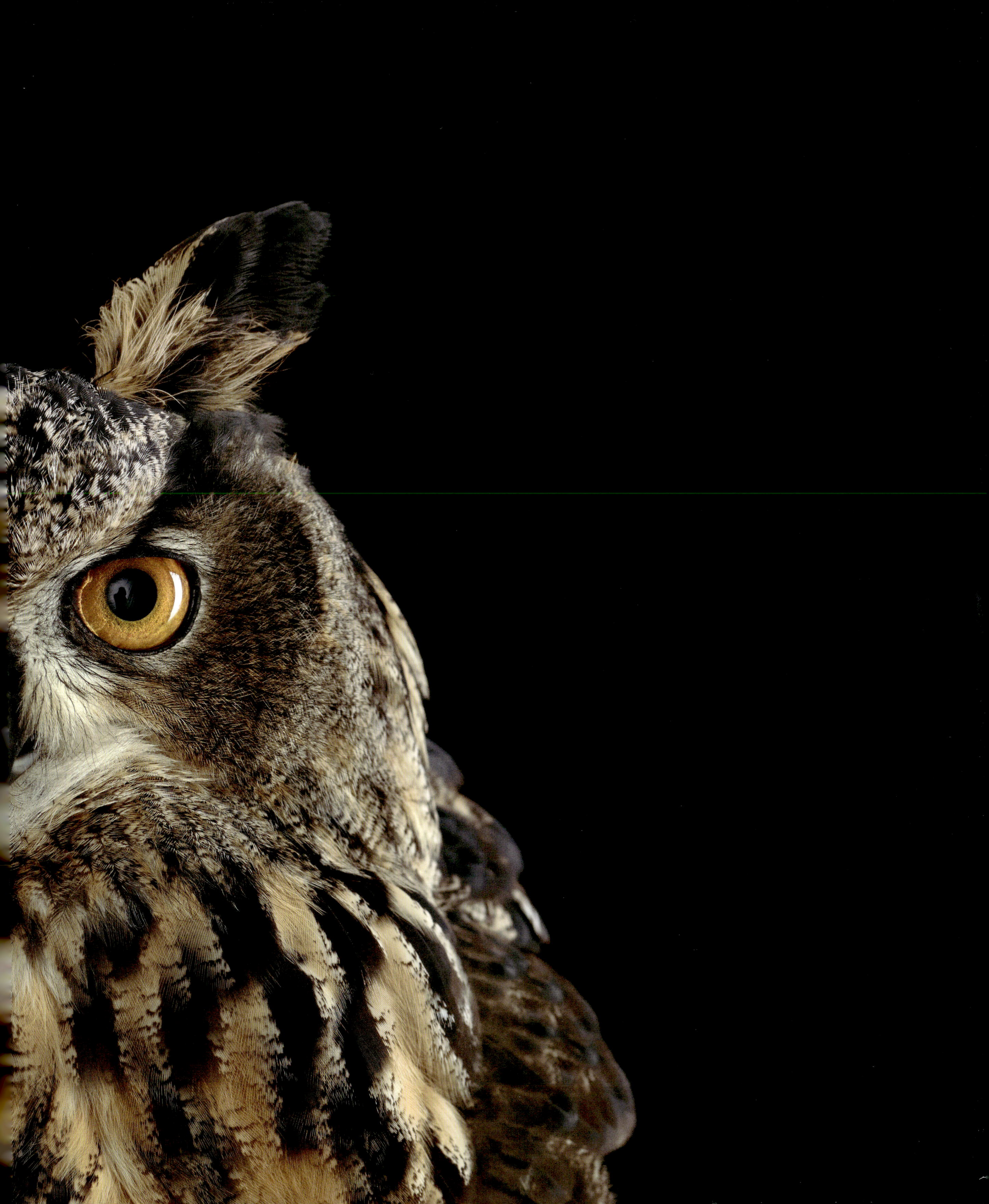

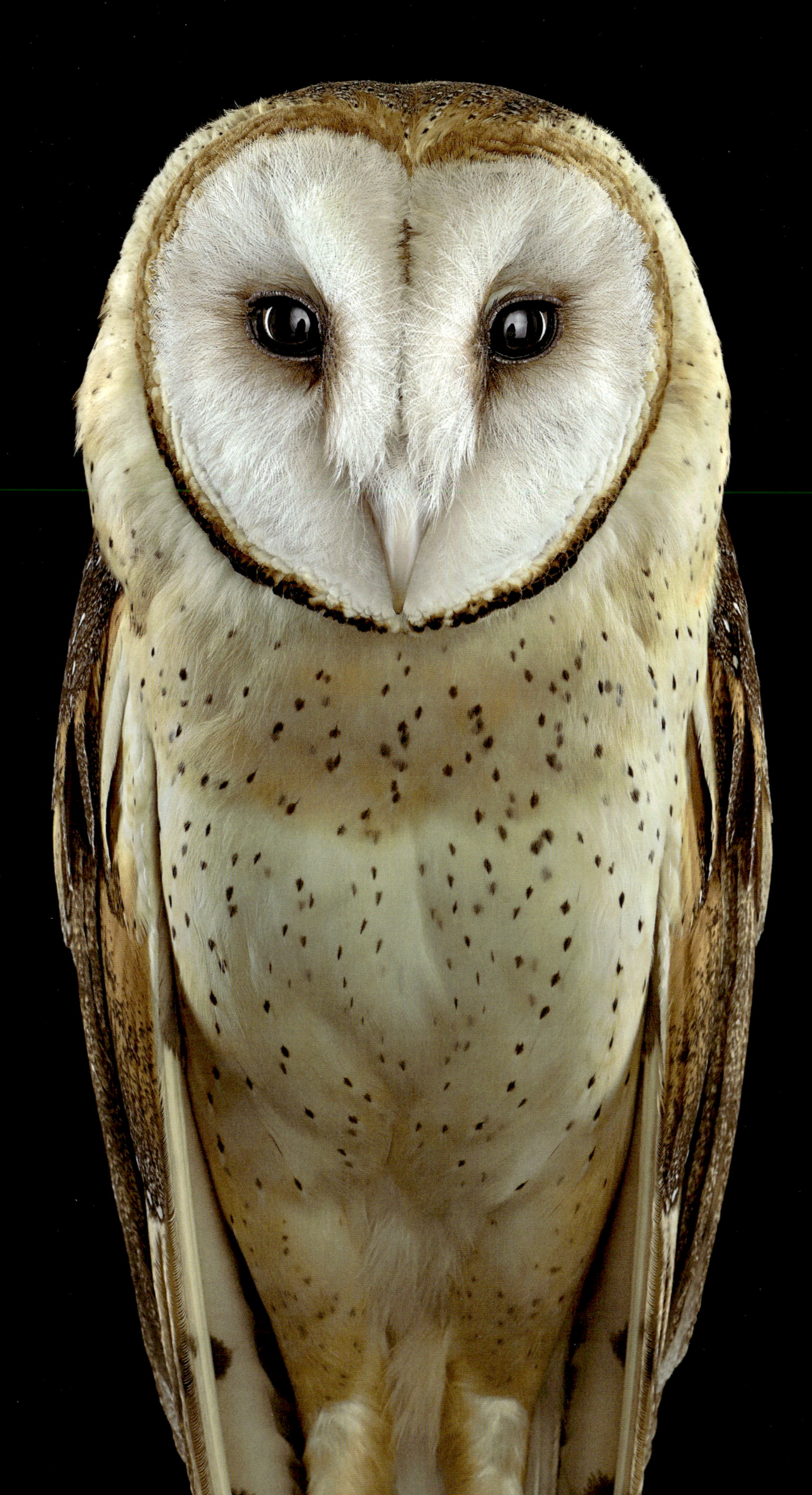

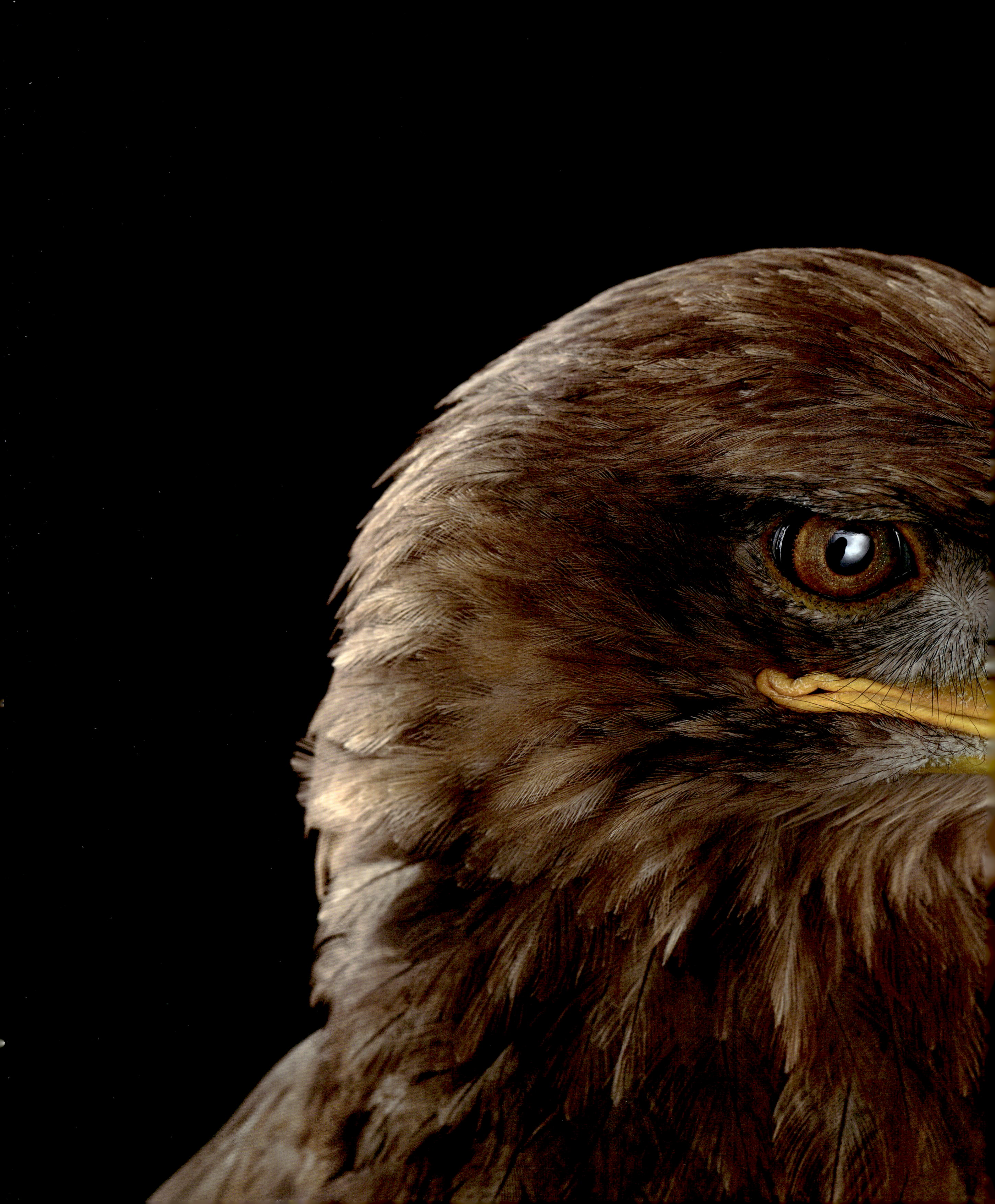

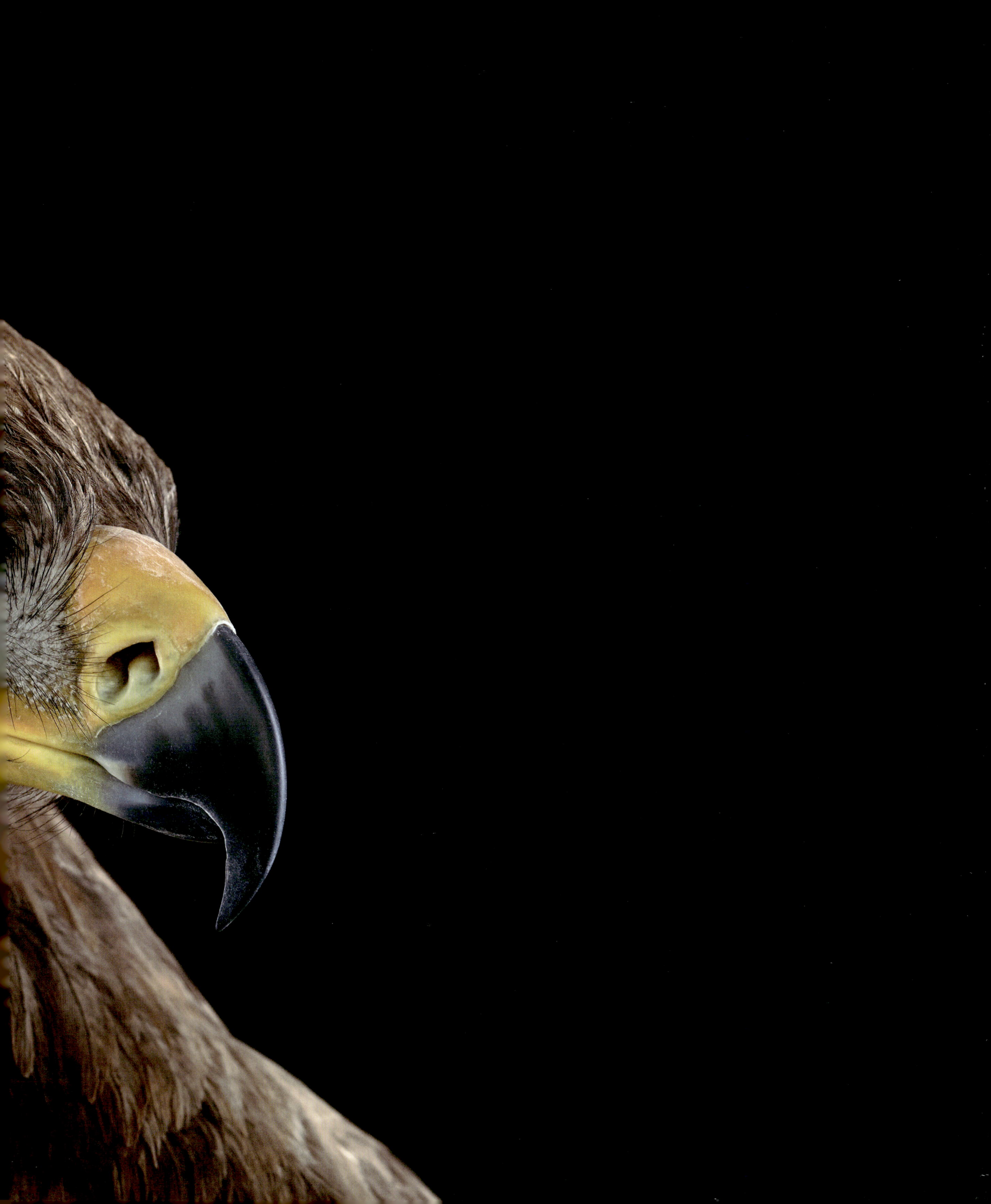

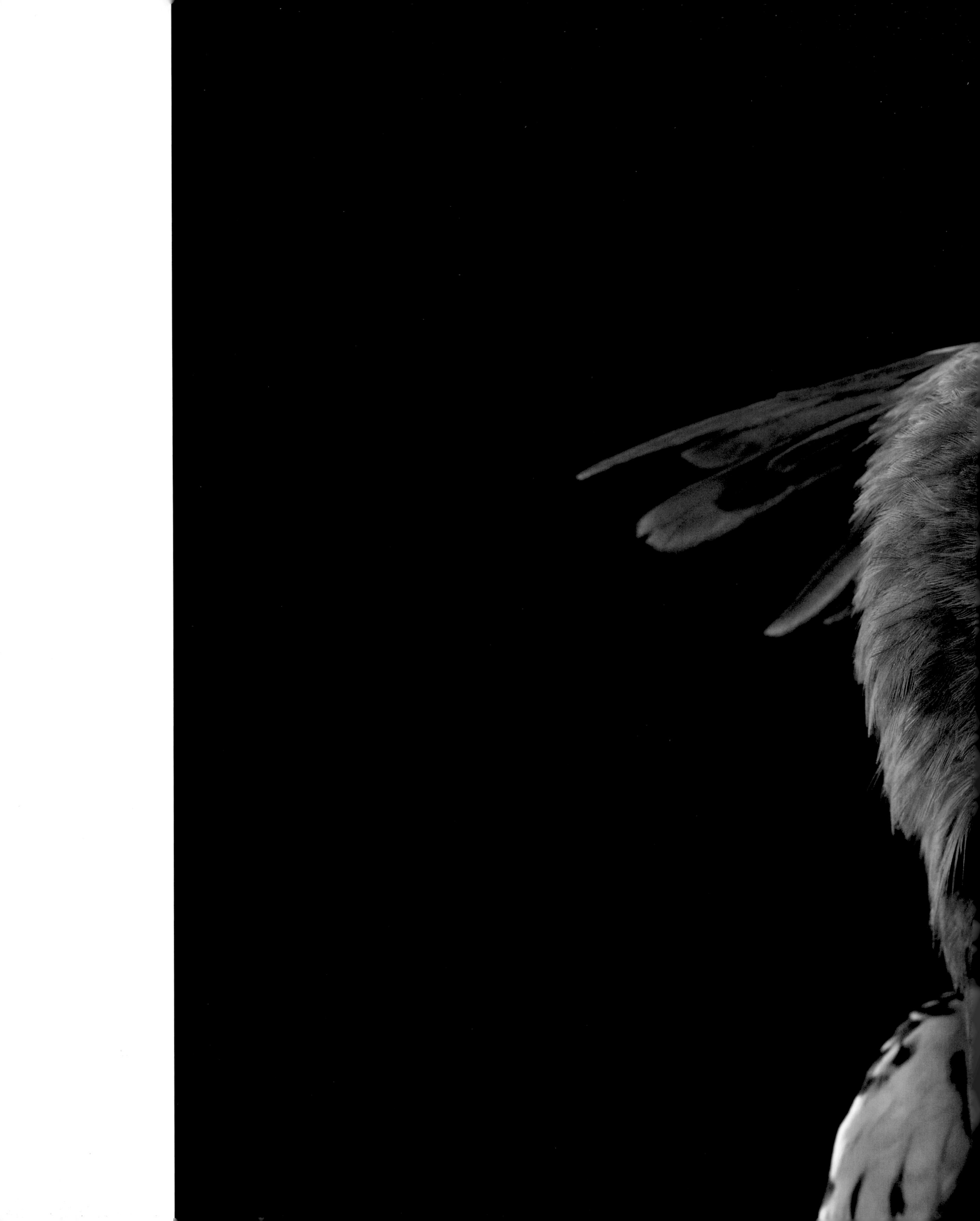

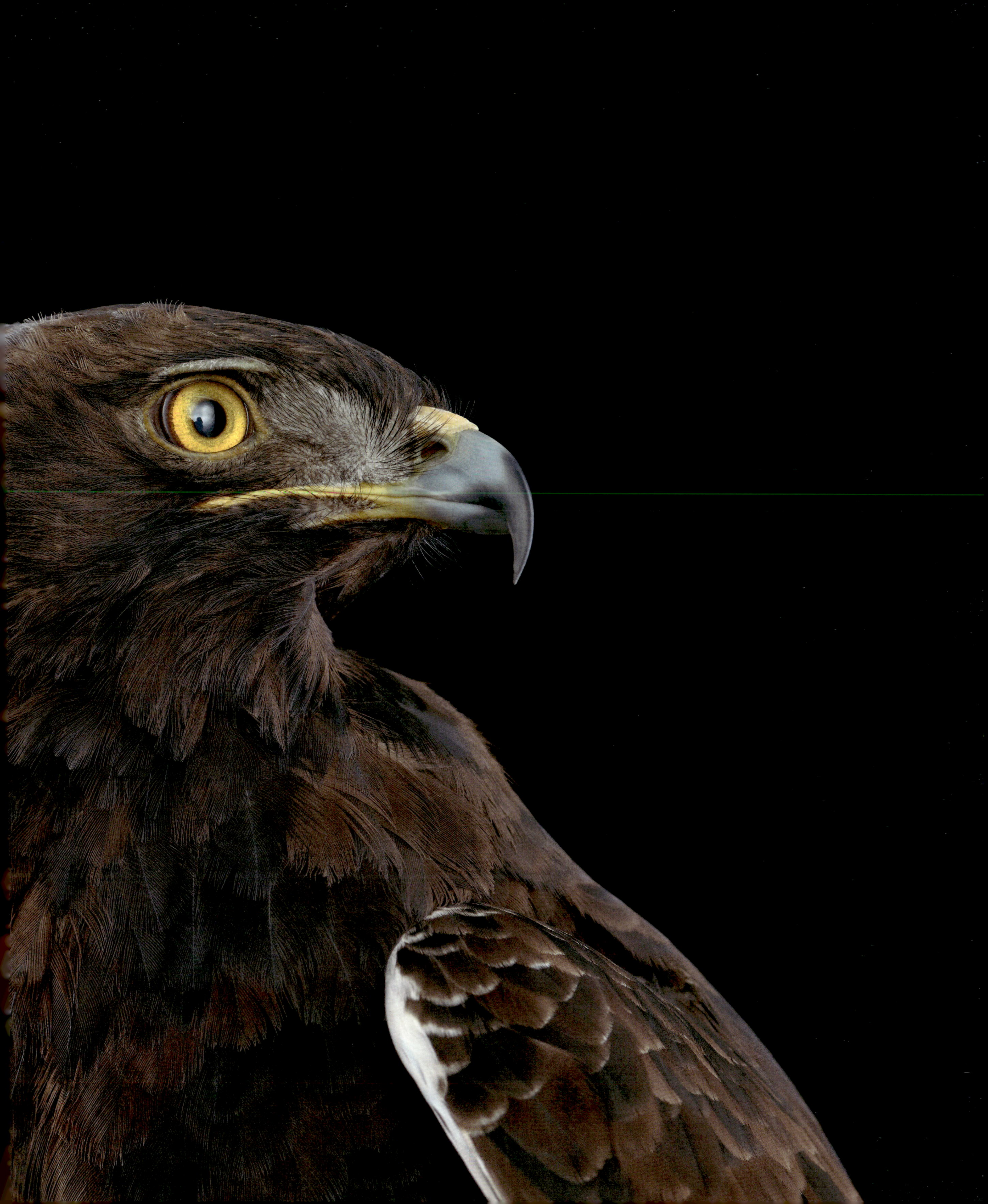

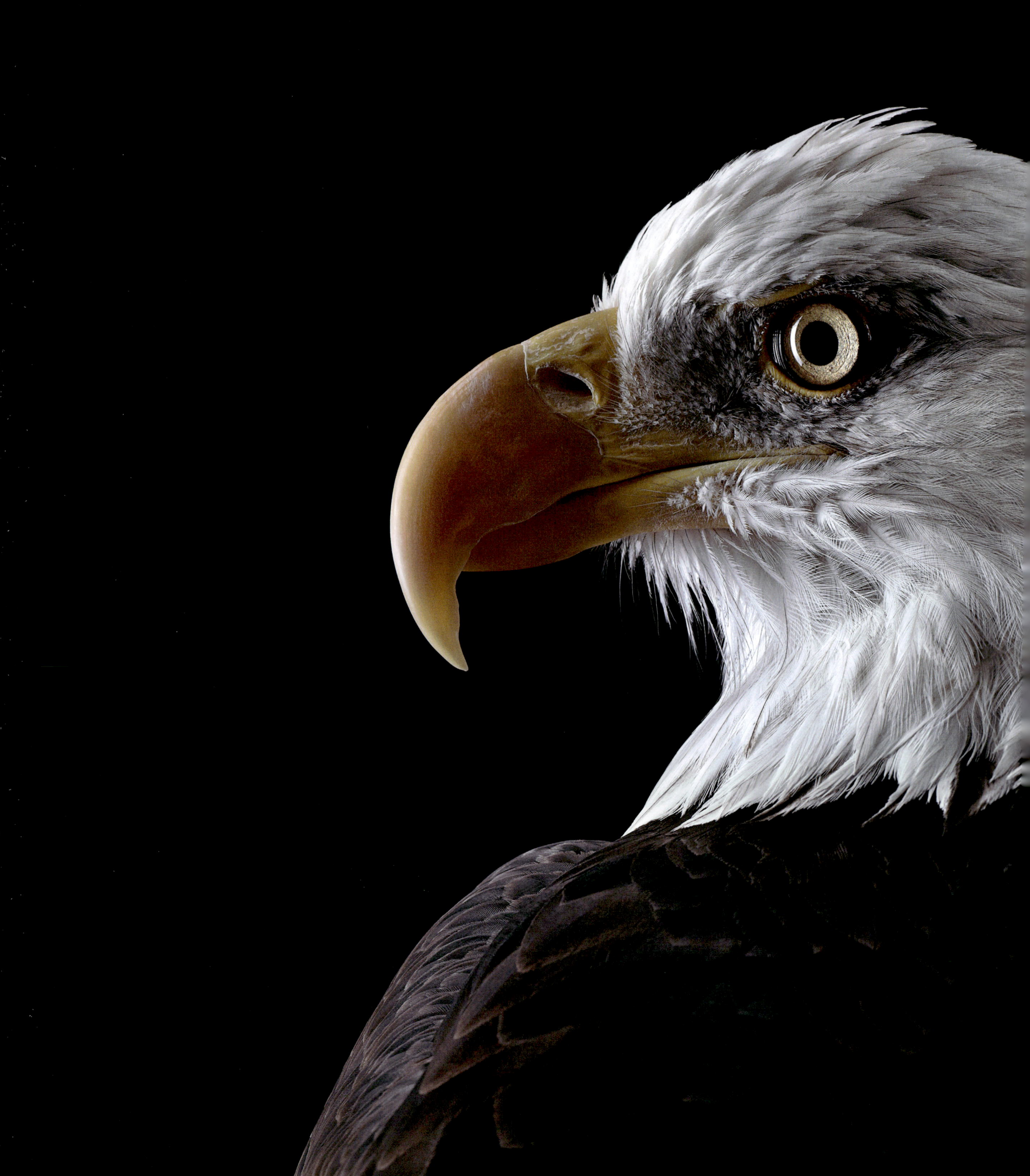

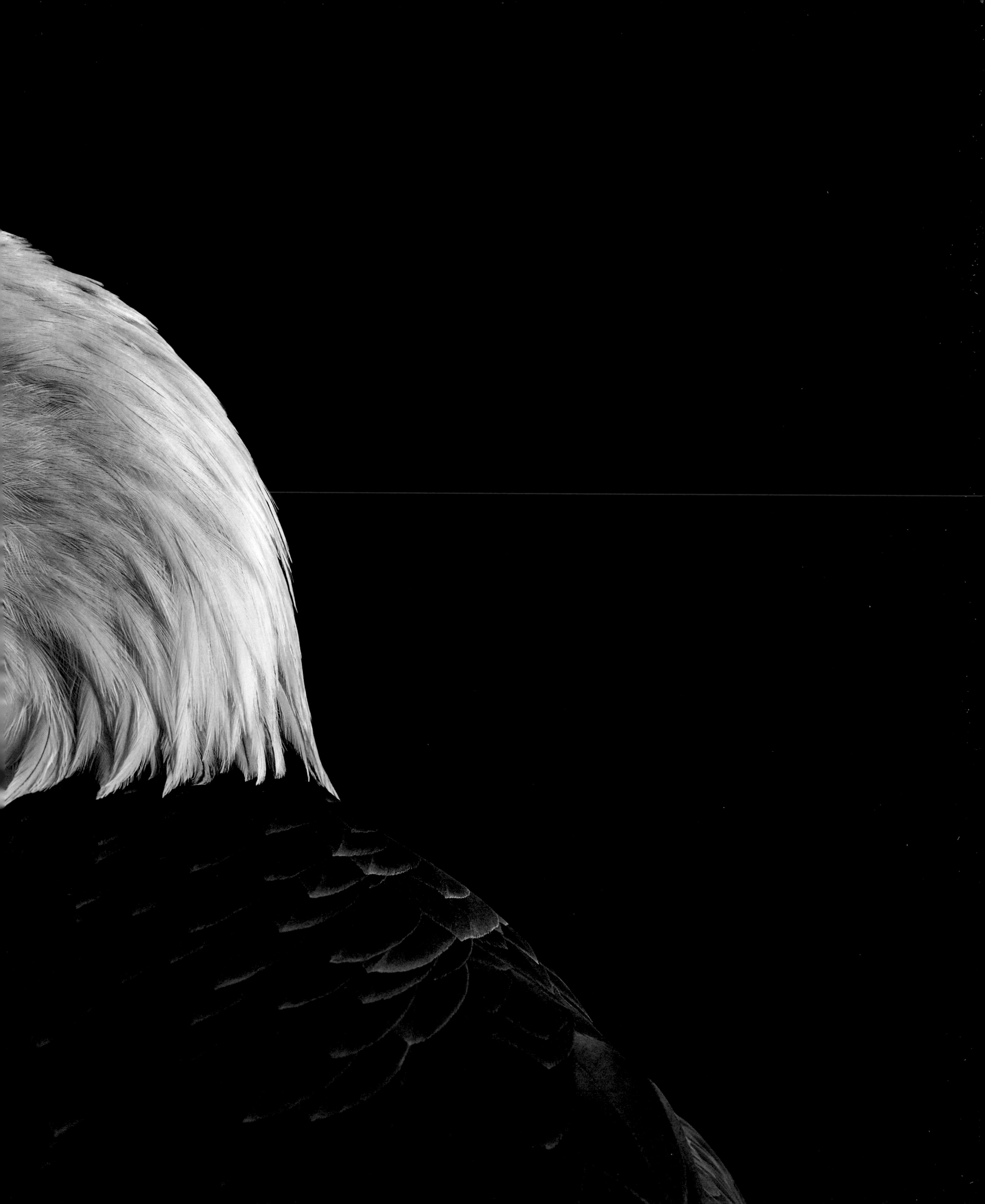

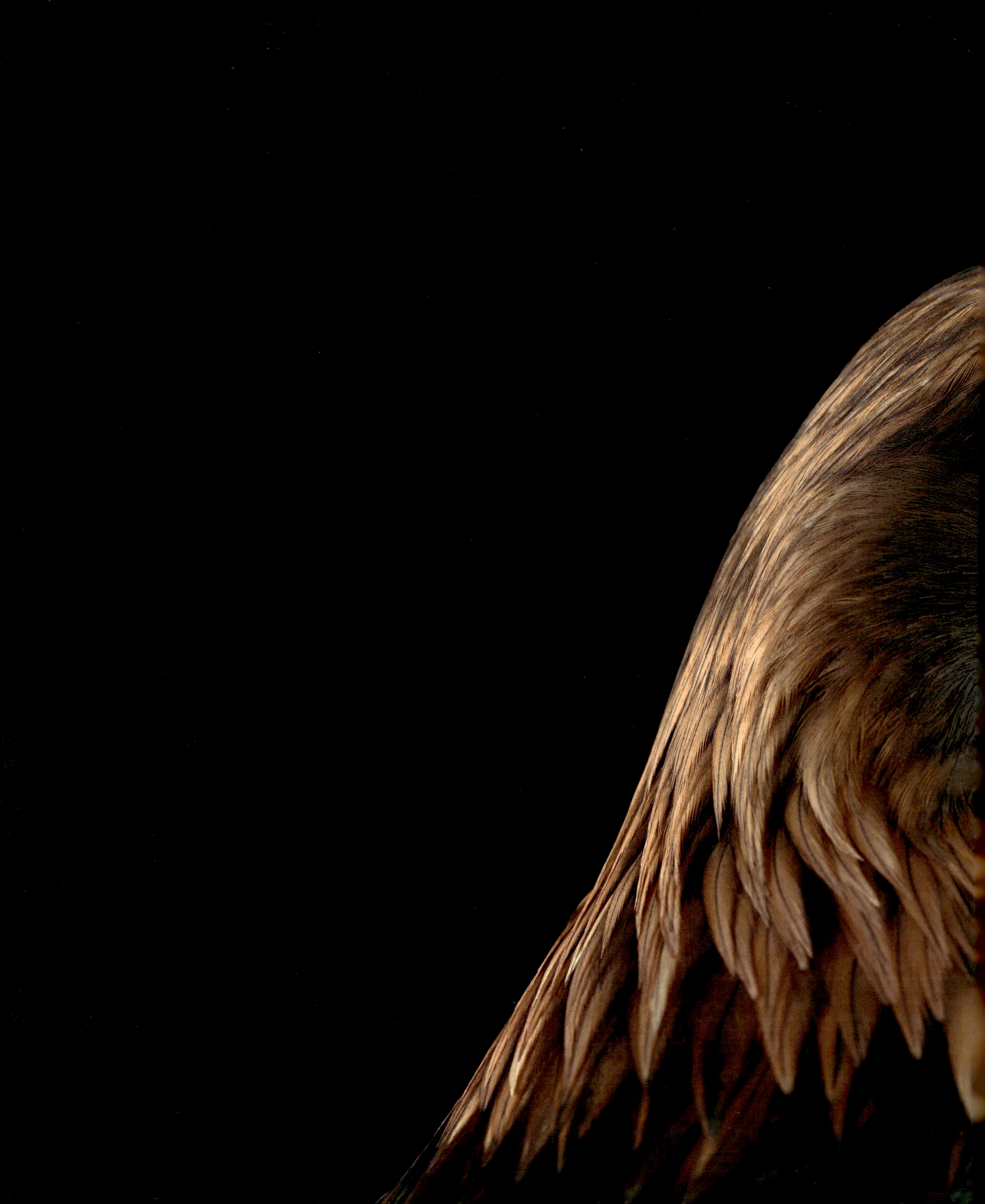

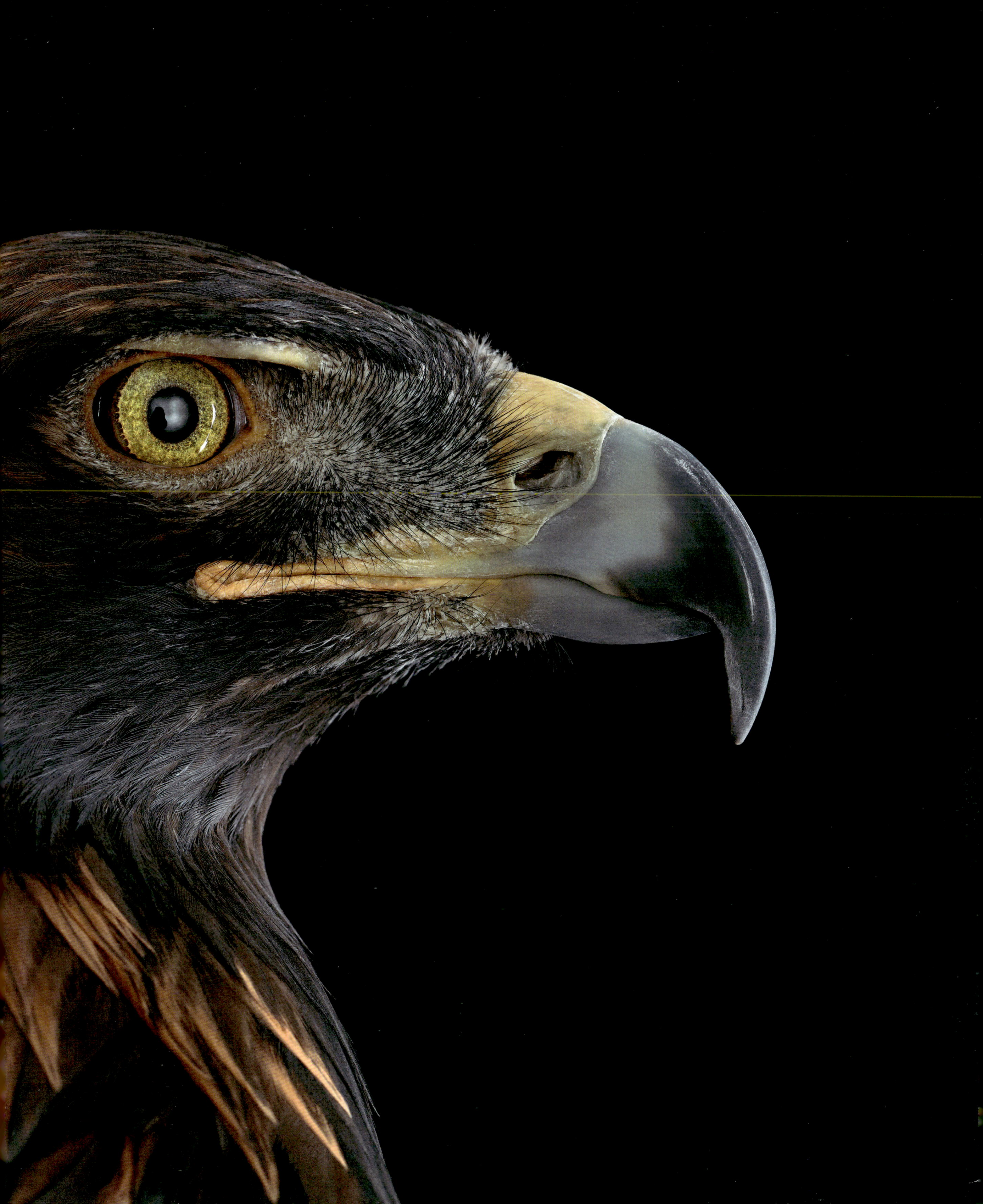

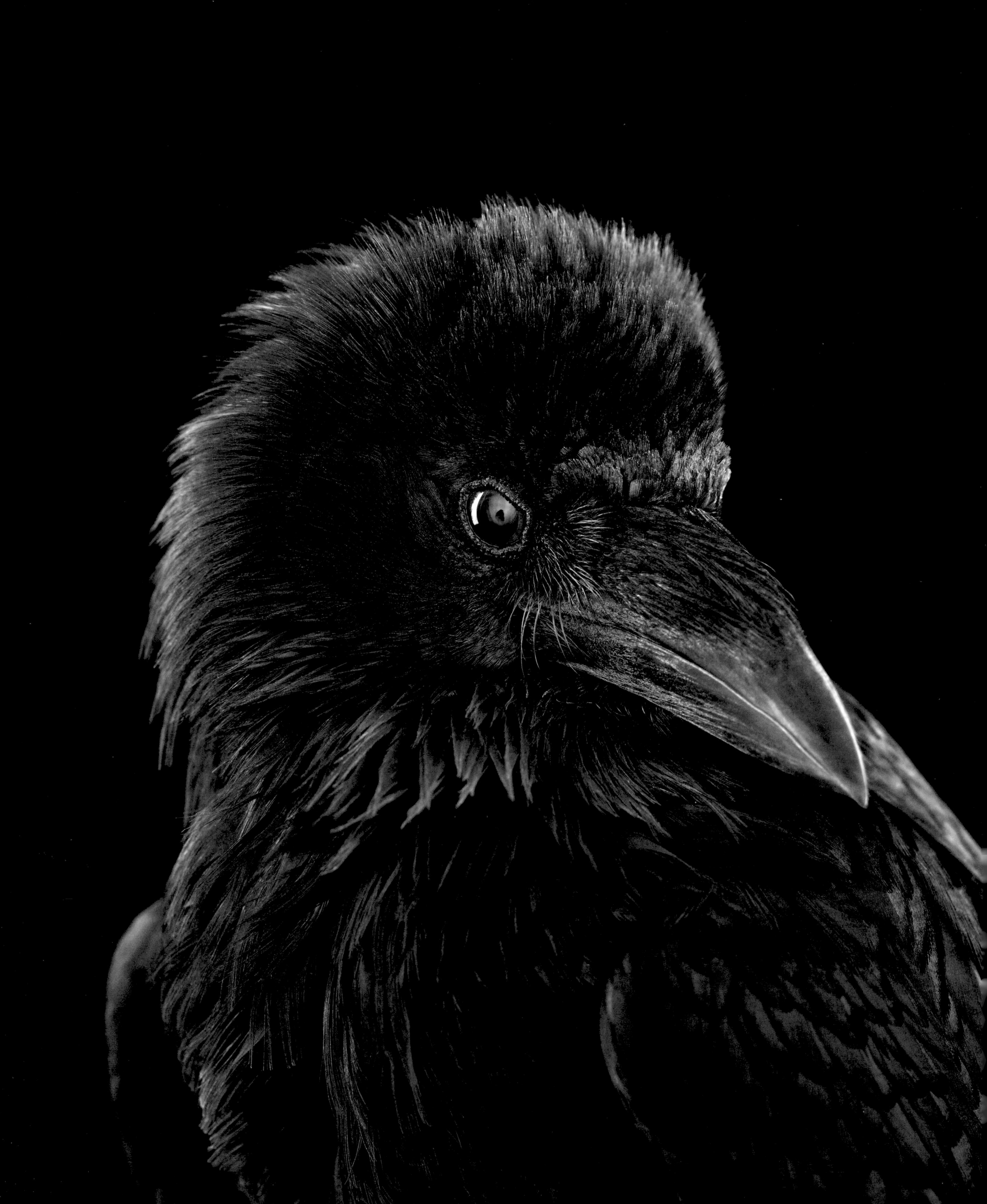

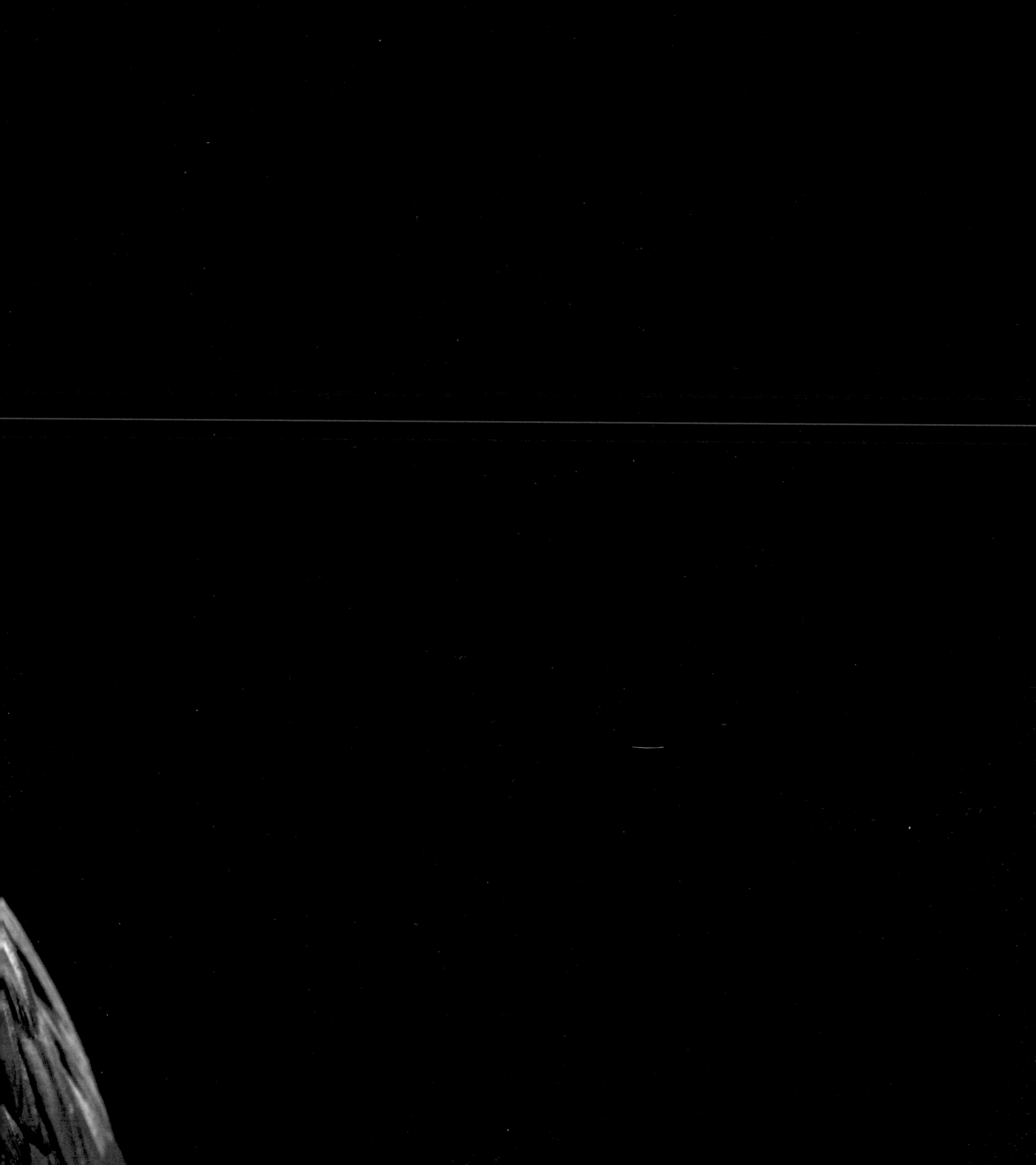

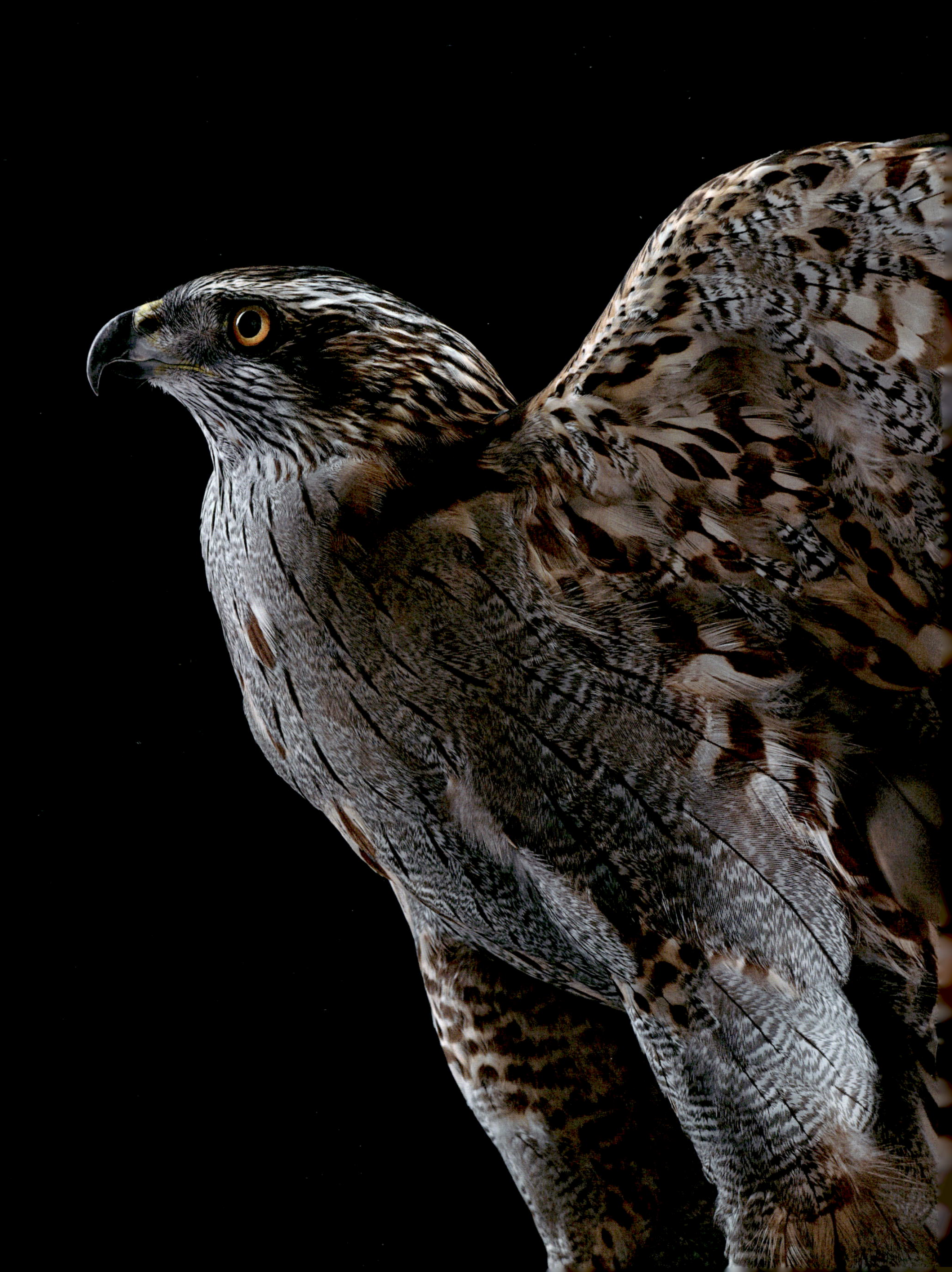

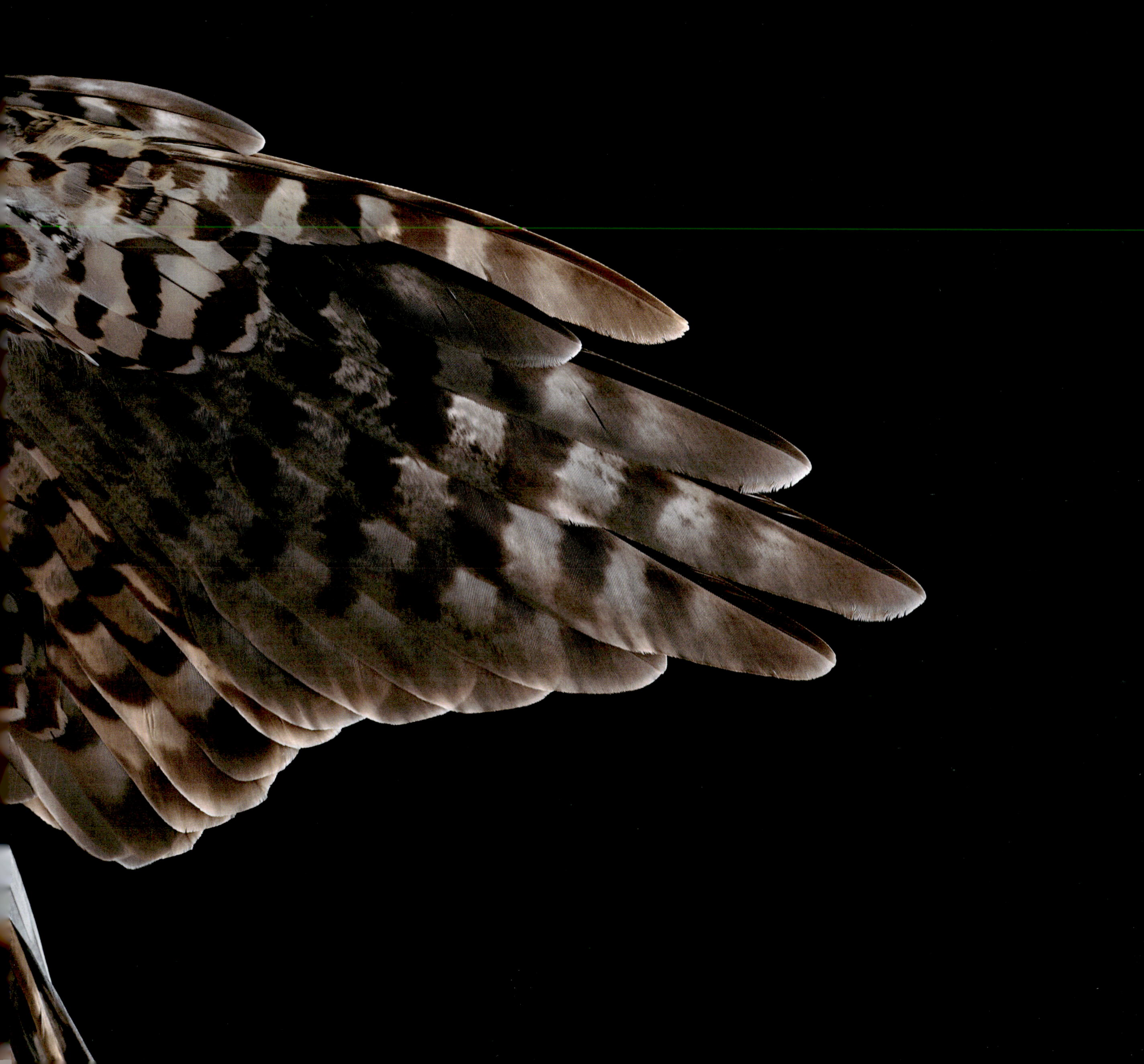

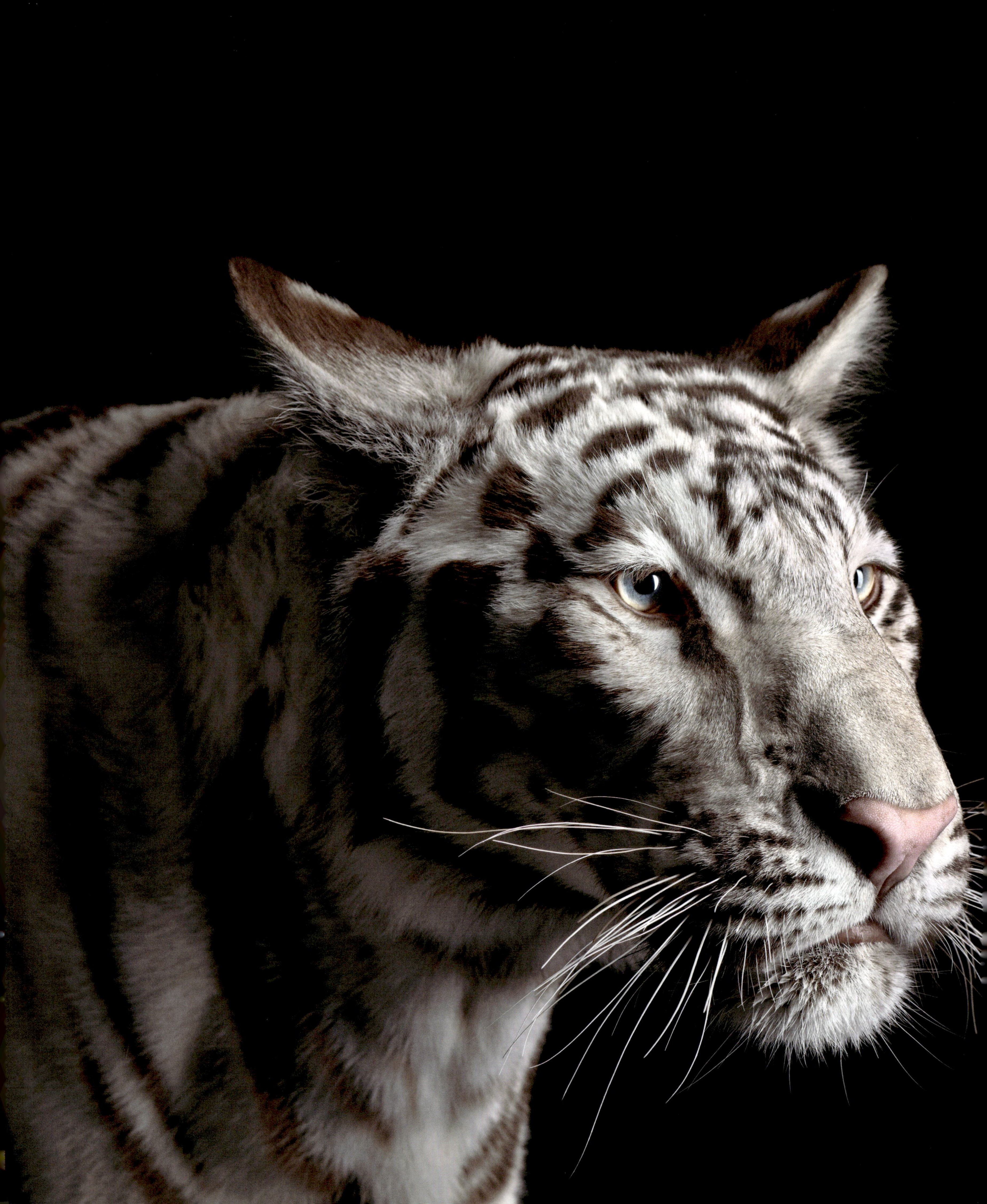

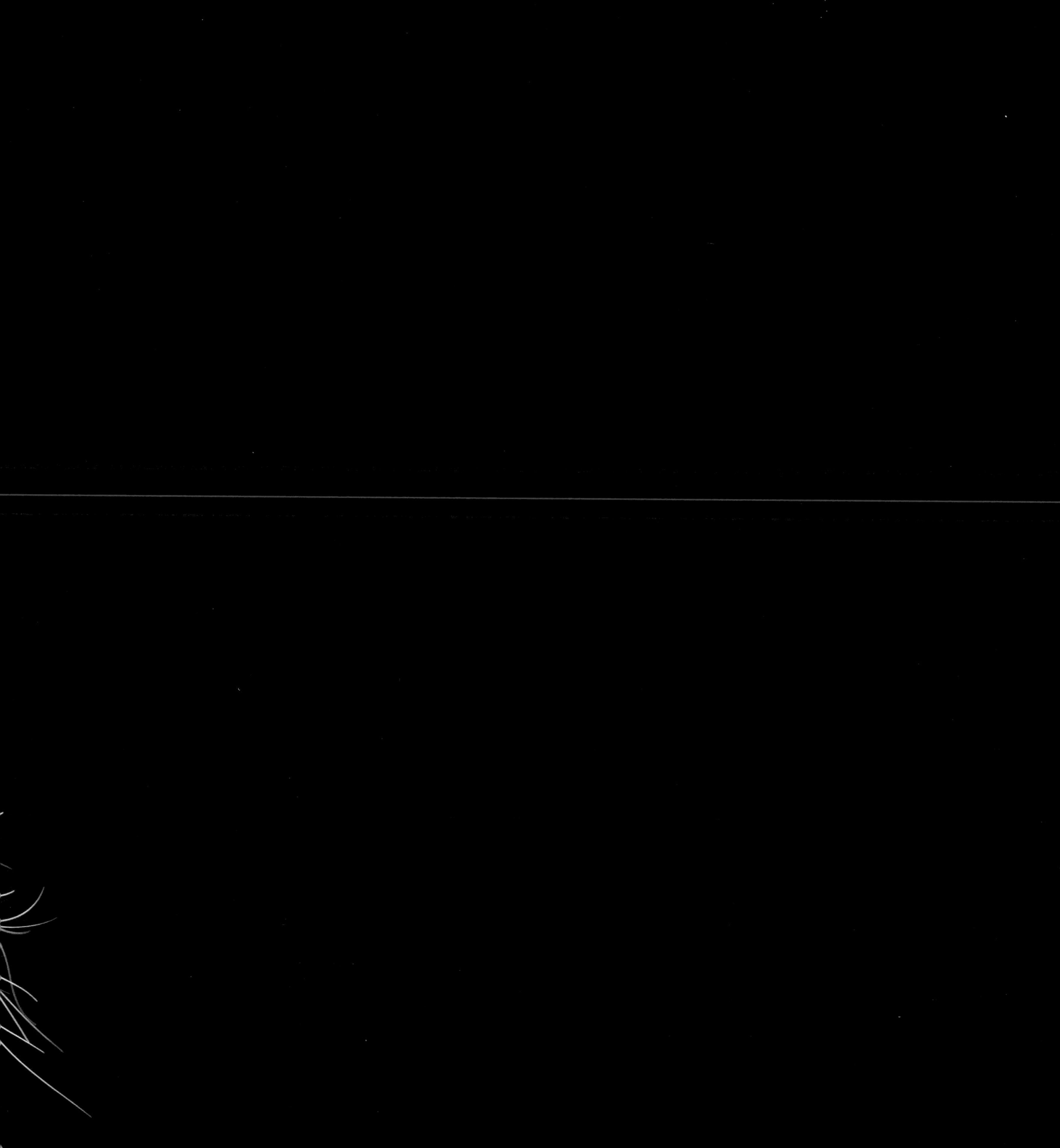

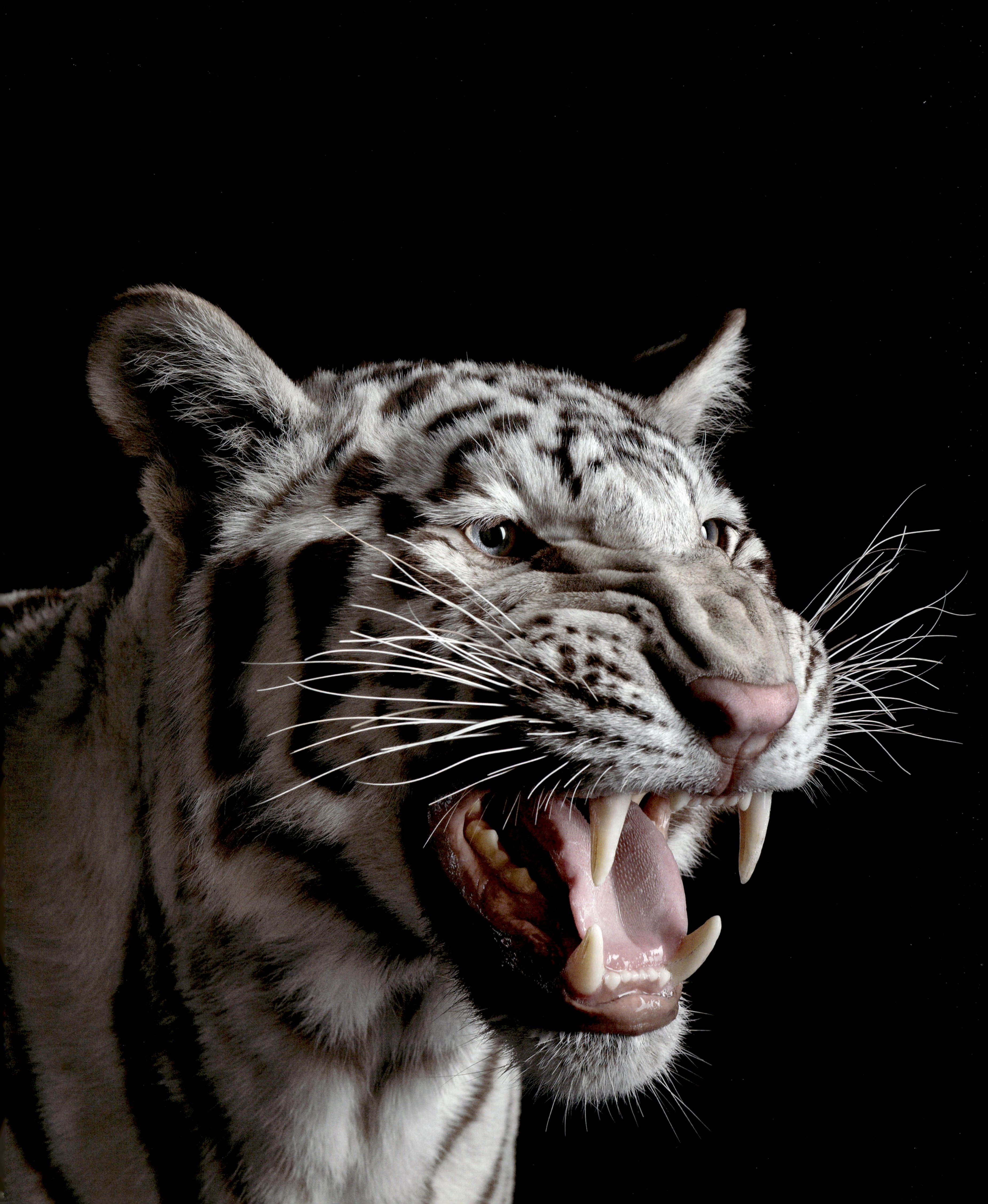

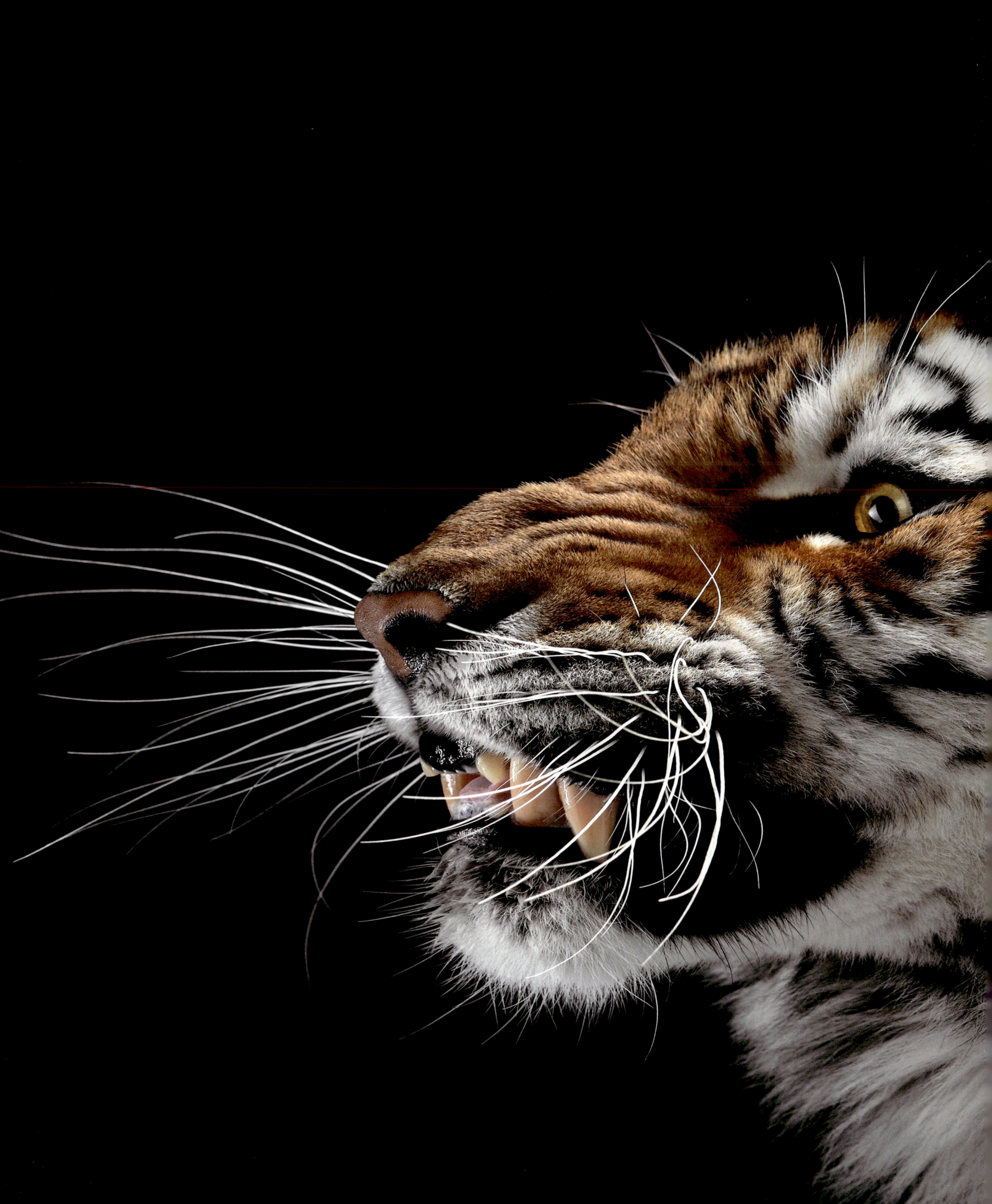

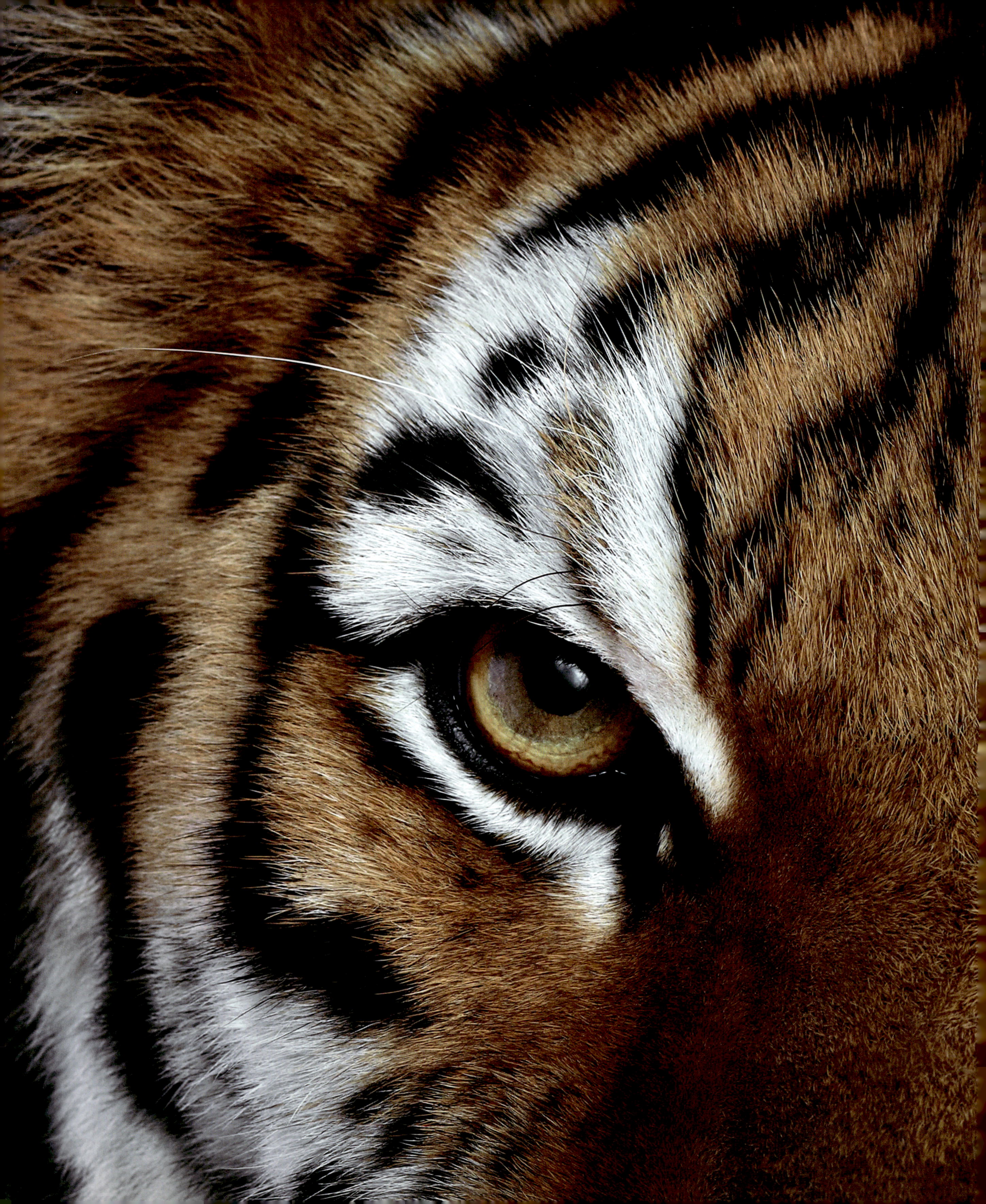

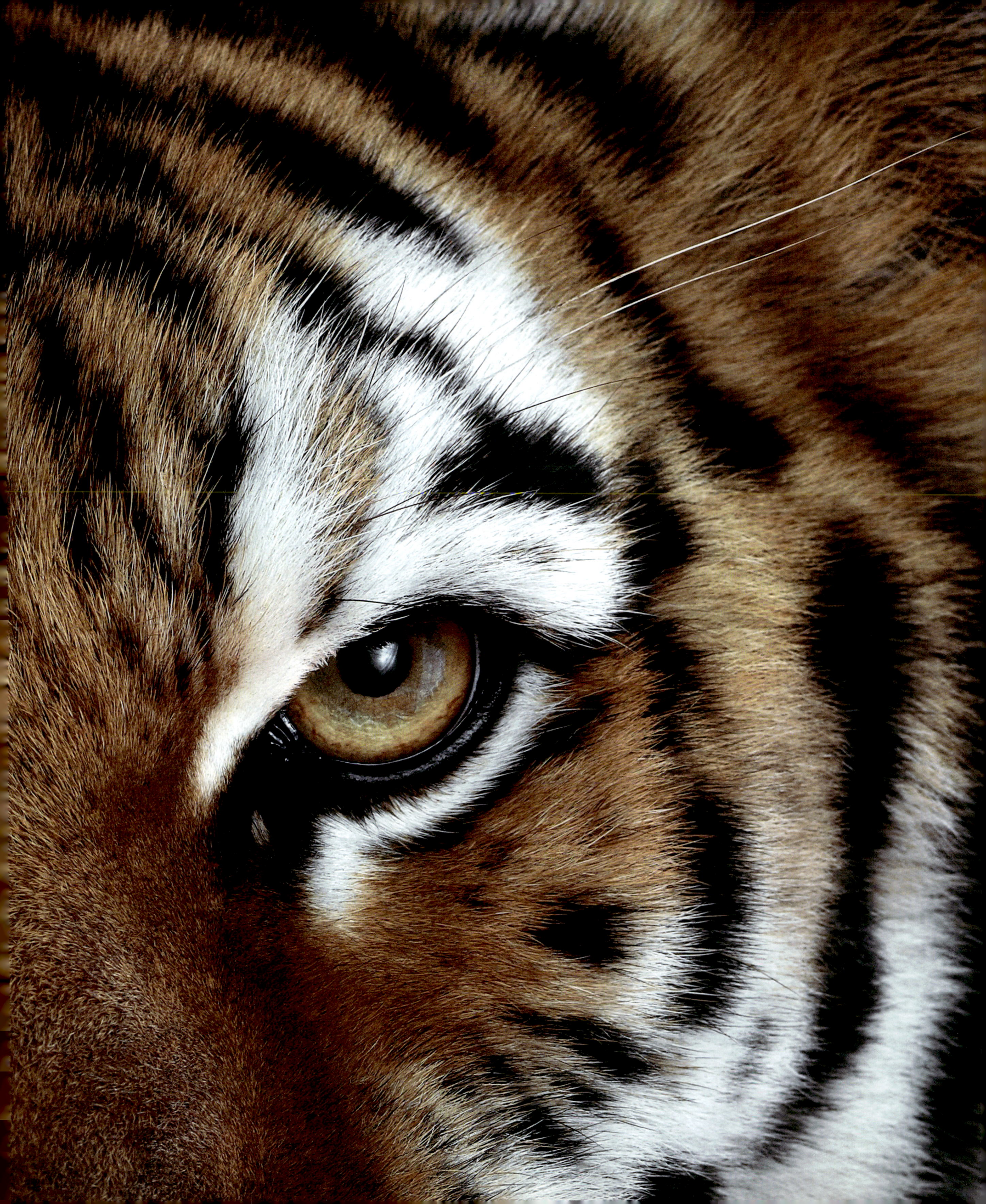

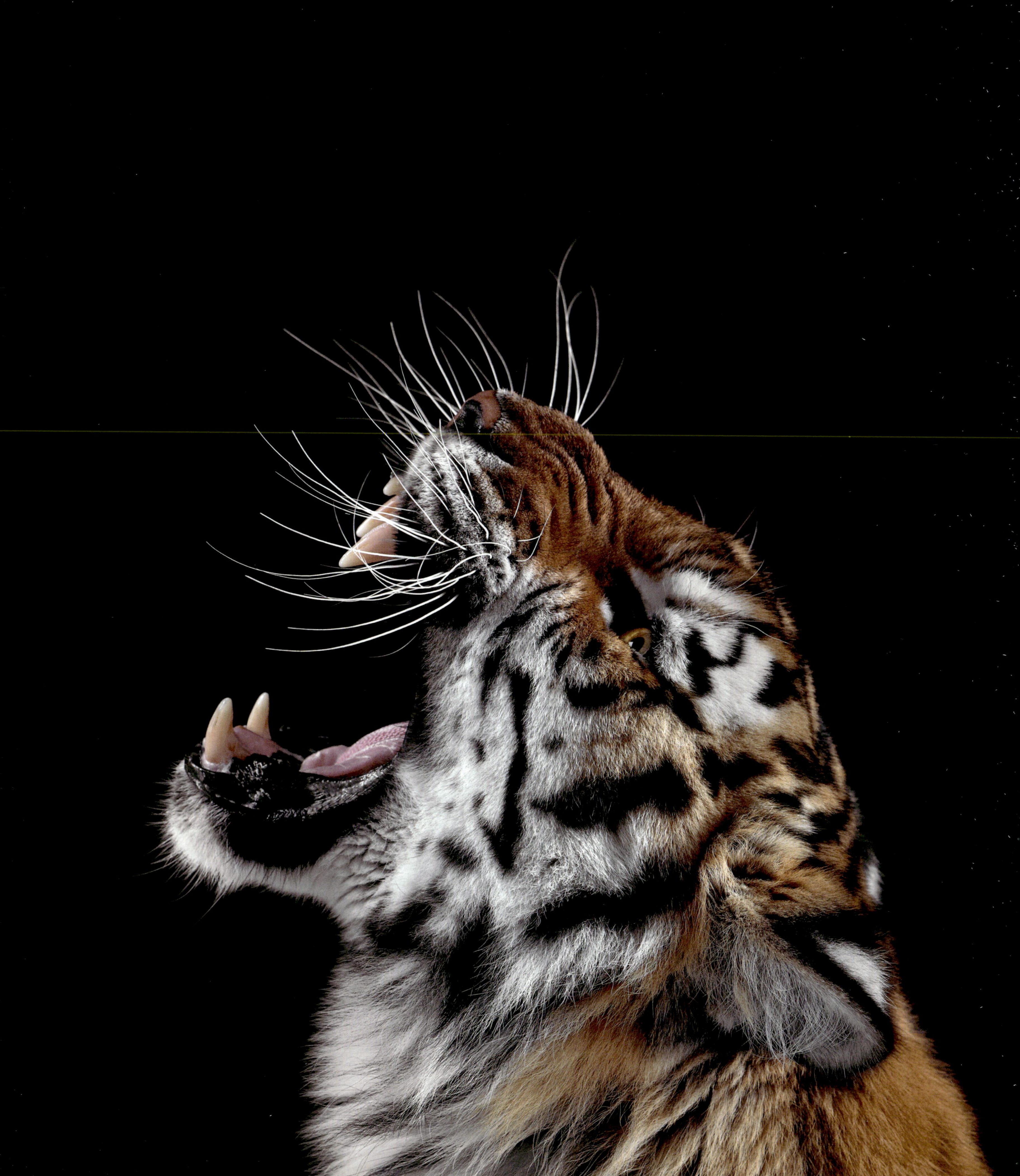

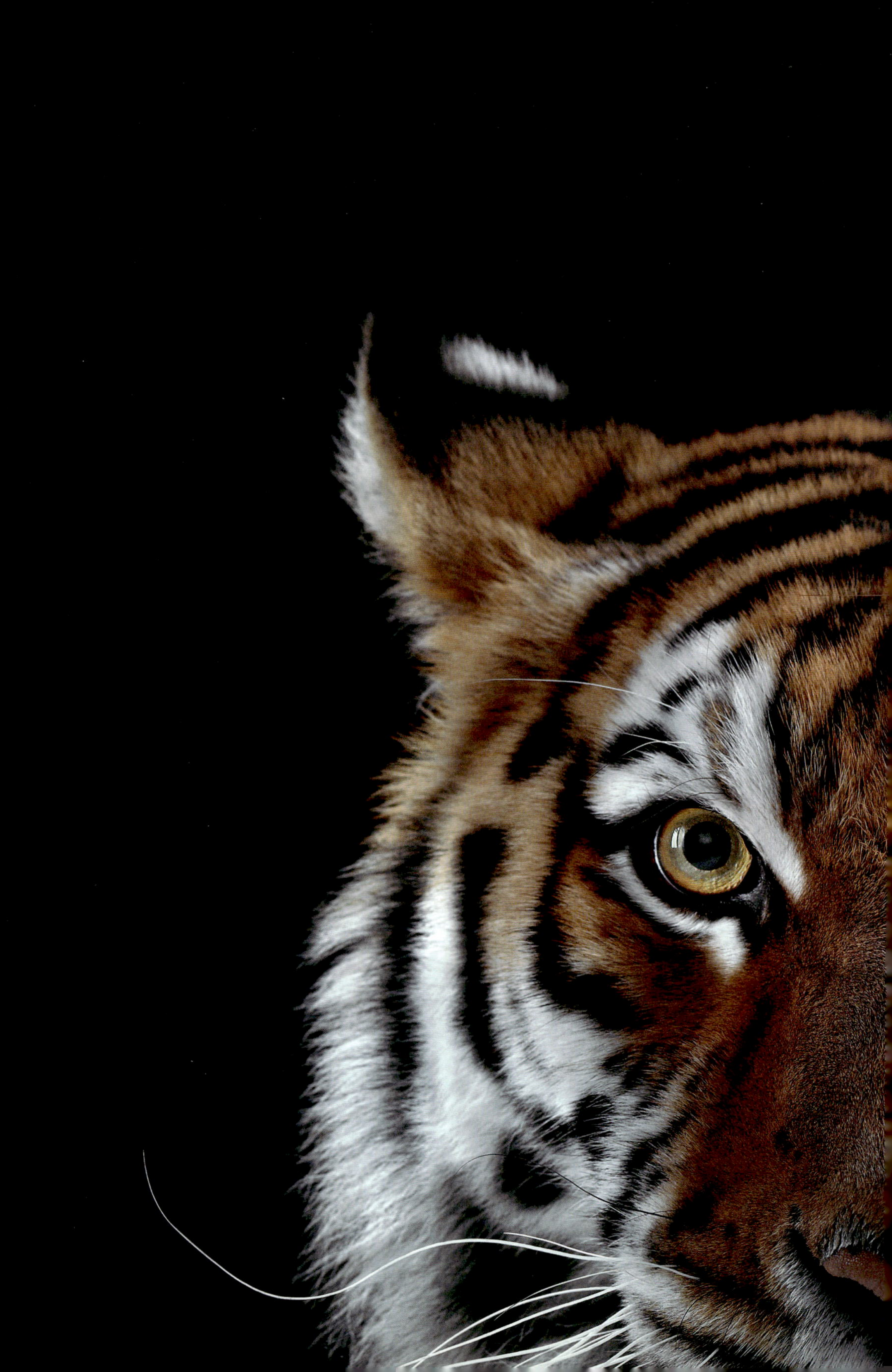

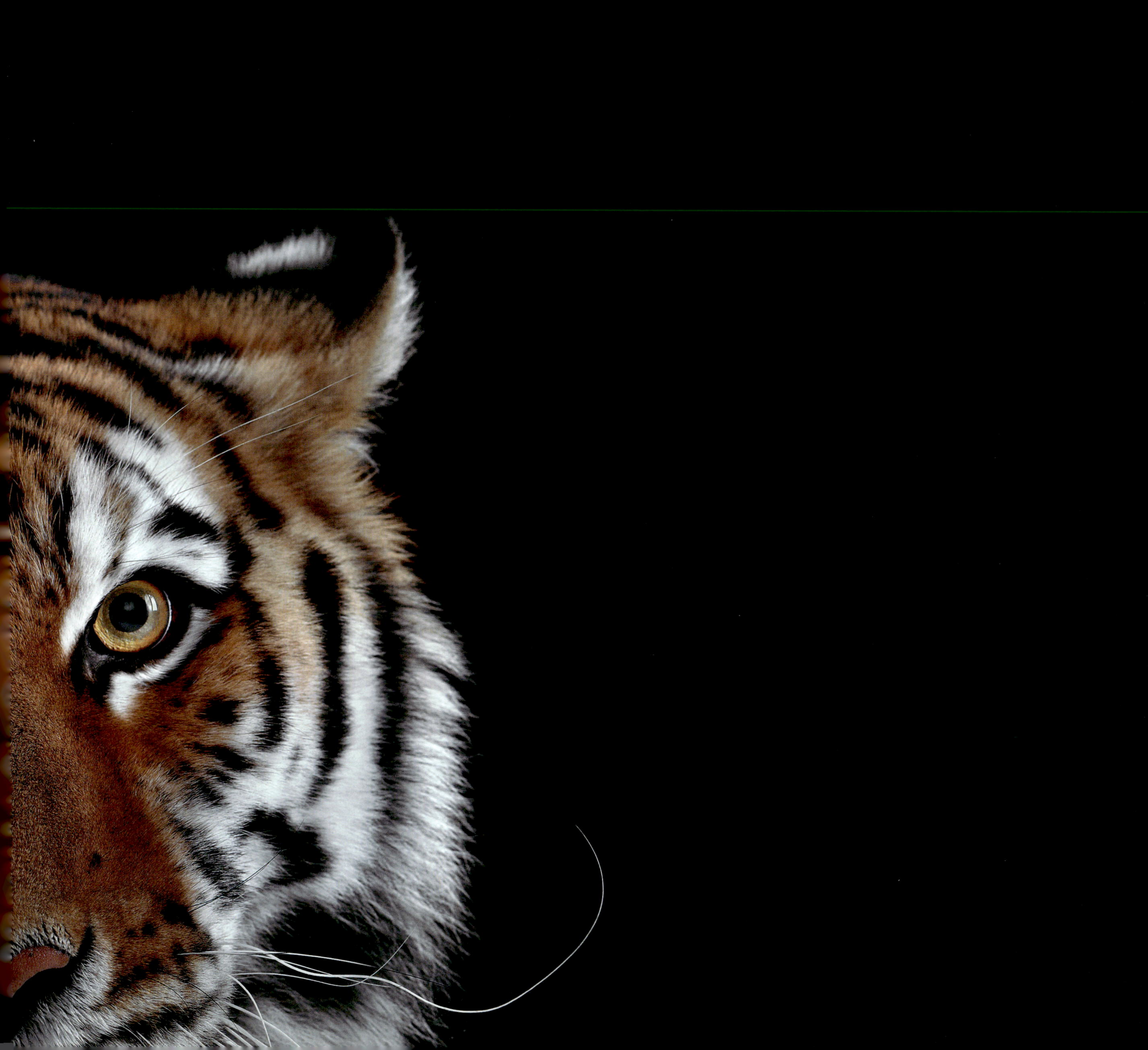

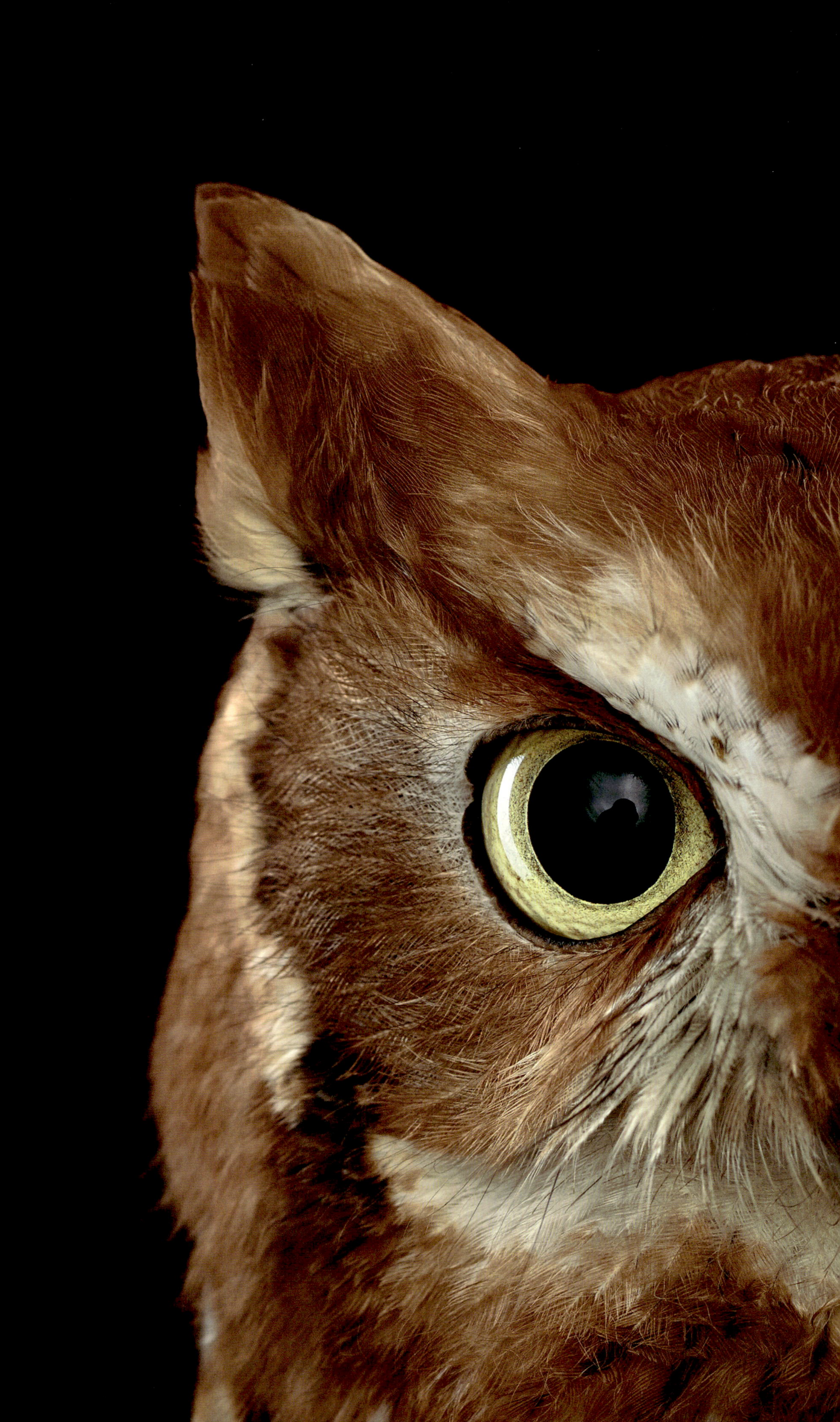

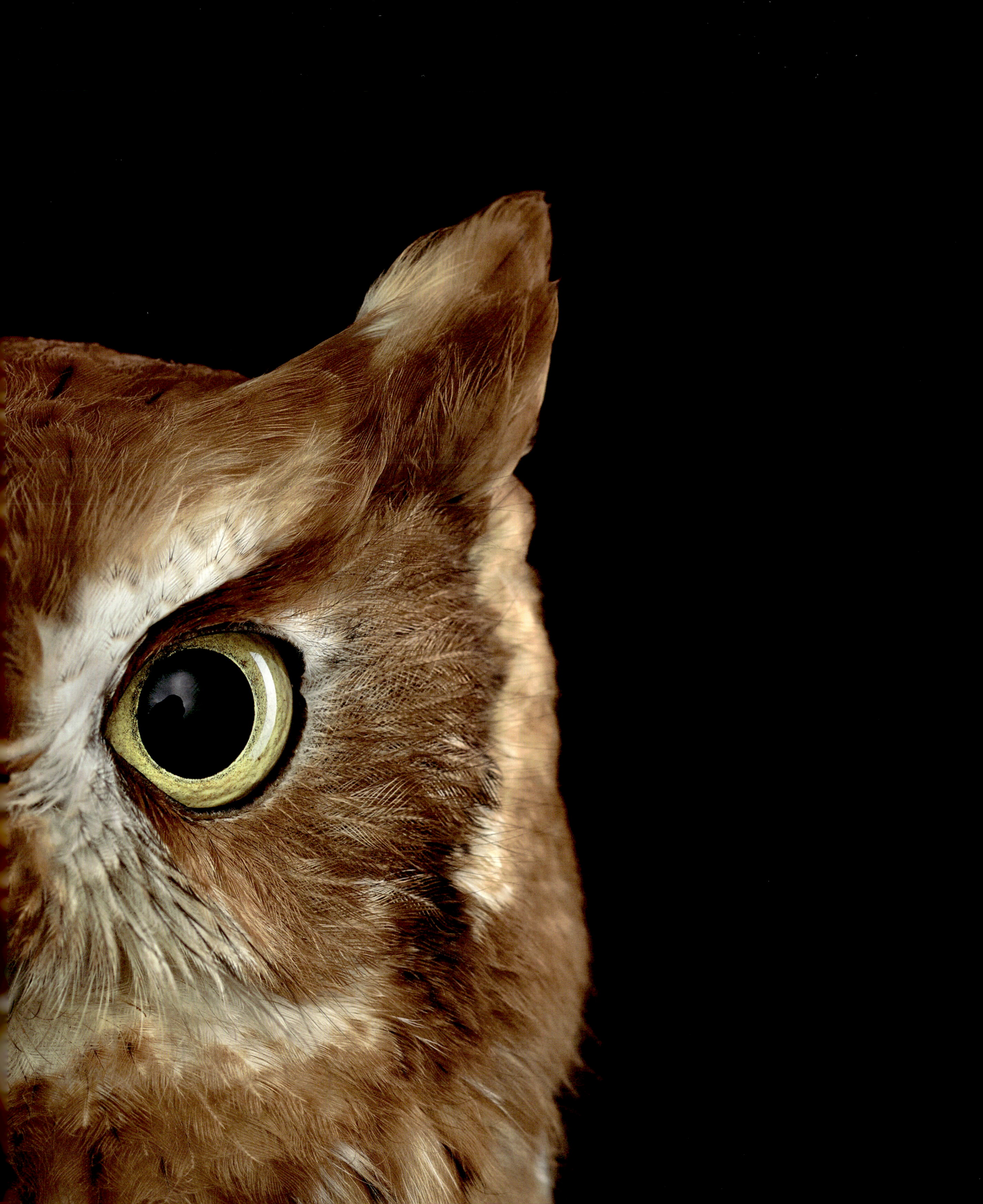

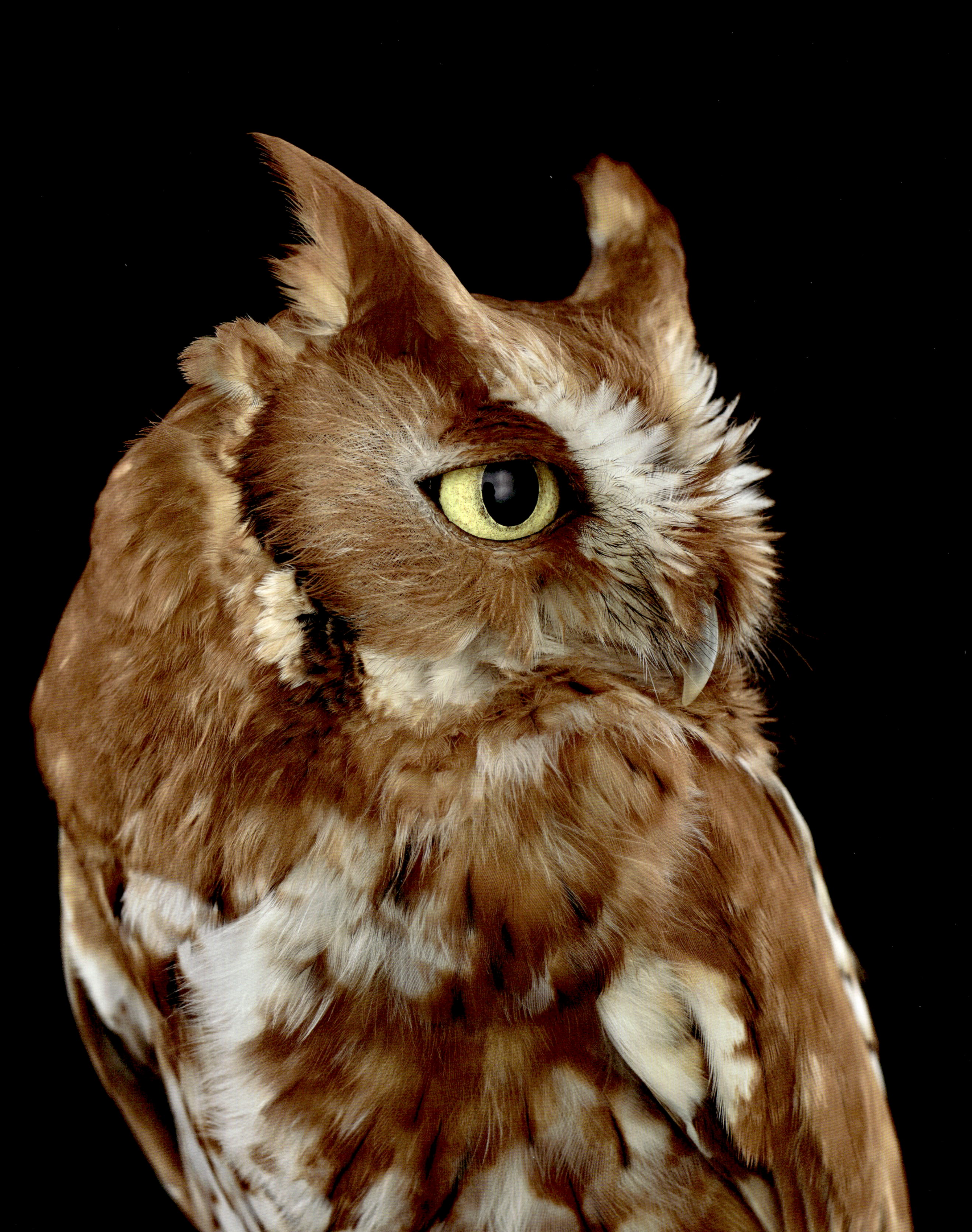

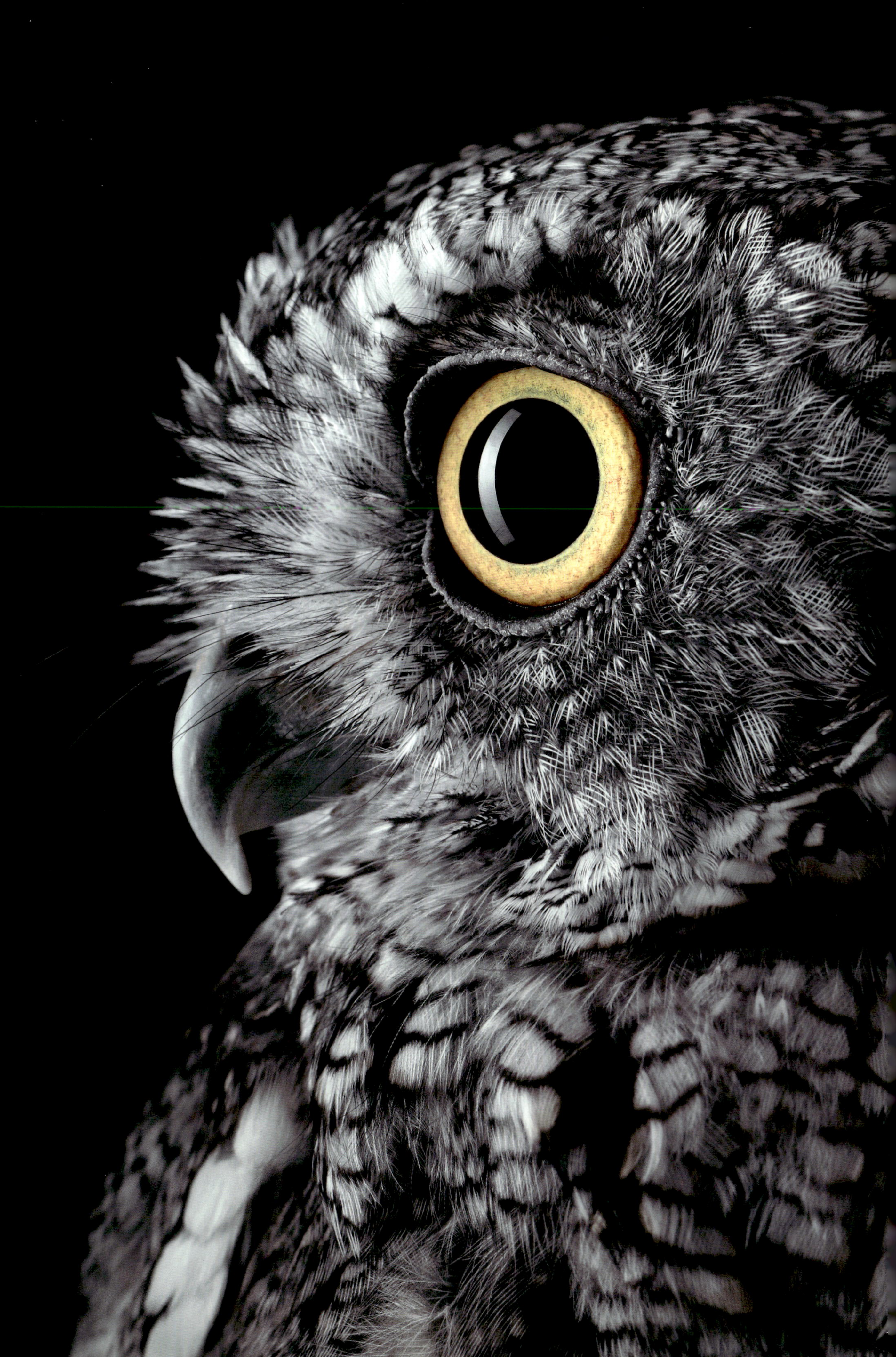

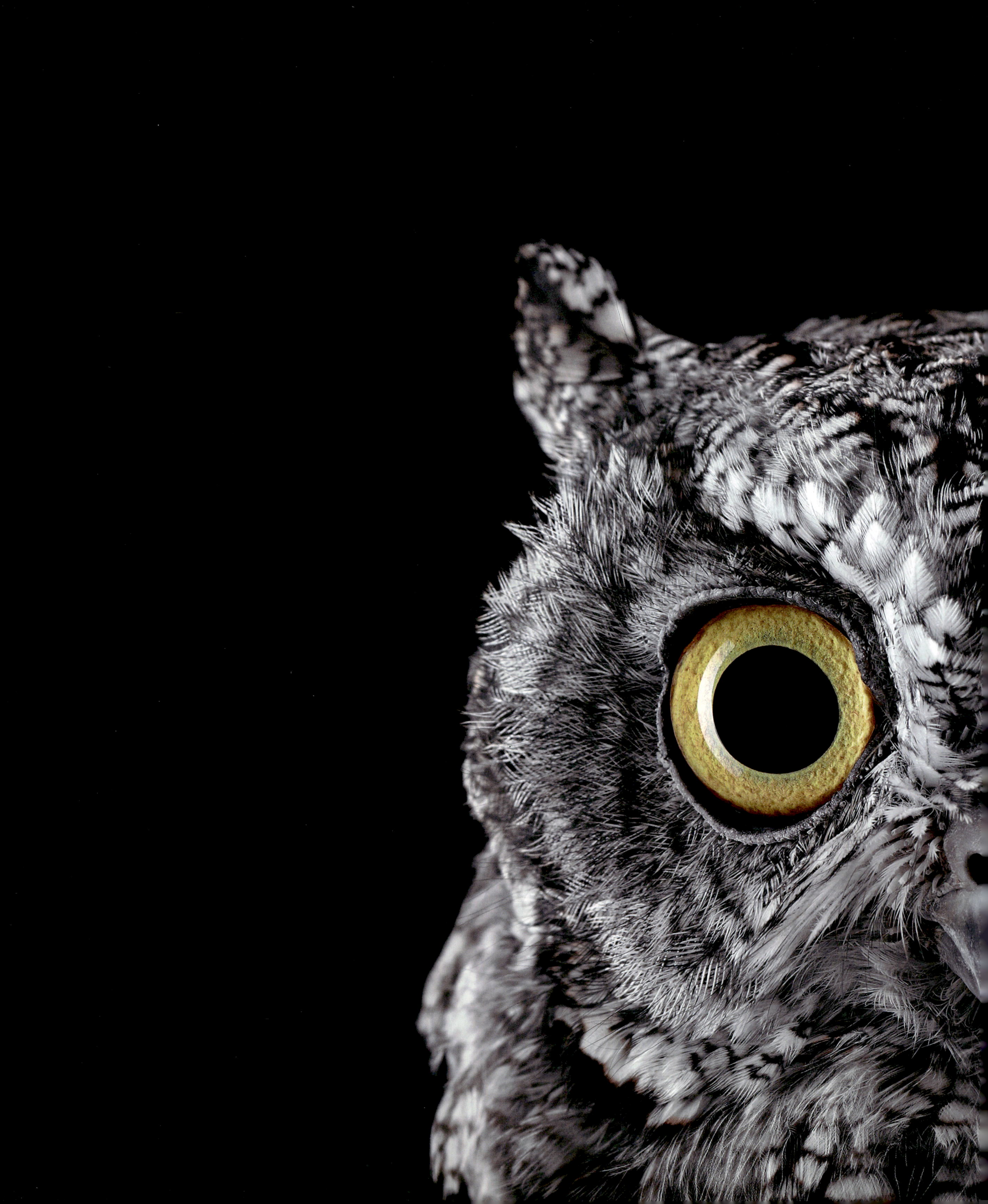

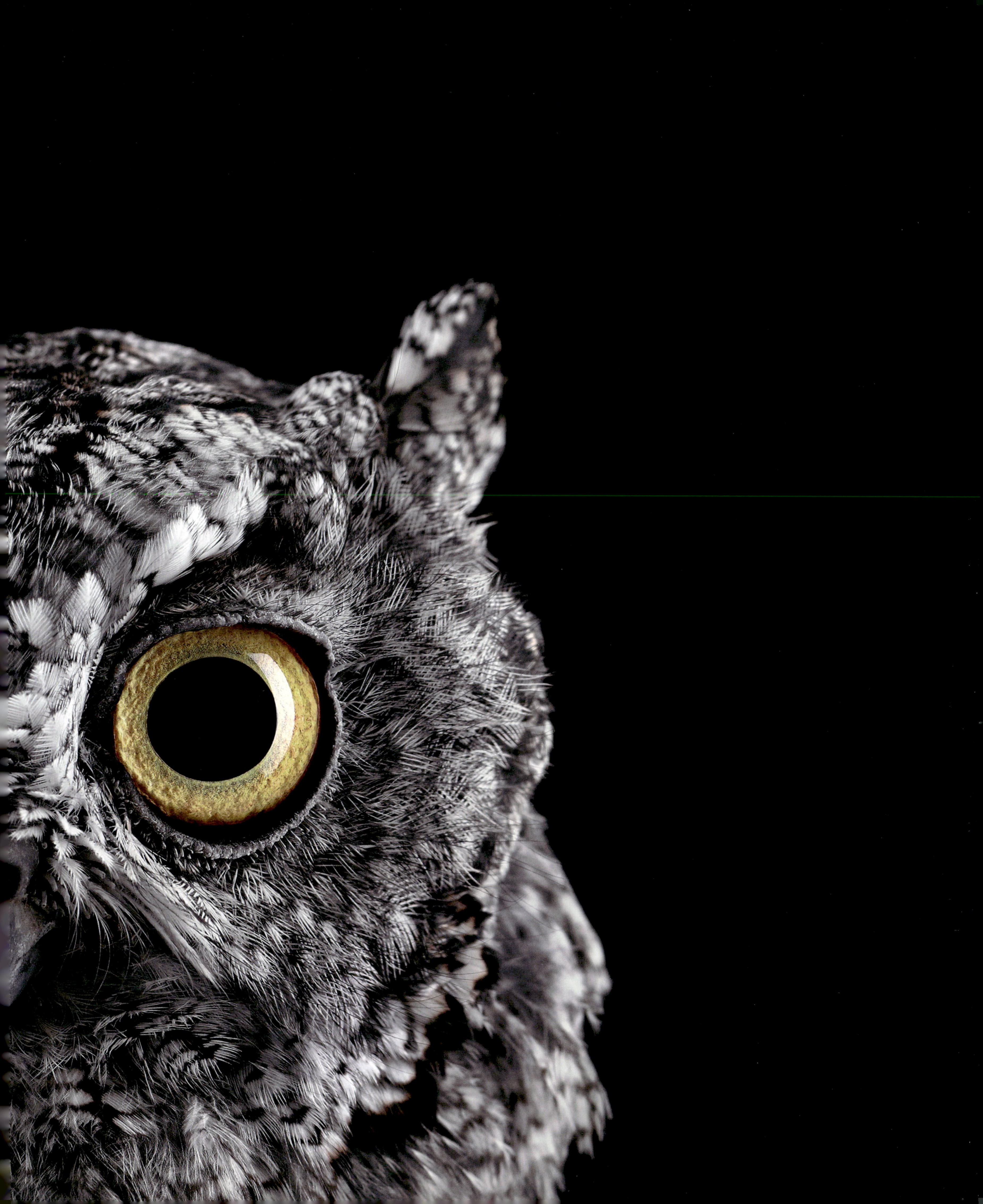

CAPTIONS

African Elephant
Scientific name: *Loxodonta africana*
Range: Sub-Saharan Africa
Conservation status: Threatened

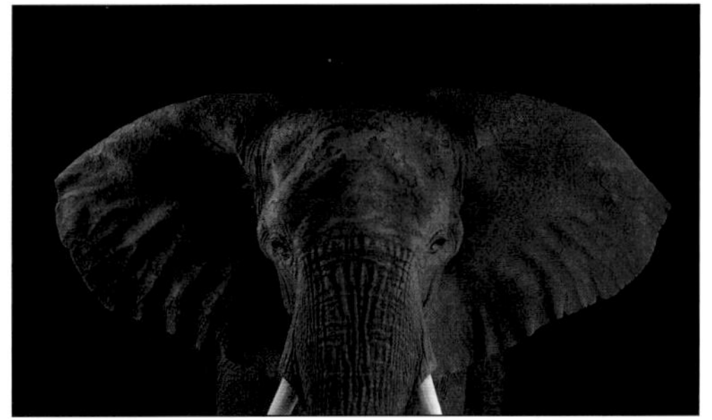

African Elephant #1, Los Angeles, CA, 2010

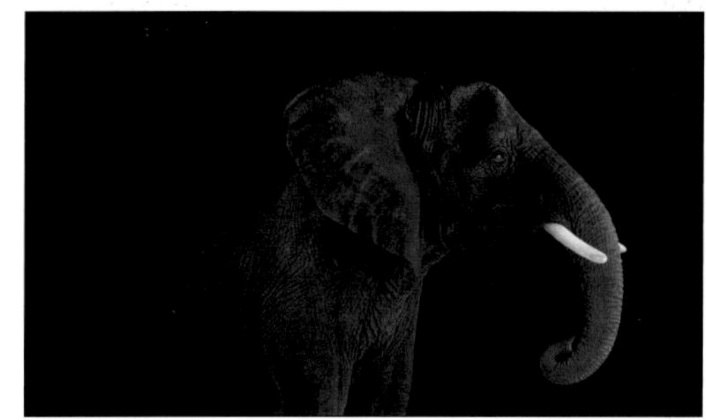

African Elephant #3, Los Angeles, CA, 2010

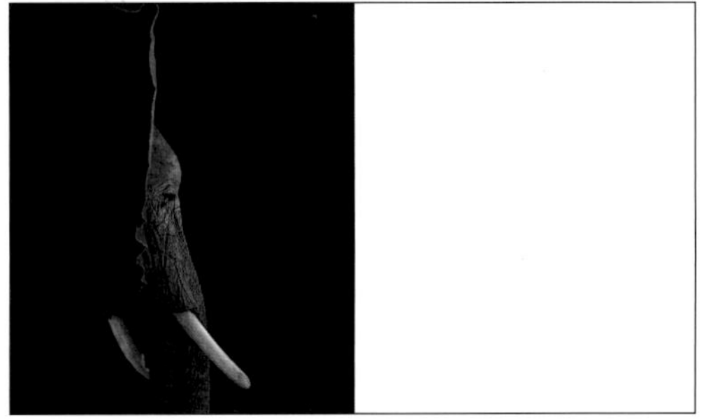

African Elephant #4, Los Angeles, CA, 2010

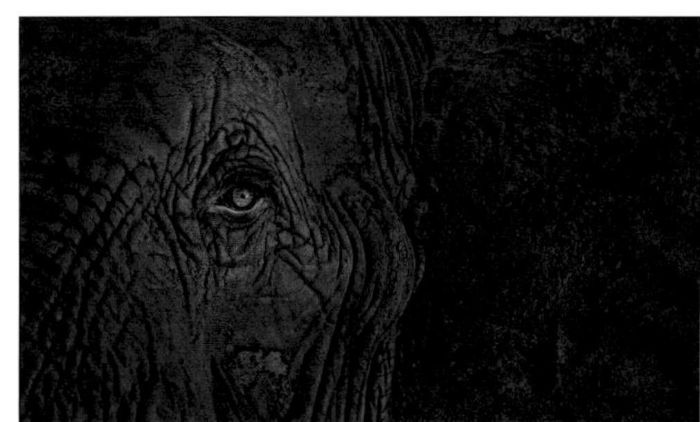

African Elephant #5, Los Angeles, CA, 2010

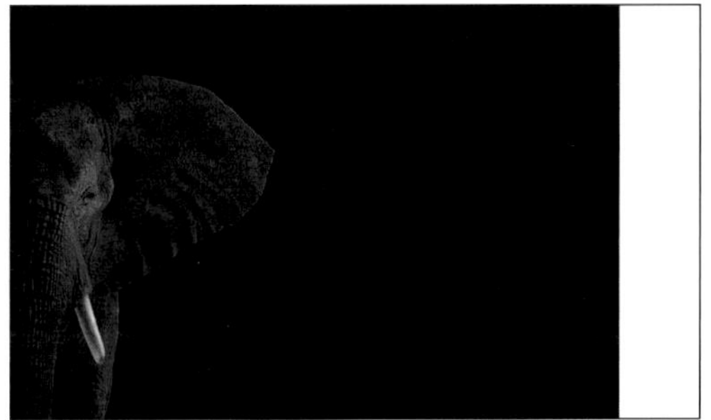

African Elephant #6, Los Angeles, CA, 2010

Chimpanzee
Scientific name: *Pan troglodytes*
Range: West and Central Africa
Conservation status: Endangered

Chimpanzee #4, Los Angeles, CA, 2010

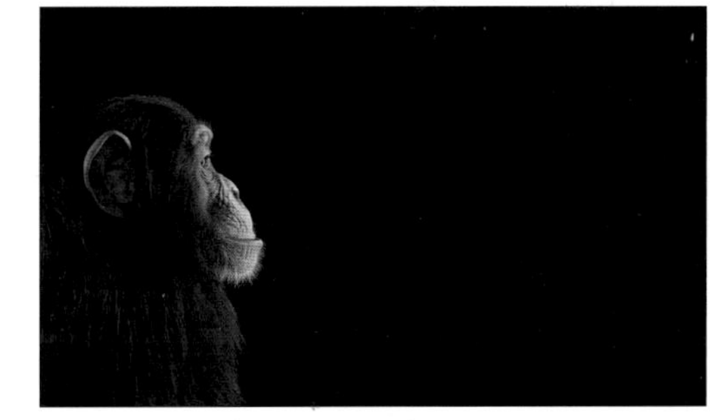

Chimpanzee #1, Los Angeles, CA, 2010

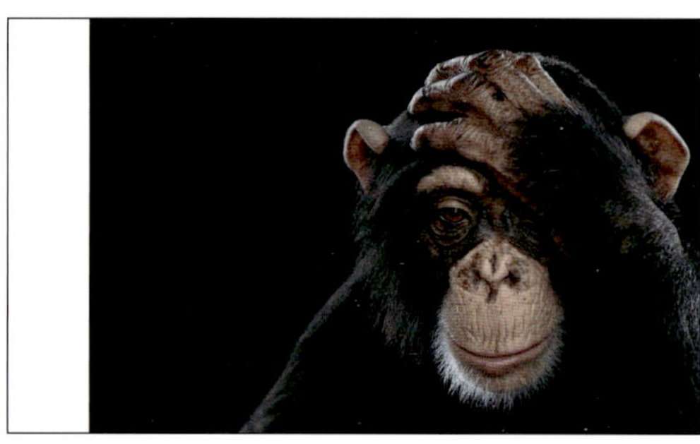

Chimpanzee #2, Los Angeles, CA, 2010

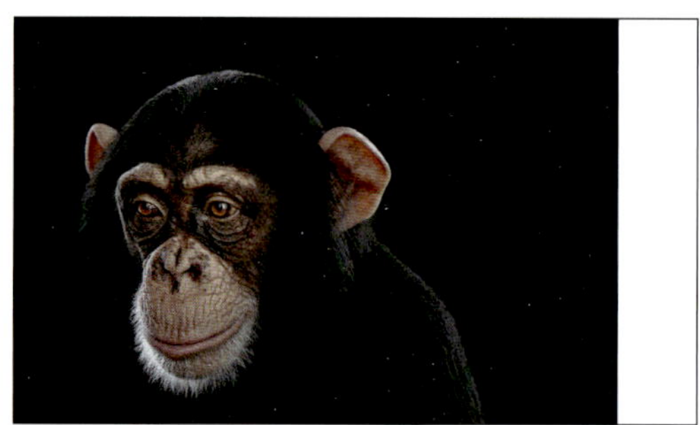

Chimpanzee #12, Los Angeles, CA, 2010

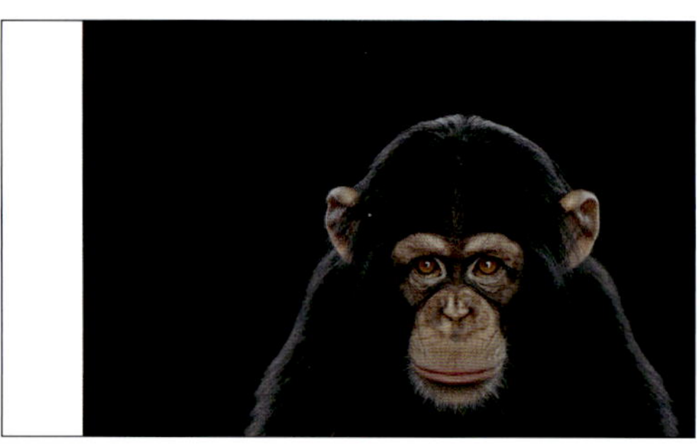

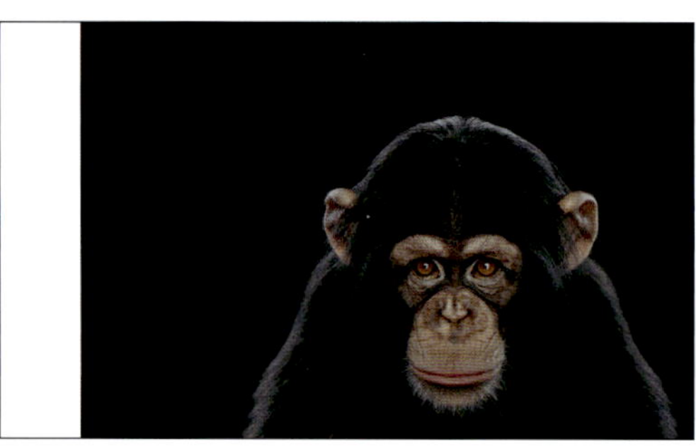

Chimpanzee #6, Los Angeles, CA, 2010

Baboon
Scientific name: *Papio anubis*
Range: North and Central Africa
Conservation status: Least threatened

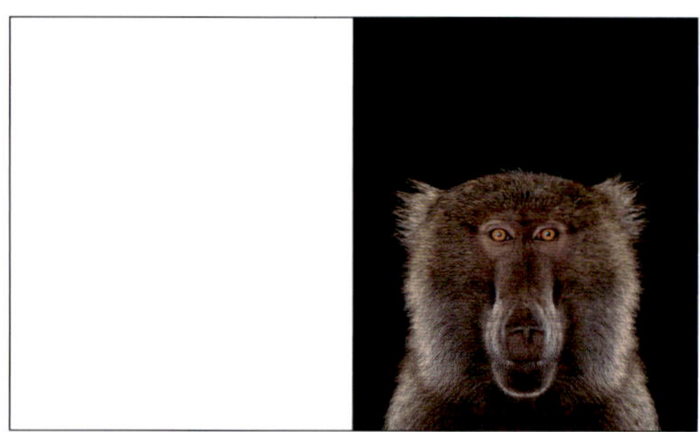

Baboon #2, Los Angeles, CA, 2011

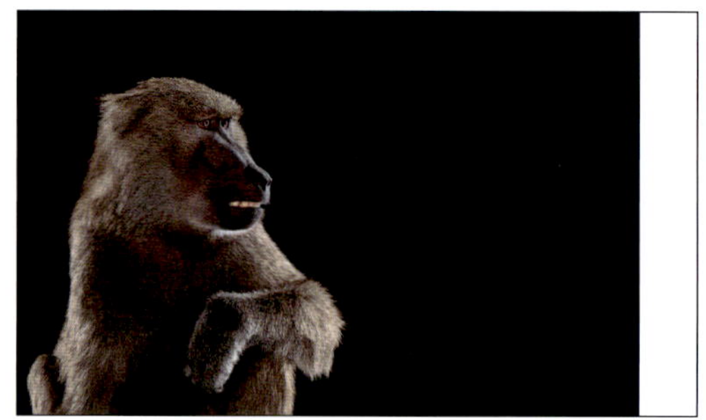

Baboon #3, Los Angeles, CA, 2011

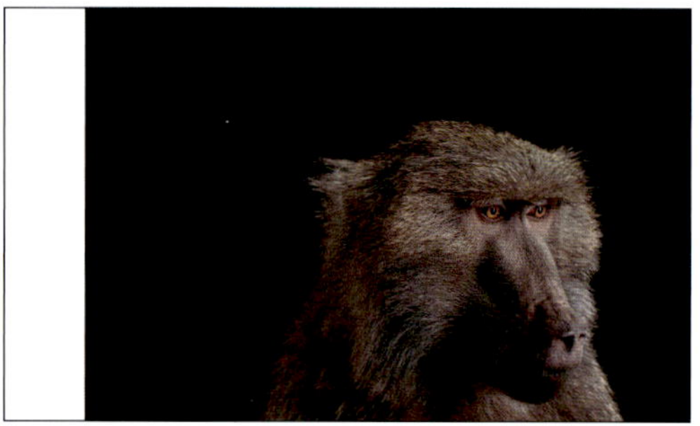

Baboon #1, Los Angeles, CA, 2011

Orangutan
Scientific name: *Pongo pygmaeus*
Range: Borneo and Sumatra
Conservation status: Endangered

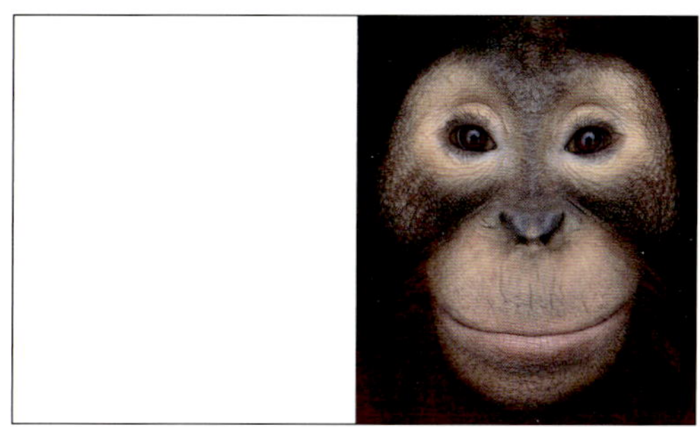
Orangutan #1, Los Angeles, CA, 2011

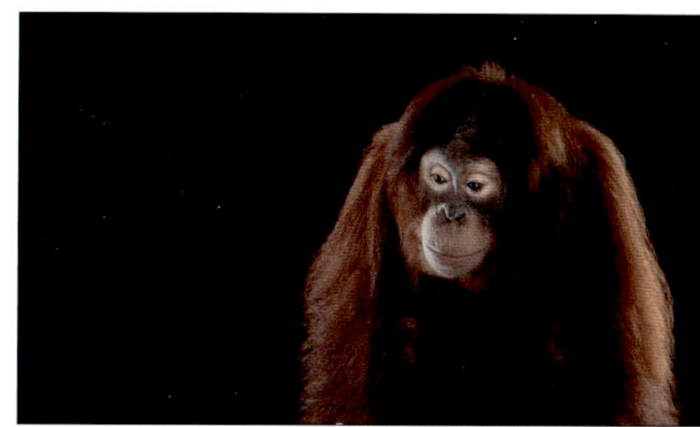
Orangutan #2, Los Angeles, CA, 2011

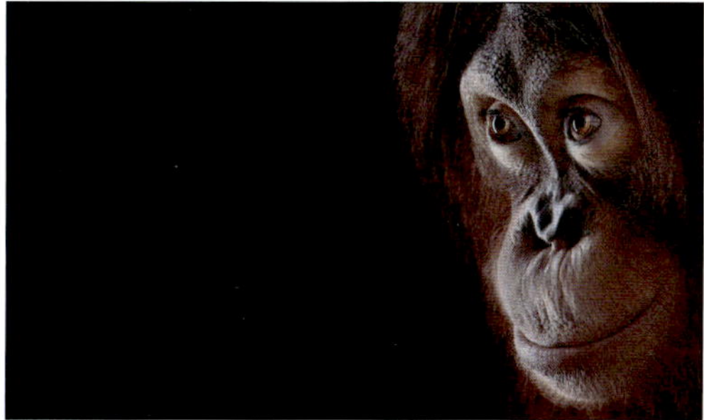
Orangutan #3, Los Angeles, CA, 2011

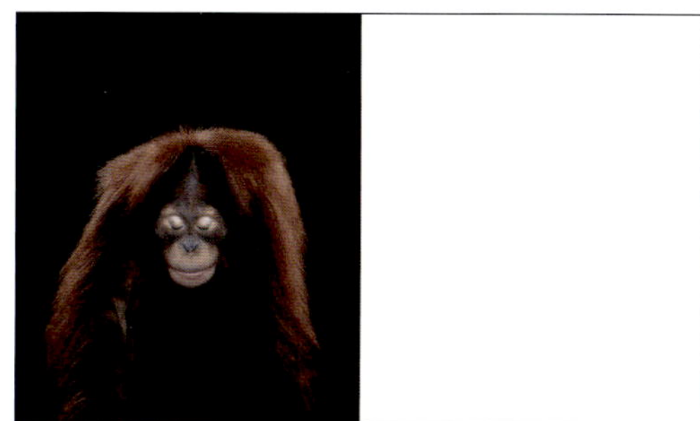
Orangutan #4, Los Angeles, CA, 2011

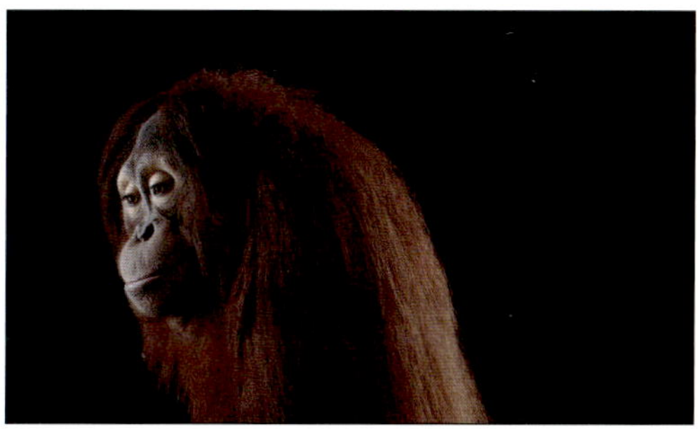
Orangutan #6, Los Angeles, CA, 2011

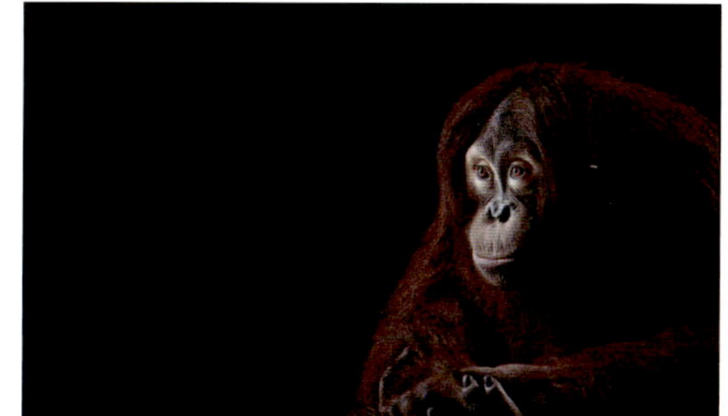
Orangutan #5, Los Angeles, CA, 2011

Lion
Scientific name: *Panthera leo*
Range: Sub-Saharan Africa
Conservation status: Threatened

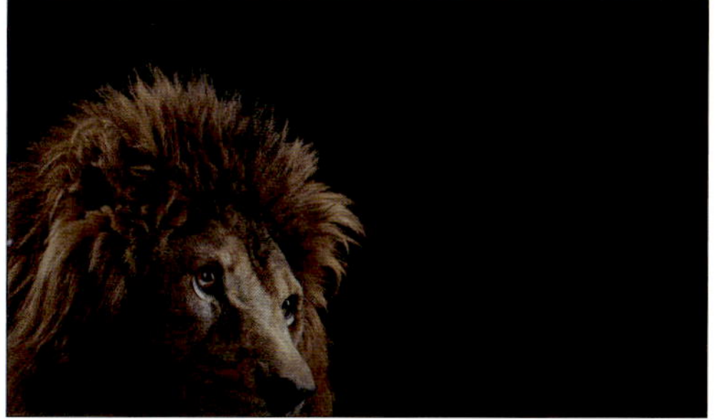
Lion #3, Los Angeles, CA, 2010

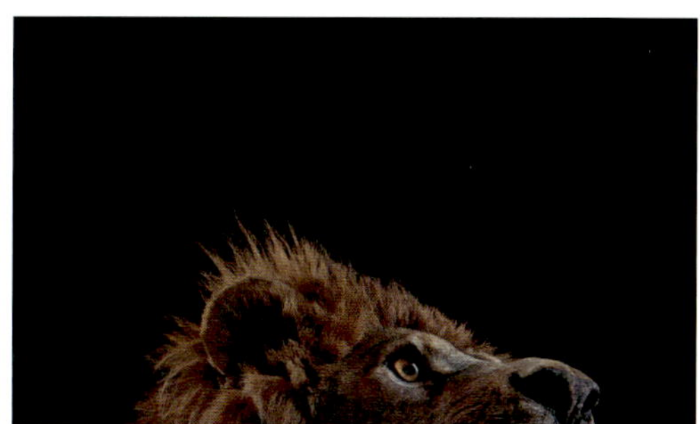
Lion #1, Los Angeles, CA, 2010

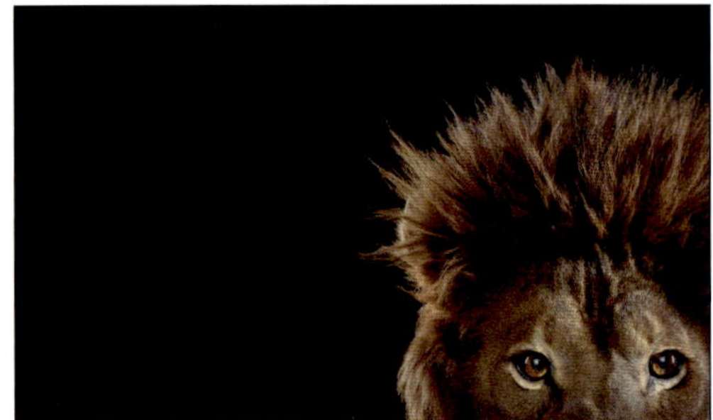

Lion #5, Los Angeles, CA, 2010

Zebra
Scientific name: *Equus quagga*
Range: Eastern and Southern Africa
Conservation status: Least threatened

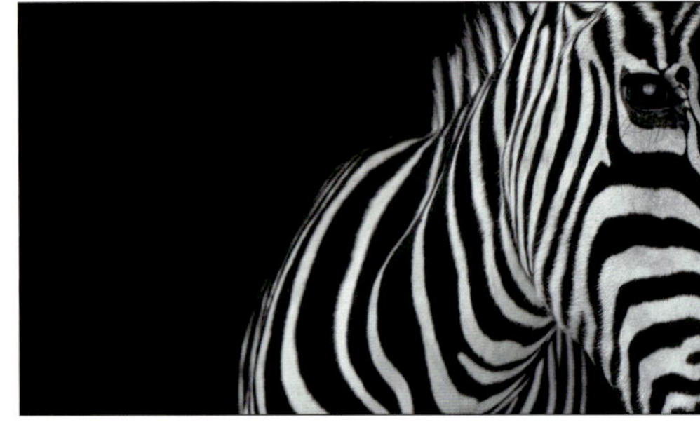

Zebra #1, Los Angeles, CA, 2010

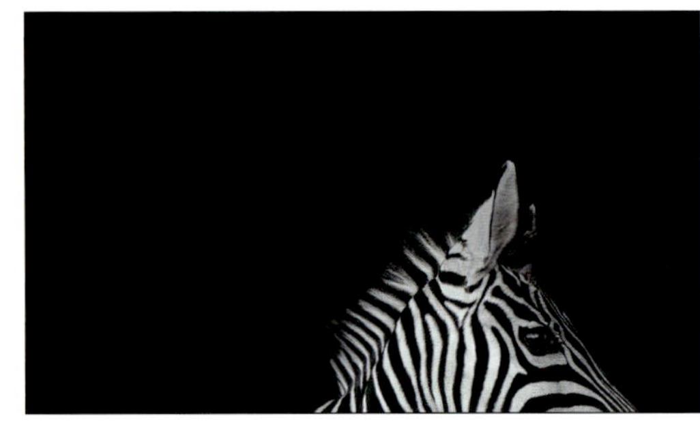

Zebra #2, Los Angeles, CA, 2010

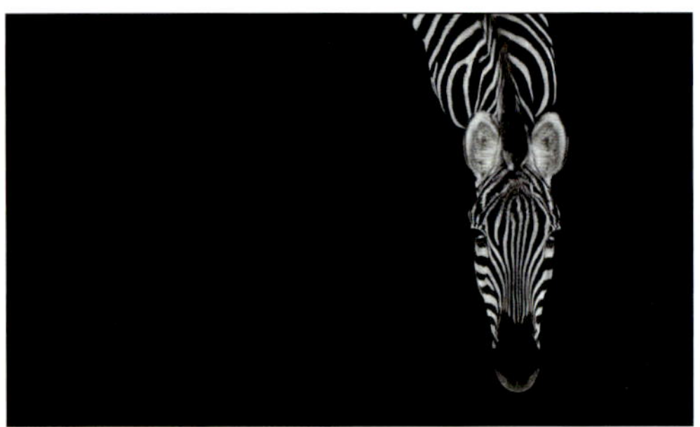

Zebra #3, Los Angeles, CA, 2010

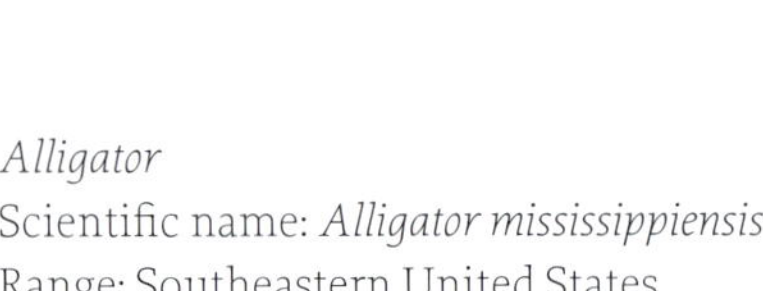

Alligator
Scientific name: *Alligator mississippiensis*
Range: Southeastern United States
Conservation status: Least threatened

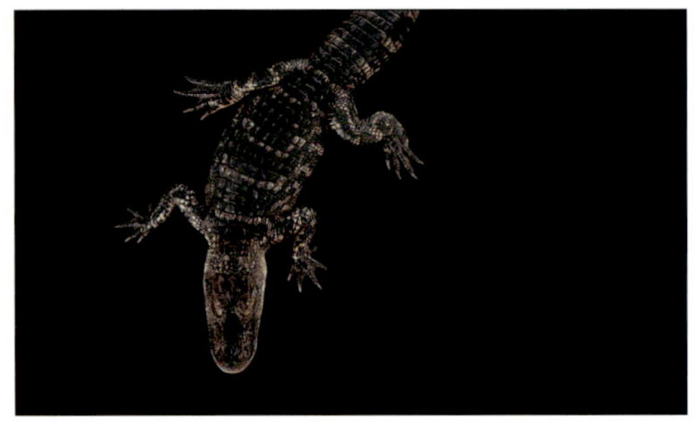

Alligator #3, Los Angeles, CA, 2011

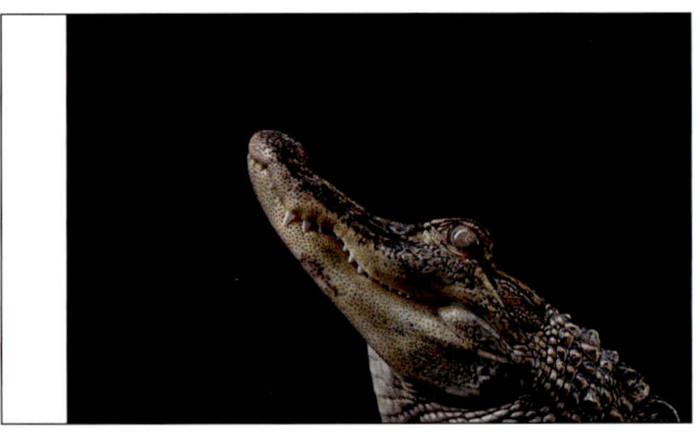

Alligator #1, Los Angeles, CA, 2011

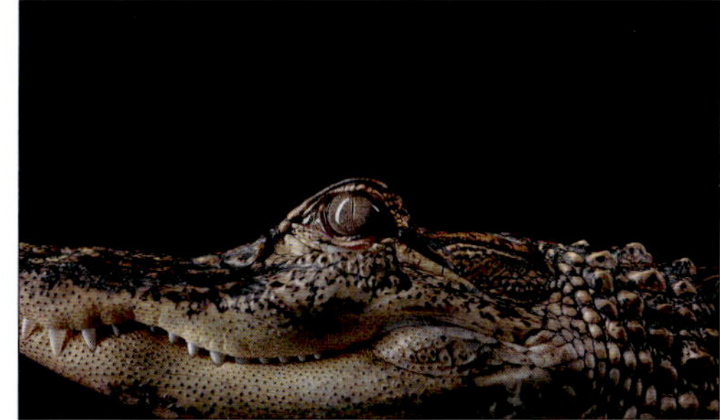

Alligator #2, Los Angeles, CA, 2011

Mountain Lion
Scientific name: *Puma concolor*
Range: North and South America
Conservation status: Least threatened

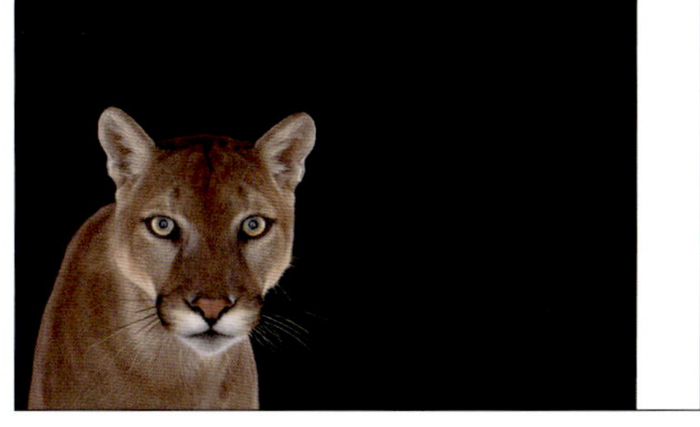

Mountain Lion #1, Los Angeles, CA, 2011

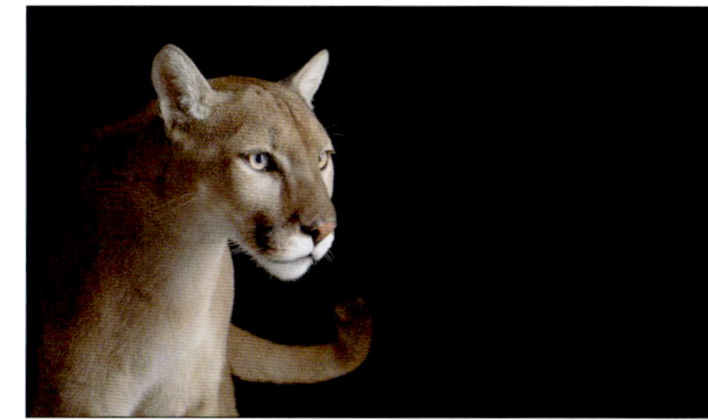

Mountain Lion #4, Los Angeles, CA, 2011

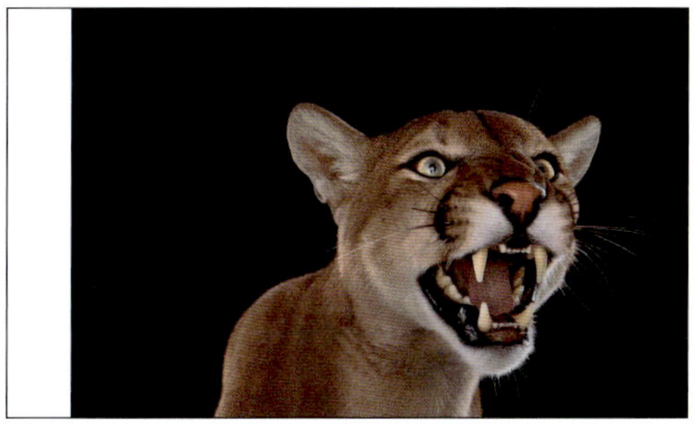

Mountain Lion #3, Los Angeles, CA, 2011

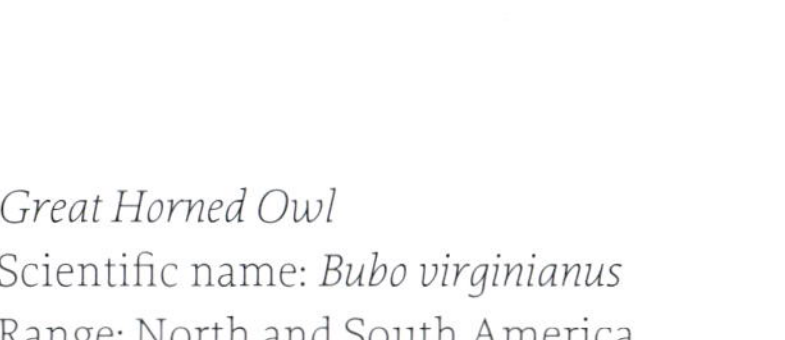

Great Horned Owl
Scientific name: *Bubo virginianus*
Range: North and South America
Conservation status: Least threatened

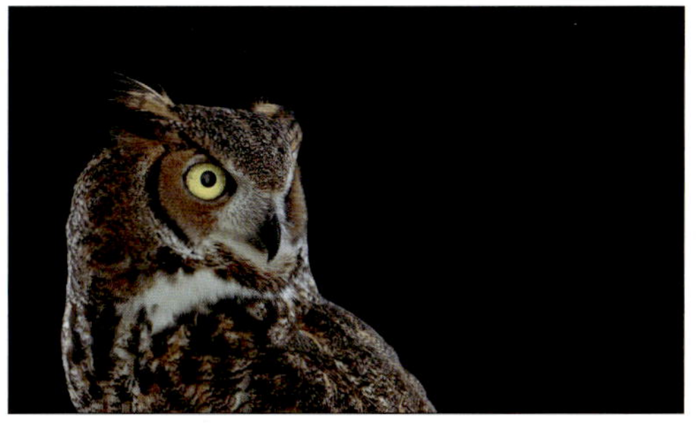

Great Horned Owl #2, St. Louis, MO, 2012

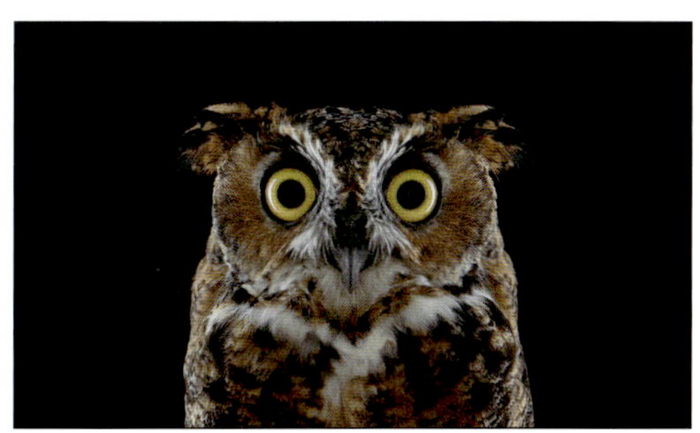

Great Horned Owl #3, Espanola, NM, 2011

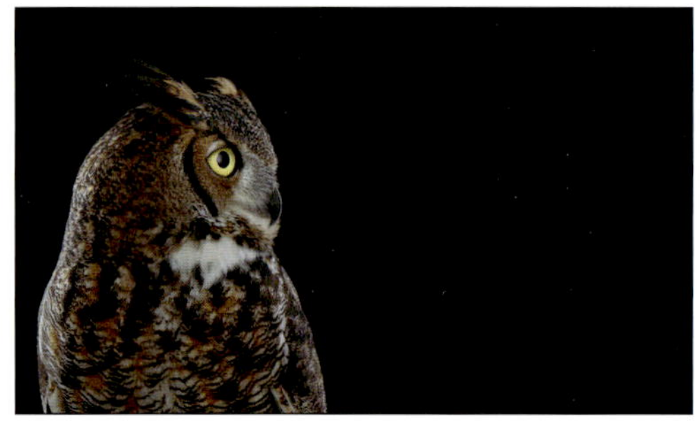

Great Horned Owl #5, St. Louis, MO, 2012

Serval
Scientific name: *Leptailurus serval*
Range: Sub-Saharan Africa
Conservation status: Least threatened

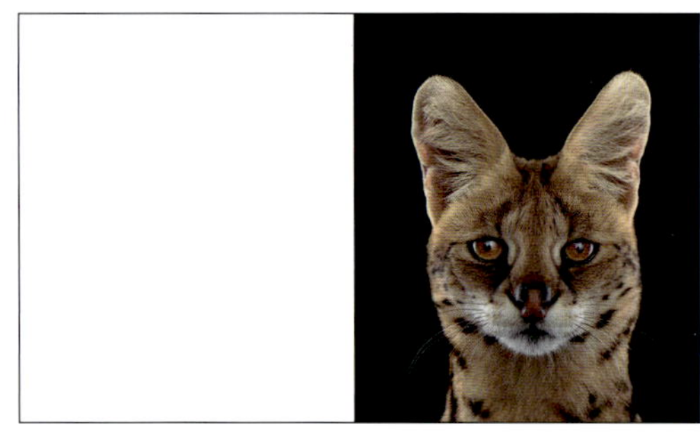

Serval #1, Albuquerque, NM, 2013

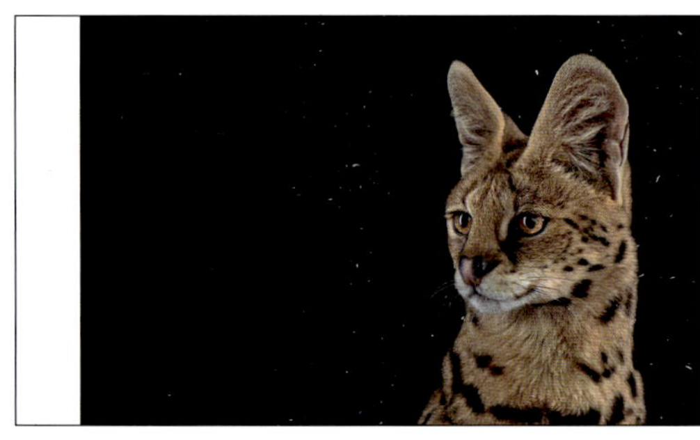

Serval #2, Albuquerque, NM, 2013

Jaguar
Scientific name: *Panthera onca*
Range: Southwestern United States, Central and South America
Conservation status: Near threatened

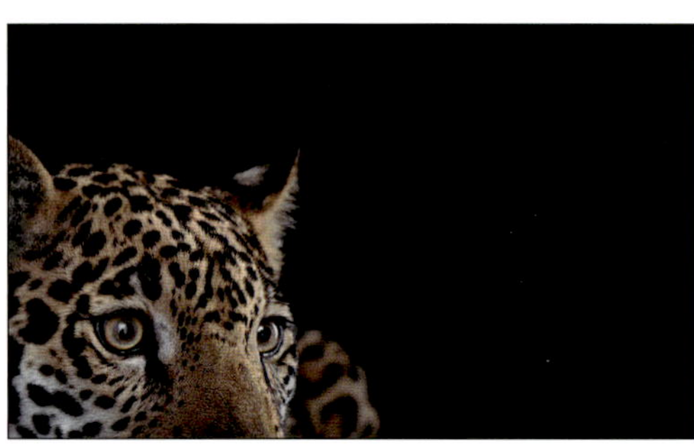

Jaguar #1, Los Angeles, CA, 2011

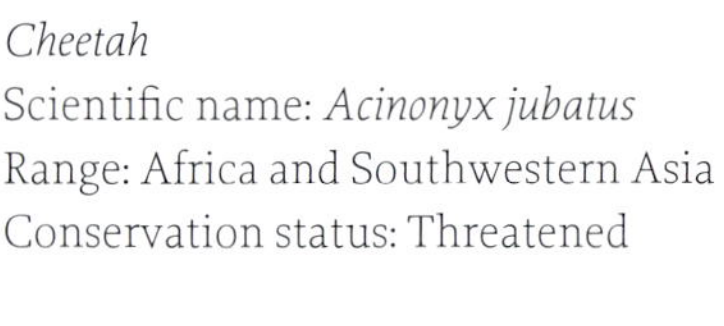

Cheetah
Scientific name: *Acinonyx jubatus*
Range: Africa and Southwestern Asia
Conservation status: Threatened

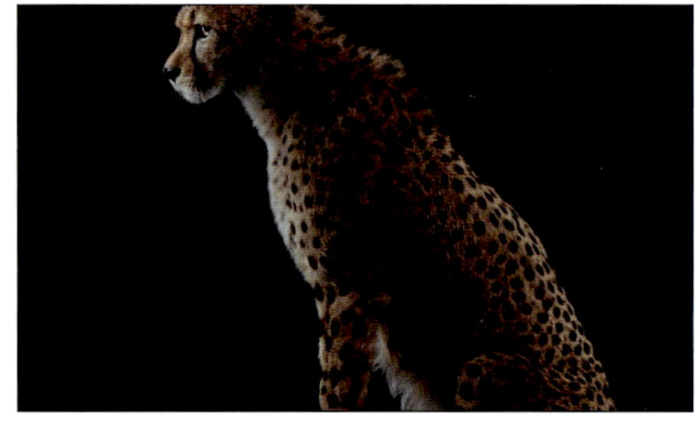

Cheetah #1, Los Angeles, CA, 2011

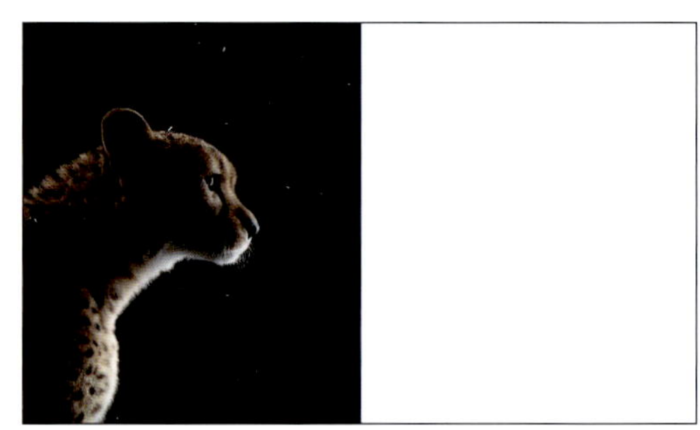

Cheetah #2, Los Angeles, CA, 2011

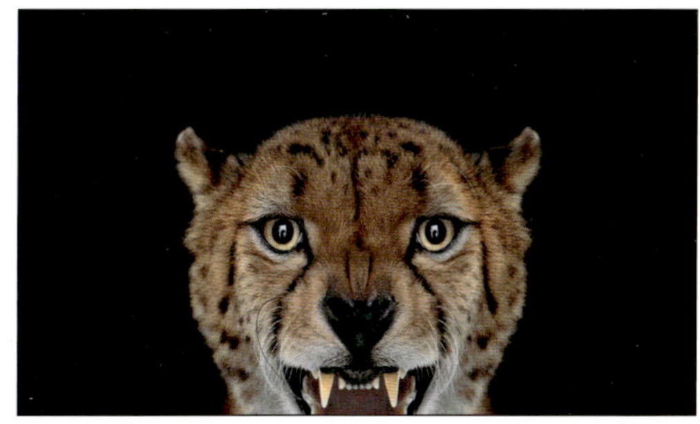

Cheetah #3, Los Angeles, CA, 2011

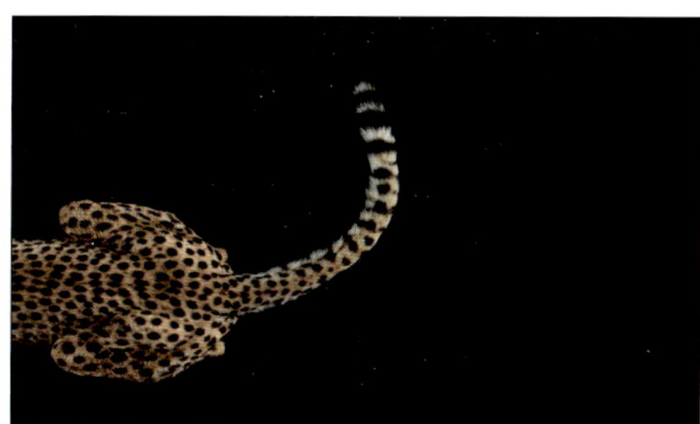

Cheetah #4, Los Angeles, CA, 2011

Bull
Scientific name: *Bos taurus*
Range: Worldwide
Conservation status: Not threatened

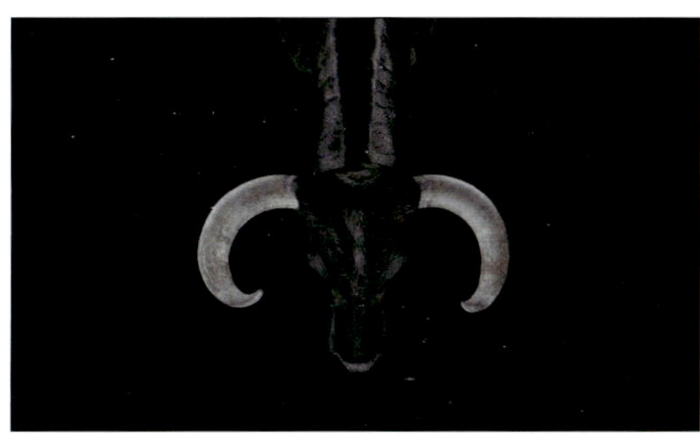

Bull #2, Los Angeles, CA, 2011

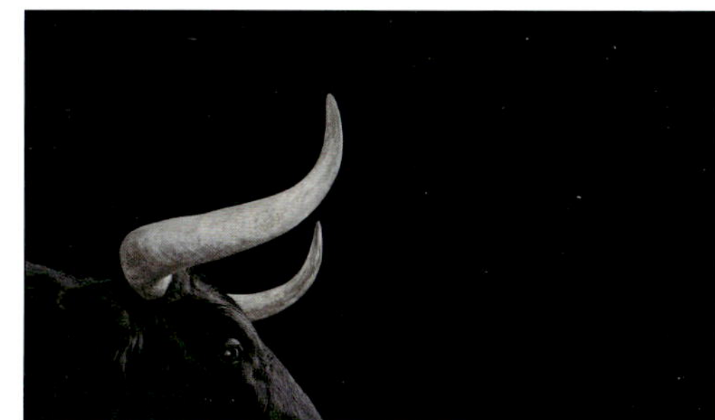

Bull #1, Los Angeles, CA, 2011

White Rhinoceros
Scientific name: *Ceratotherium simum*
Range: Southern Africa
Conservation status: Near threatened

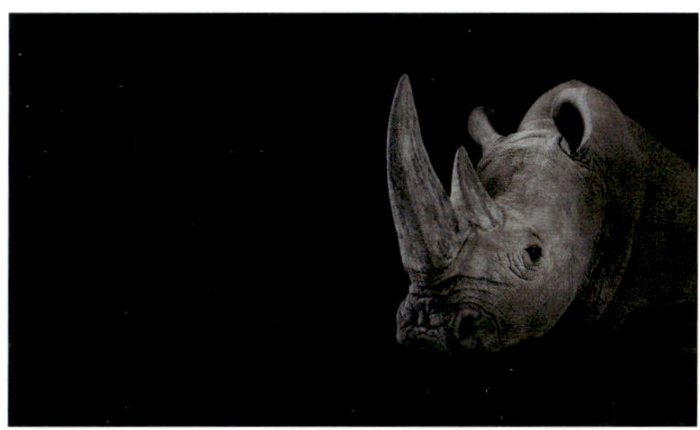

White Rhinoceros #1, Albuquerque, NM, 2013

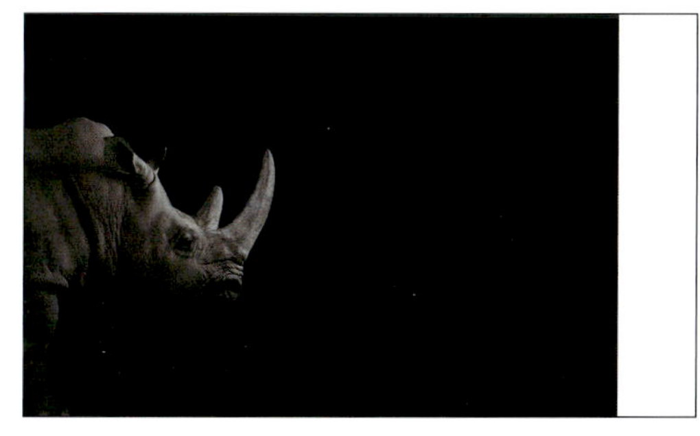

White Rhinoceros #2, Albuquerque, NM, 2013

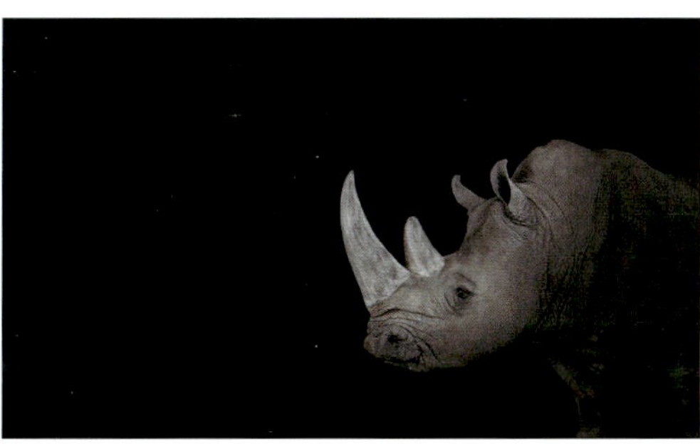

White Rhinoceros #3, Albuquerque, NM, 2013

Giraffe
Scientific name: *Giraffa camelopardalis*
Range: Sub-Saharan Africa
Conservation status: Least threatened

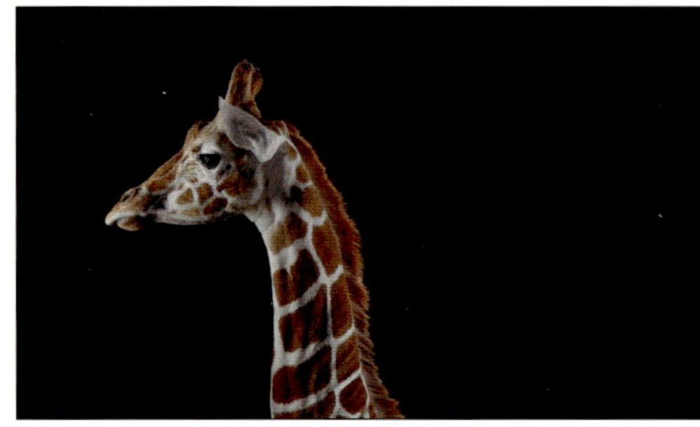

Giraffe #1, Los Angeles, CA, 2011

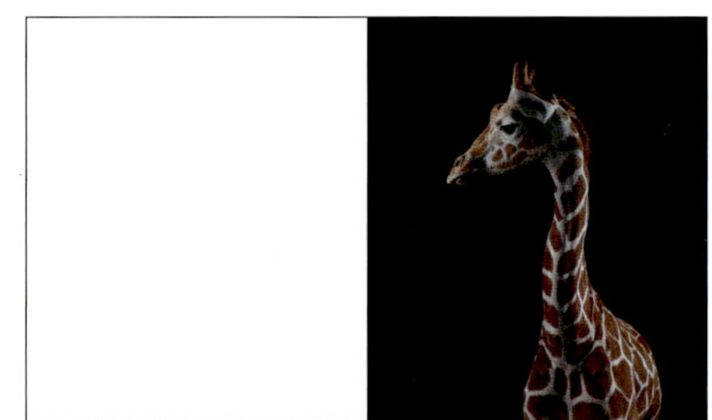

Giraffe #3, Los Angeles, CA, 2011

Kangaroo
Scientific name: *Macropus rufus* (Red Kangaroo)
Range: Australia and Tasmania
Conservation status: Least threatened

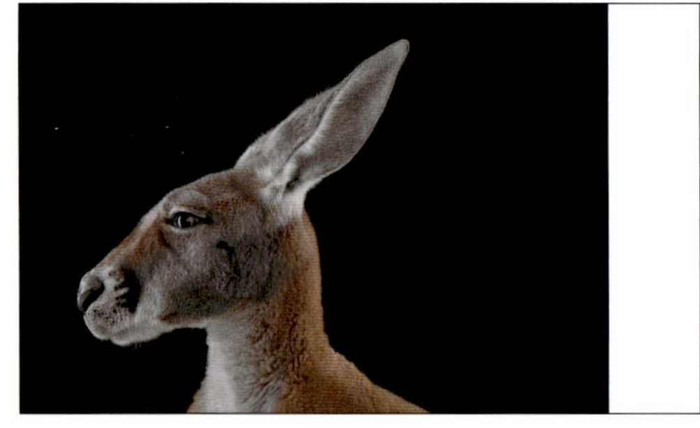

Kangaroo #1, Los Angeles, CA, 2011

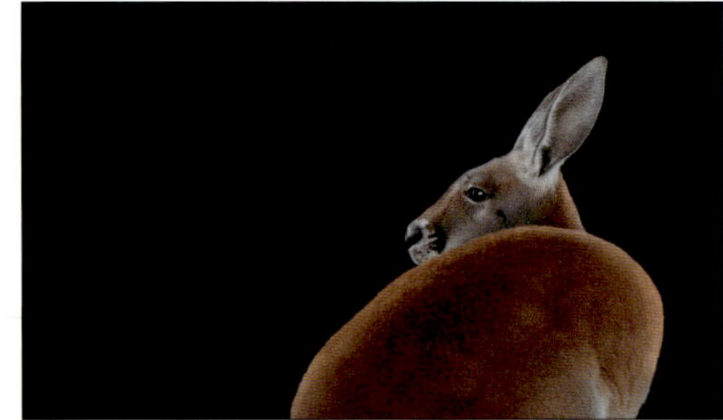

Kangaroo #2, Los Angeles, CA, 2011

Bateleur Eagle
Scientific name: *Terathopius ecaudatus*
Range: Sub-Saharan Africa
Conservation status: Near threatened

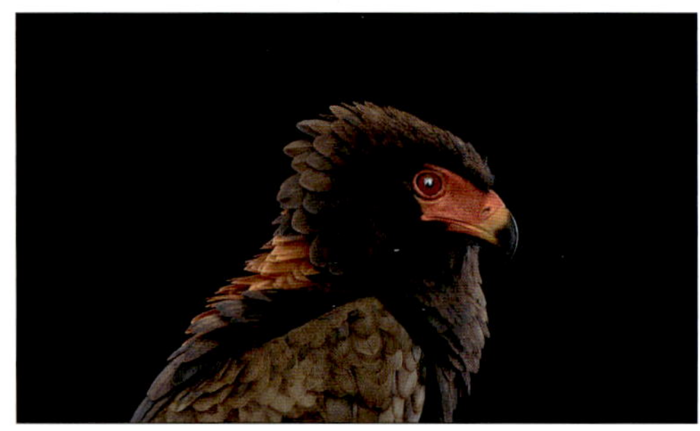

Bateleur Eagle #1, St. Louis, MO, 2012

African Crowned Crane
Scientific name: *Balearica regulorum*
Range: Sub-Saharan Africa
Conservation status: Endangered

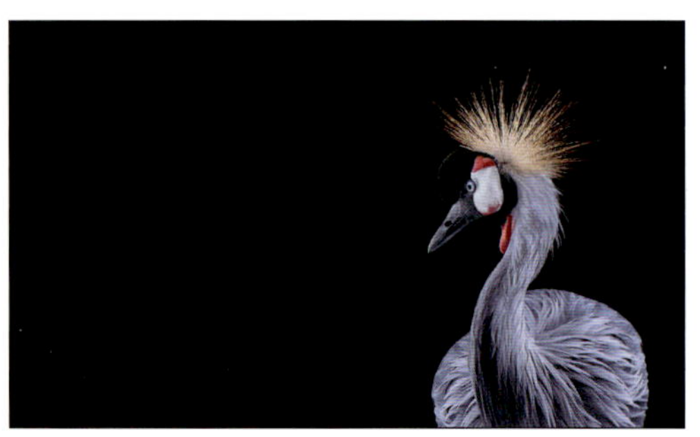

African Crowned Crane #1, Los Angeles, CA, 2011

Spider Monkey
Scientific name: *Ateles geoffroyi*
(Geoffroy's Spider Monkey)
Range: Central and South America
Conservation status: Endangered

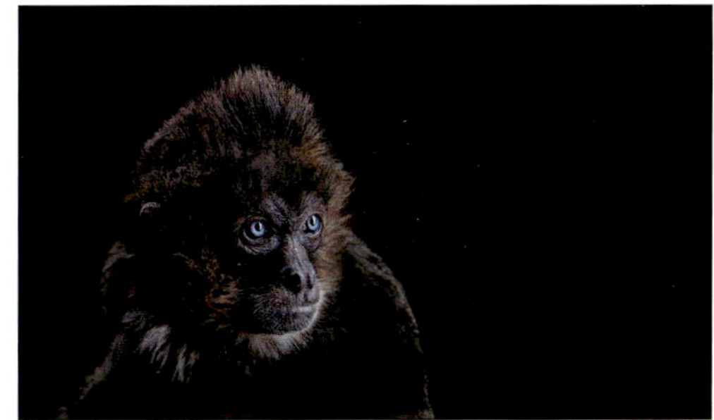

Spider Monkey #1, Los Angeles, CA, 2011

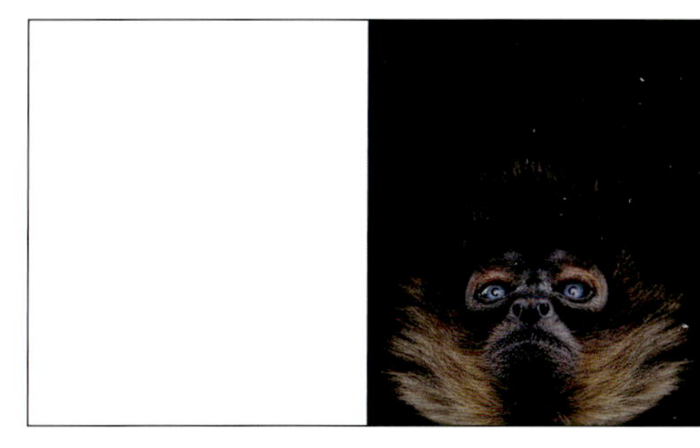

Spider Monkey #2, Los Angeles, CA, 2011

Capuchin Monkey
Scientific name: *Cebus apella*
(Brown Capuchin Monkey)
Range: Central and South America
Conservation status: Near threatened

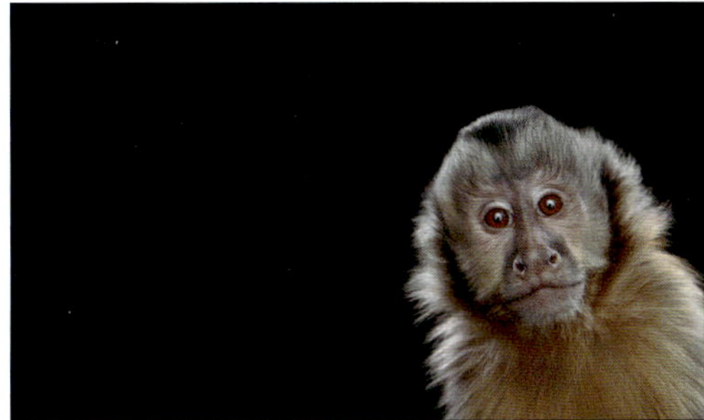

Capuchin Monkey #2, Los Angeles, CA, 2010

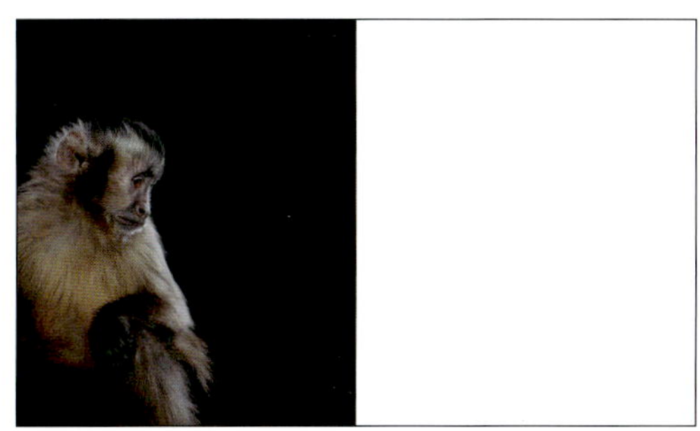

Capuchin Monkey #3, Los Angeles, CA, 2010

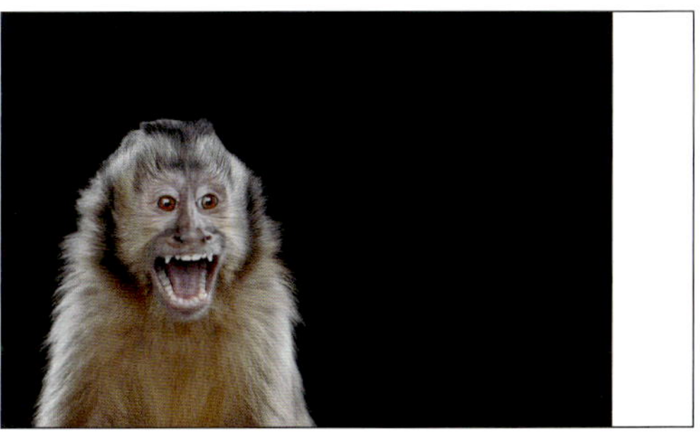

Capuchin Monkey #4, Los Angeles, CA, 2010

Long-Eared Owl
Scientific name: *Asio otus*
Range: North America, Europe, and Asia
Conservation status: Least threatened

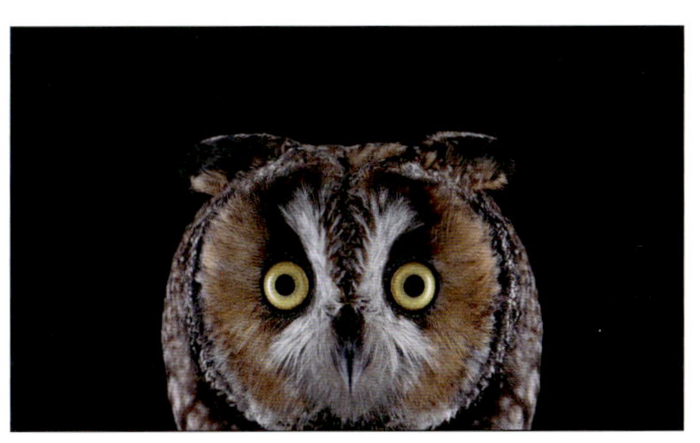

Long-Eared Owl #1, Espanola, NM, 2011

Spectacled Owl
Scientific name: *Pulsatrix perspicillata*
Range: Central and South America
Conservation status: Least threatened

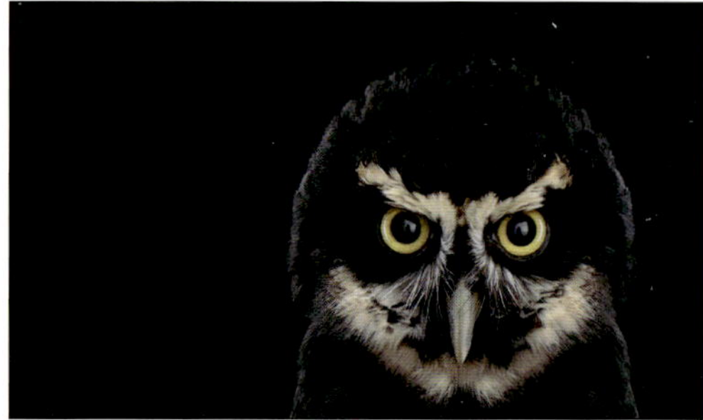

Spectacled Owl #1, St. Louis, MO, 2012

Mexican Spotted Owl
Scientific name: *Strix occidentalis*
Range: Western U.S. and Northern Mexico
Conservation status: Near threatened

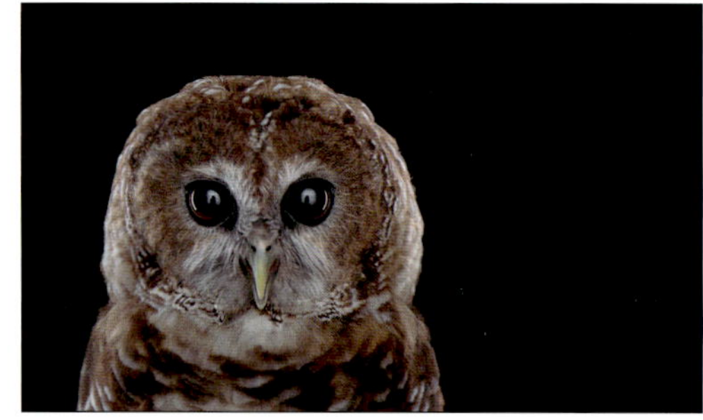

Mexican Spotted Owl #1, Espanola, NM, 2011

Burrowing Owl
Scientific name: *Athene cunicularia*
Range: North and South America
Conservation status: Least threatened

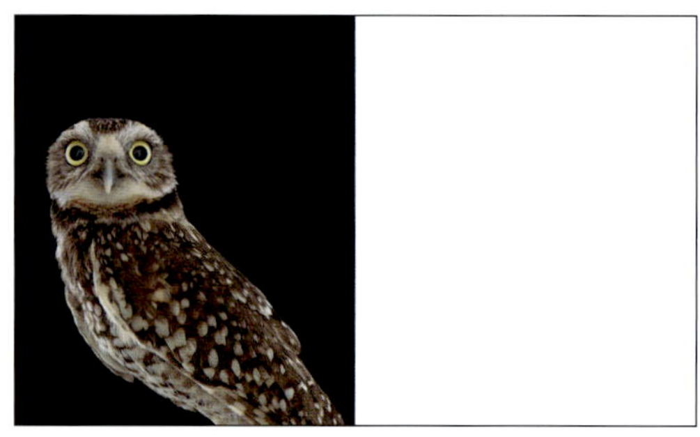

Burrowing Owl #1, Espanola, NM, 2013

Eurasian Eagle Owl
Scientific name: *Bubo bubo*
Range: Europe and Asia
Conservation status: Least threatened

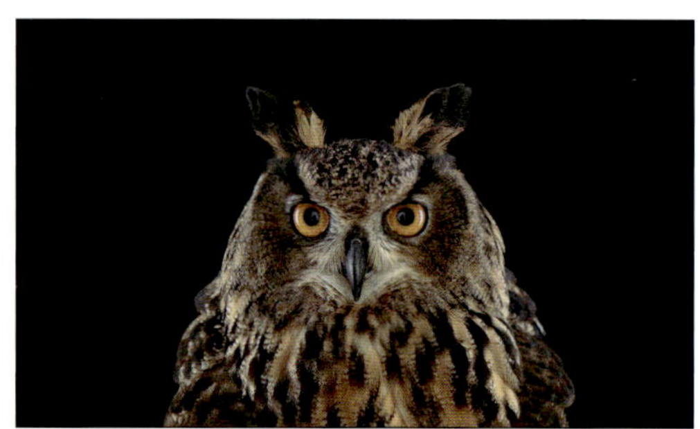

Eurasian Eagle Owl #1, St. Louis, MO, 2012

Barn Owl
Scientific name: *Tyto alba*
Range: Worldwide
Conservation status: Least threatened

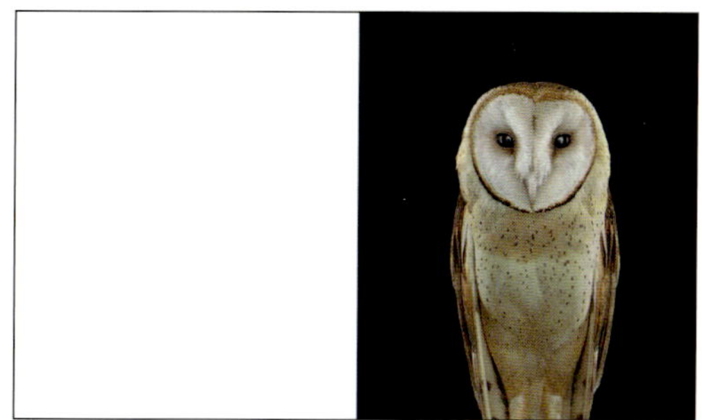

Barn Owl #1, St. Louis, MO, 2012

Tawny Eagle
Scientific name: *Aquila rapax*
Range: Africa, Asia, and India
Conservation status: Least threatened

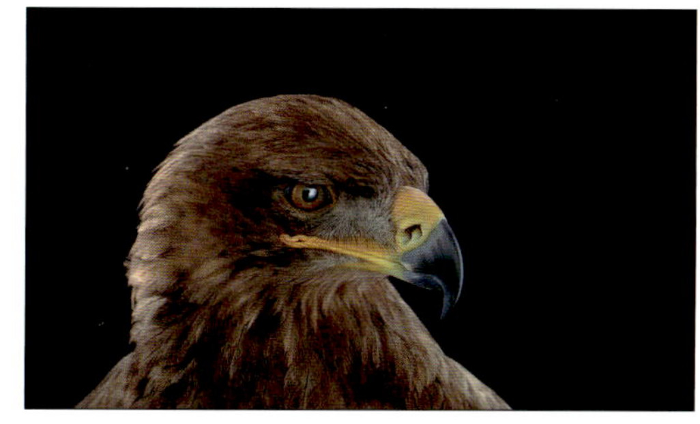

Tawny Eagle #1, St. Louis, MO, 2012

Crested Eagle
Scientific name: *Morphnus guianensis*
Range: Central and South America
Conservation status: Near threatened

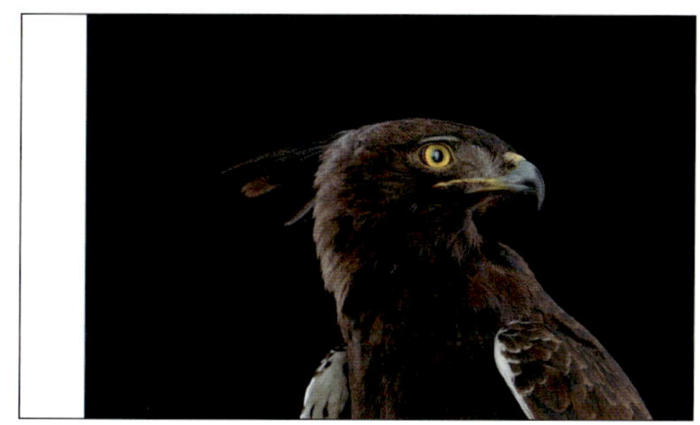

Crested Eagle #1, St. Louis, MO, 2012

Bald Eagle
Scientific name: *Haliaeetus leucocephalus*
Range: North America
Conservation status: Least threatened

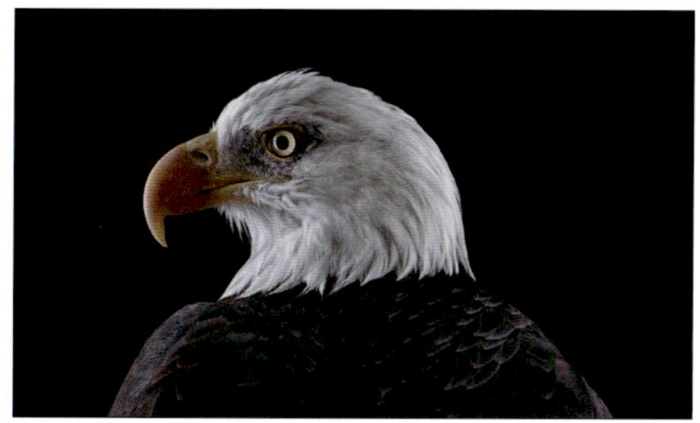

Bald Eagle #1, Espanola, NM, 2011

Golden Eagle
Scientific name: *Aquila chrysaetos*
Range: North America, Europe, and Asia
Conservation status: Least threatened

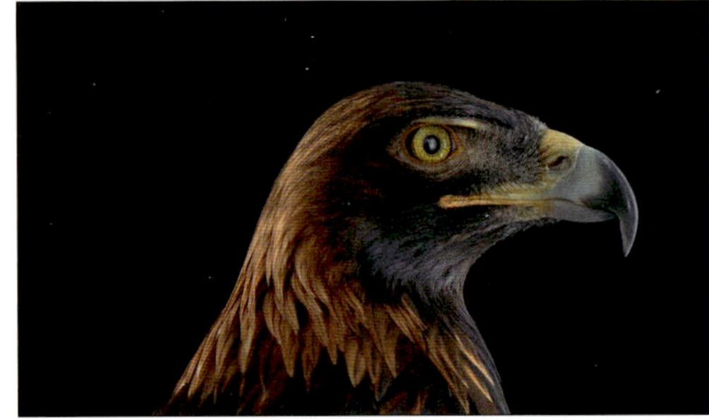

Golden Eagle #1, St. Louis, MO, 2012

Raven
Scientific name: *Corvus cryptoleucus*
(Chihuahuan Raven)
Range: North America, Europe, and Asia
Conservation status: Least threatened

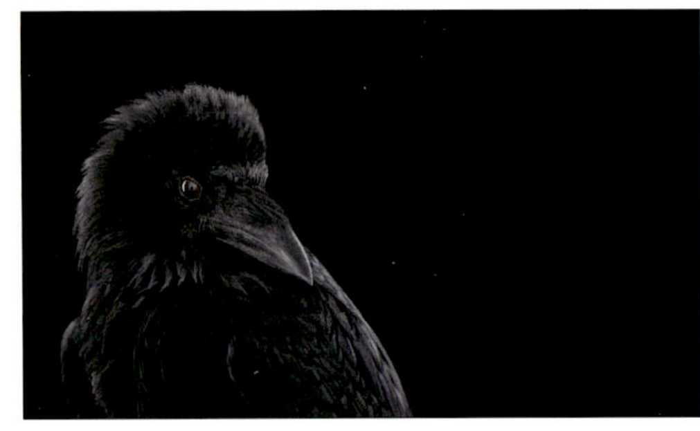

Raven #2, Albuquerque, NM, 2013

Northern Goshawk
Scientific name: *Accipiter gentilis*
Range: North America, Europe, and Asia
Conservation status: Least threatened

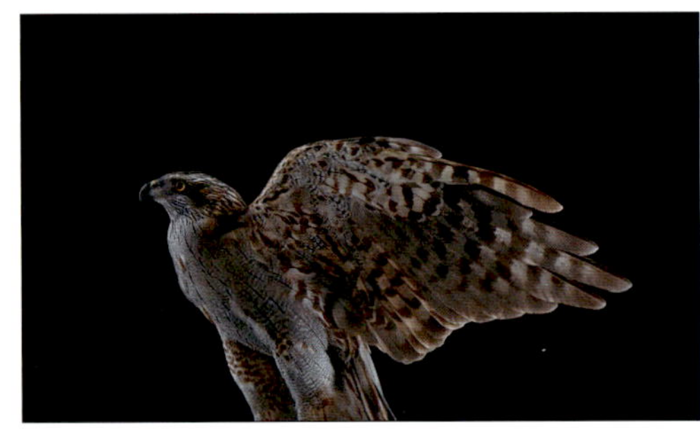

Northern Goshawk #1, Espanola, NM, 2011

White Tiger
Scientific name: *Panthera tigris tigris* (Bengal tiger)
Range: India and Asia
Conservation status: Endangered

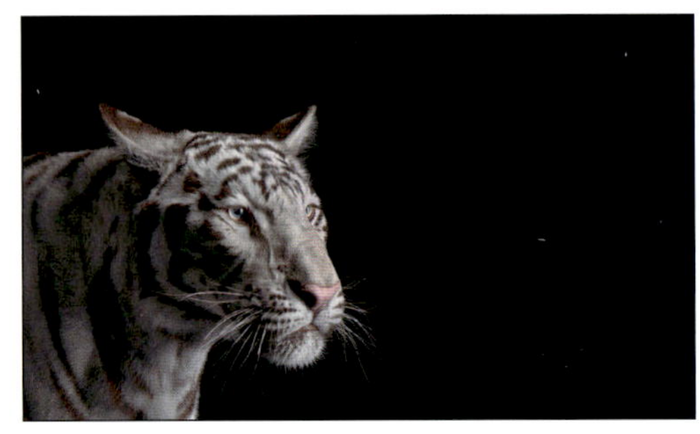

White Tiger #1, Los Angeles, CA, 2011

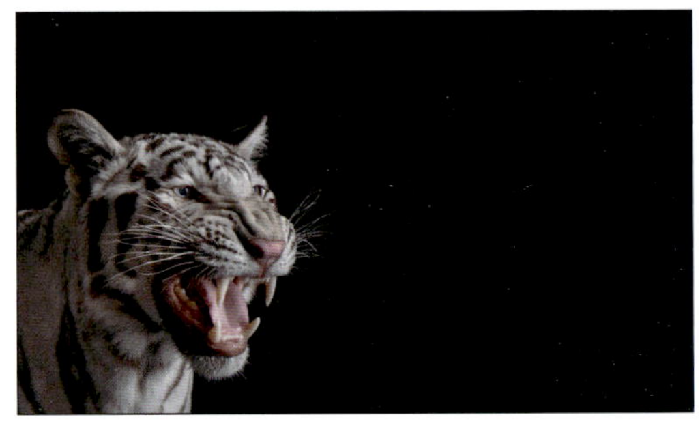

White Tiger #2, Los Angeles, CA, 2011

Siberian Tiger
Scientific name: *Panthera tigris altaica*
Range: Eastern Russia
Conservation status: Endangered

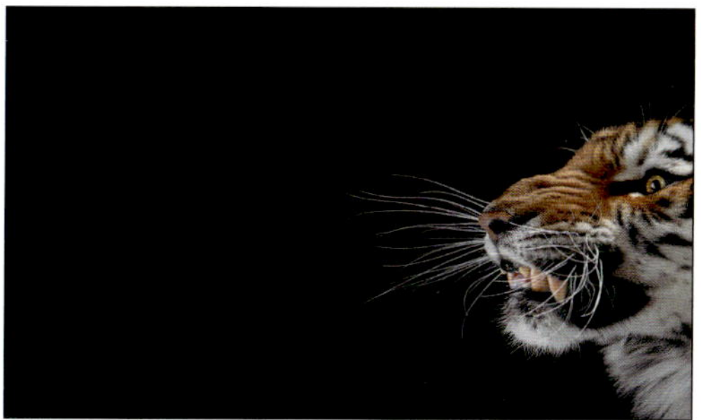
Siberian Tiger #1, Los Angeles, CA, 2010

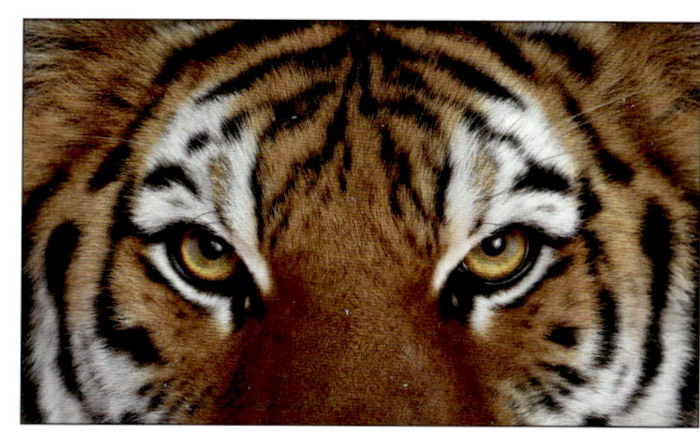
Siberian Tiger #4, Los Angeles, CA, 2010

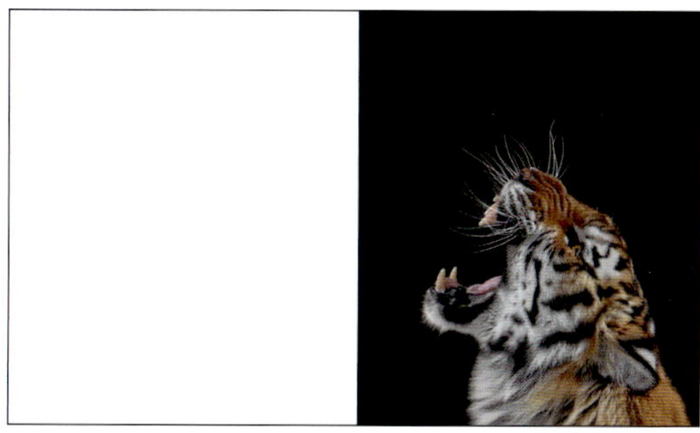
Siberian Tiger #3, Los Angeles, CA, 2010

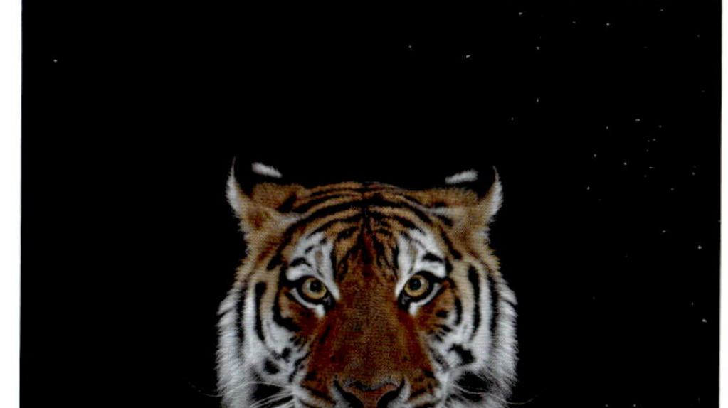
Siberian Tiger #6, Los Angeles, CA, 2010

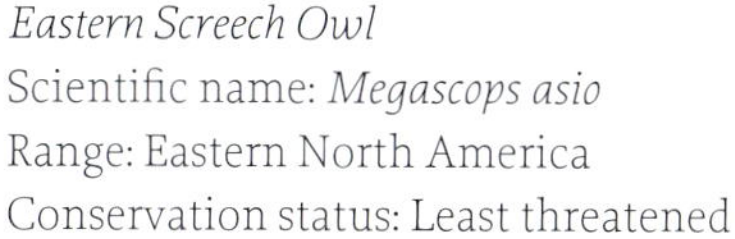

Eastern Screech Owl
Scientific name: *Megascops asio*
Range: Eastern North America
Conservation status: Least threatened

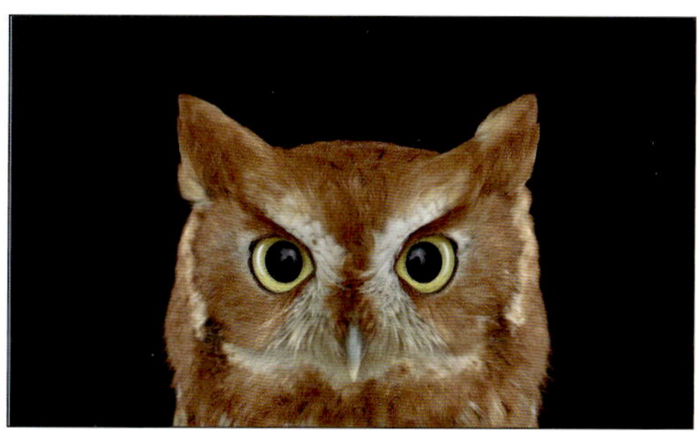
Eastern Screech Owl #1, St. Louis, MO, 2012

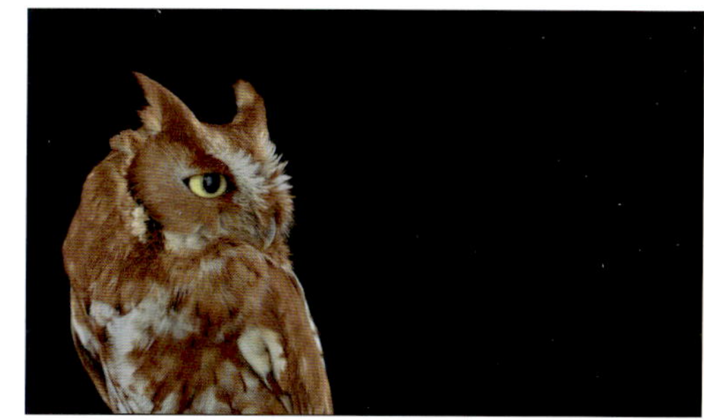
Eastern Screech Owl #2, St. Louis, MO, 2012

Western Screech Owl
Scientific name: *Megascops kennicottii*
Range: North and Central America
Conservation status: Least threatened

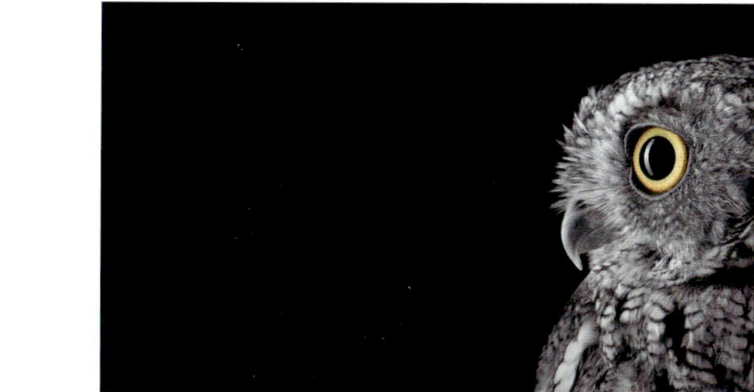
Western Screech Owl #2, Espanola, NM, 2011

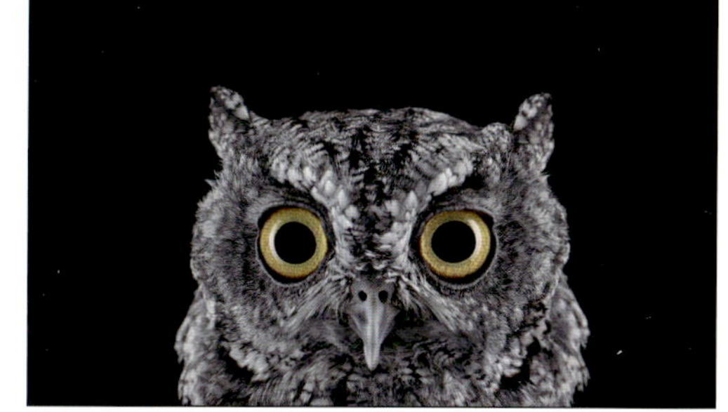
Western Screech Owl #1, Espanola, NM, 2011

Acknowledgments

First and foremost, I would like to thank Didier Doinel of Doinel Gallery in London. He believed in these photographs even before I did. Without his unwavering support of my work, this series would never have come to fruition. Thank you for accompanying me on this unexpected, yet very rewarding journey. I would also like to thank Pilar Lerma, Inma Cumplido Valverde, and Gina Traboulsi for all their hard work at various exhibitions and art fairs around Europe and Asia.

Secondly, I would like to express my gratitude to everyone at Prestel Publishing, especially Andrew Hansen and Curt Holtz, for their support of my vision and for their invaluable assistance in bringing this book to life.

Also, a special thank you to Desmond Morris for writing the introduction. It is an honor to have your unique thoughts and insights included.

And to John Vokoun at Fire Dragon Color, thanks for your refined eye, exceptional attention to detail, and theoretical perspective. Your insights helped me recognize new and important aspects of this work.

In addition, I would like to thank the many dedicated individual trainers, sanctuary workers, and zookeepers who helped me produce these shoots. Without their patience and expertise, this project would not have been possible.

Finally, to the many animals whose images grace these pages, it was a rare privilege to share a few moments of your lives. Although you will not remember me, I will remember you.

Brad Wilson, Santa Fe, March 2014

Front Cover: *African Elephant # 6*, Los Angeles, CA, 2011
Back Cover: *Mountain Lion # 1*, Los Angeles, CA, 2011

Prestel Verlag, Munich
A member of Verlagsgruppe Random House GmbH

Prestel Verlag
Neumarkter Strasse 28
81673 Munich
Tel. +49 (0)89 4136-0
Fax +49 (0)89 4136-2335

Prestel Publishing Ltd.
14-17 Wells Street
London W1T 3PD
Tel. +44 (0)20 7323-5004
Fax +44 (0)20 7323-0271

Prestel Publishing
900 Broadway, Suite 603
New York, NY 10003
Tel. +1 (212) 995-2720
Fax +1 (212) 995-2733

www.prestel.com

Library of Congress Control Number is available; British Library Cataloguing-in-Publication Data: a catalogue record for this book is available from the British Library; Deutsche Nationalbibliothek holds a record of this publication in the Deutsche Nationalbibliografie; detailed bibliographical data can be found under: http://www.dnb.de

Prestel books are available worldwide. Please contact your nearest bookseller or one of the above addresses for information concerning your local distributor.

Editorial direction: Curt Holtz
Copyediting: Jonathan Fox, Barcelona
Design and layout: Joana Niemeyer, Studio April, London
Production: Friederike Schirge
Origination: Reproline Genceller, Munich
Printing and binding: TBB, a.s., Banská Bystrica

Printed in Slovakia

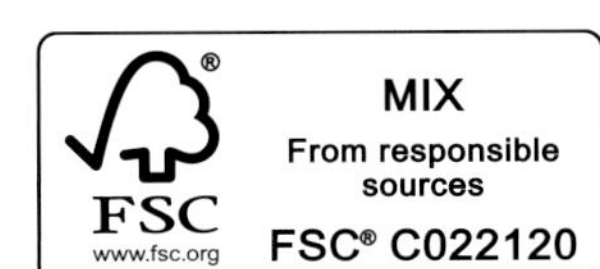

Verlagsgruppe Random House FSC® N001967
The FSC® -certified paper Profisilk has been supplied by Igepa, Germany

ISBN 978-3-7913-4892-6